Rethinking Secondary Education

Rethinking Secondary Education:

A Human-Centred Approach

Scherto R. Gill
Garrett M. Thomson

Harlow, England • London • New York • Boston • San Francisco • Toronto • Sydney • Auckland • Singapore • Hong Kong
Tokyo • Seoul • Taipei • New Delhi • Cape Town • São Paulo • Mexico City • Madrid • Amsterdam • Munich • Paris • Milan

Pearson Education Limited
Edinburgh Gate
Harlow
Essex CM20 2JE
England

and Associated Companies throughout the world

Visit us on the World Wide Web at:
www.pearson.com/uk

First published 2012

ISBN 978-1-4082-8478-0

British Library Cataloguing-in-Publication Data
A catalogue record for this book is available from the British Library

Library of Congress Cataloguing-in-Publication Data
A catalog record for this book is available from the Library of Congress

10 9 8 7 6 5 4 3 2 1
16 15 14 13 12

Typeset in 11.25/14pt Minion by 35
Printed in Great Britain by Henry Ling Ltd, at the Dorset Press, Dorchester, Dorset

Contents

Acknowledgements

First and foremost, we would like to express our deep gratitude to the board and staff of the Guerrand-Hermès Foundation for Peace (GHFP) whose work has been generously sponsored by Simon Guerrand-Hermès. The GHFP has made this project possible by supporting our work in many ways. The book was conceived and implemented for and by the GHFP, and the original ideas of human-centred education were inspired by many conversations with our colleagues and friends. Amongst these individuals are Simon Guerrand-Hermès, Sharif and Astuti Horthy, Prof. Patrice Brodeur, Alexandra Asseily, Prof. Ivor Goodson, Muhammad Ridwan and Hardin Tibbs.

We have also benefited from conversations and discussions with fellow educators and thinkers. Those whom we would like to thank in particular are Prof. Michael Fielding (Institute of Education), Mike Davies (Bishop Park College), Prof. Adrian Moore (University of Oxford), Virginia Thomas (Susila Dharma International), Jane Thomas (Human Scale Education) and Liz Thomson (British Council).

We would also like to thank the staff and students of the state schools in the UK which we visited as part of our research and the student researchers who inspired us with their energy and enthusiasm. We regret that we cannot name the schools nor the young people involved in our research due to confidentiality. However, we do want to thank one particular young person, Sophia Campbell, who was a huge inspiration throughout our project.

We would also like to mention the staff and students of other schools that we have visited and worked with over the years, especially Bishops Park College in Essex, UK; Colegio Amor in Bogota, Colombia; Lewes New School in the UK; Bina Cita Utama School in Indonesia and Yes Quest, a worldwide youth project.

Finally, we would like to thank our immediate families who have had to live with this project: Helena, Tony, Toto, Verena, Susana and Robert.

Introduction

This book originated from our work for the Guerrand-Hermès Foundation for Peace. The Foundation supports educational projects around the world, many of which embody alternative educational practices, and it has organised various international conferences to explore innovative education.

After reflection on these experiences, two important points struck us with great force. The first was how alternative schools usually stand outside the state structure, a world apart in terms of thinking, culture and everyday practice. (The term 'alternative schools' refers to a wide-ranging category of educational institutions that include progressive schools, free schools, democratic schools, and schools following an alternative educational ethos and pedagogy such as Steiner schools, Montessori schools, and so forth.) Through this dawning realisation, we started to frame a question which seemed especially relevant in the context of a country with a highly developed state education system such as Britain: 'How can the two ways of thinking and acting better relate to each other?' We became convinced that, in order to improve, public education needs to take a sideways step. To continue on the current trajectory is to risk turning it into a huge social machine tuned for better national economic performance, with pre-set targets and pre-packaged educational goals. At the same time, alternative schools seem to be locked into relative isolation, appealing to relatively wealthy parents who want their children to escape the modernised and depersonalised worldview that appears to be embodied in most state education.

Stepping back from this duality, however, we felt both approaches – state and alternative education – had merits and demerits, and this set us the challenge of articulating the strategically key strengths and weaknesses of both. Theoretically, how can they be reconciled and combined? Practically, how can they contribute to each other, and work symbiotically? After some searching, we reformulated our main question as: 'How can the best aspects of alternative education benefit the state educational system?'

The best practices of alternative education are usually rooted in the idea that the individual child should be at the centre of education. Drawing sustenance from that root, those practices treat a child's development in a holistic and individualised manner that allows each person to become more fully him- or herself. The ideas behind such practices may not be entirely clear, and yet they have inspired schools in countries such as Thailand, Colombia and Indonesia, within whose culture children are happy and able to transcend their extremely difficult socio-economic situations. In countries such as the UK, why should these benefits only be available to wealthier children? The secrets of the success of some alternative schools need to be available to, and find a home in, the state sector. Education has the power to dramatically improve our lives.

The second point that hit us concerned secondary compared to primary educa-tion. In the latter, there already is some dialogue comparing the ideas and prac-tices of alternative and state conceptions of education. This interchange extends back to the formation of nurseries and kindergartens, where the culture of schools is often influenced, perhaps indirectly, by the thought and practice of Montessori, Steiner and Pestalozzi. As a result, state primary schools are often very considerate of the children they care for.

However, this contrasts sharply with aspects of the culture of many secondary schools. Secondary schools are often regarded as focusing primarily on grades and public examinations. They are places where childhood ends rather dram-atically; young people are confronted head-on with the hard realities of (and preparation for) adult life. According to this idea of the system, young people need to knuckle down in order to be better prepared for the rigours of the work-force and market place, and for the so-called 'harsh world'. It is therefore not so easy for secondary educational institutions to embrace an alternative ethos in day-to-day teaching and learning.

For these reasons, we realised that it would be more fruitful and challenging to direct our question 'How can the best aspects of alternative education benefit the state educational system?' specifically towards secondary schooling. We decided to direct our attention largely but not exclusively to the secondary edu-cation of children between the ages of 14–16.

In summary, this book is intended to build a bridge between, on the one hand, the ever-changing principles of state secondary education in England and, on the other, the myriad forms of alternative education. We have tried to do this with an eye that is both critical and appreciative, and with the feeling that romanticism and cynicism are equal failures to wed vision with reality.

In working on the values and concerns that ideally ought to motivate a second-ary educational system, we found that the phrase 'human-centred education' captured the essential meanings central to our thought, and distilled the inno-vative practices that we had observed. Thus, part of our challenge is to explain the idea of human-centred education and its significance especially for secondary state education.

Because this book is in part about the aims that the system *should be* directed towards, and the principles that underlie those aims, it is a work in philosophy. Roughly, this means that it tries to establish conclusions through thoughtful argument. However, to answer the questions that drive our investigation, we need to make practical recommendations about curriculum, teaching, assess-ment and the organisation of schools, and this requires a good knowledge of teachers and students, and of the many things that they do together. This means that the book is also about educational practice. Therefore, our work is inter-disciplinary. It addresses conceptual questions such as: 'What are the aims of education?', 'What is learning?' and 'What is human flourishing?' in order to develop a theoretical framework for human-centred education. It also contains an investigation of empirical questions such as: 'How do young people experi-ence adolescence at this age?', 'What do young people think of their experiences in secondary schools?', 'How are young people taught in secondary schools?' and 'What is a typical school day like for a young person?' We investigated these questions by visiting schools in the UK and other countries, by talking to teachers and head-teachers and by interviewing young people about adolescence and education. We will describe the research methodology we have employed in later chapters.

There are many assumptions that we have made, but one needs to be mentioned from the outset. We have adopted a mildly objectivist view about value claims. This means that such claims that affirm that one state of affairs is better than another can be true or false. However, this does not imply that such claims are absolutely true or false independently of context, and that there is always one absolute true answer to all value questions. (For more explanation and some defence of this position, see Thomson, 2002.)

Since, in some respects, the vision of education that we have developed is relatively new, we hope that our readers will enjoy a theoretical argument about the nature of education. In the second half of the book, we have tried to show how the new theory impinges on and transforms practice. We examine curriculum, pedagogy and assessment, as well as the school as a learning institution.

Although our focus has been primarily on the English secondary education system, our discussion will be applicable to other contexts because it is largely directed to the principles upon which such education should be founded.

We believe that this book will appeal to a wide readership, including academic researchers, teacher educators, students of education, and educational practitioners and policy makers.

1
Towards human-centred education

Much of this book is about what counts as good educational standards. Parents want the best education for their children; the public is worried that education standards are falling. Such concerns are clearly value-laden and mean little without some clarification of what is meant by those evaluations. For instance, there is little point in talking about how effective a course is without specifying what the relevant end results are and should be. Words such as 'effective', 'better', 'falling' and 'failing' presume ends, and these involve value judgements.

Furthermore, it is not sufficient to merely postulate some ends, and simply state that these are our goals. The fact that teachers have certain purposes in mind for their students, and the fact that the Government has a programme of outcomes established by law does not mean that educational theory should simply accept those ends as given. There must be some reason why some objectives are better or more appropriate than others, at least in a given context. We argue that what constitutes better and more appropriate objectives must take into consideration the development and flourishing of human beings.

Therefore, the core of this book is that educational standards can and should be more human-centred. Human-centred education treats all those involved in education equally as humans and helps individuals develop to the fullest as happy human beings. Throughout this book, we often employ the term 'human' because it has richer and wider connotations than 'person'. As well as indicating autonomy, free thought and self-consciousness, which are usually associated with the Enlightenment idea of being a person, it also includes other qualities, such as being noble, humane, sensitive and inquisitive. It also carries the idea of an embodied being, who cannot sit for hours behind a desk passively listening and who needs to move, talk and laugh. The term is supposed to capture what are the best qualities of human beings in their fullness. This is one of the themes we are going to address in the first part of the book.

Human-centred education places the human being at the centre of the education process. In the words of A.S. Neill (1992), the idea is to make the educational processes and environment 'fit the child' rather than the other way around. What this simple but radical idea signifies in intellectual terms is the theme of the first part of the book, and what it might imply in practice is the main topic of the second part. In brief, though, a more human-centred education would require a new concept of learning and pedagogy within the state system, a thorough reappraisal of assessment methods (and connected concepts such as exams and grades), new principles for the construction of the curriculum, and re-visioning of the educational environment. We argue that society needs to move further away from knowledge-based schooling that is exam-driven towards the full education of a human being.

This does not mean, however, rejecting wholesale the mainstream approach and embracing whole-heartedly the so-called alternative or progressive tradition in education, which includes the holistic and child-centred approaches referred to by Neill. We shall try to retain what is good in mainstream approaches, and examine the ideas of the alternative tradition critically, as well as sympathetically.

Our objective is to understand better what educational standards a society ought to have. This involves identifying the values that ought to underpin educational activities. To identify them, we will look at broad educational aims and argue that some should have a higher priority than others. In doing this, we shall argue that mainstream views of education are based on a misunderstanding of values that distorts much current thinking about educational aims.

Although it is a common complaint that educational processes have become overly instrumentalised, the point is not often dealt with in sufficiently fundamental terms. Since instrumental reason is an extraordinarily powerful and useful mode of thought, and since edu-cational practices do serve certain purposes, it is important to clarify these points. People need instrumental rationality. There can be no question of avoiding or eliminating it. However, we need to understand what the boundaries of instrumental rationality are when applied to education. The problem is how to avoid misapplying it beyond its limits, and thereby avoid turning ourselves as human beings into tools or machines. What is the proper place for instrumental reasoning in edu-cational activities?

Furthermore, we claim that the mainstream view has a faulty con-ception of learning and relies on a mistaken view of the nature of assessment and measurement. By pointing out these misunderstand-ings and false conceptions, we will build a positive view of education centred on each person's flourishing as a human being. However, child-centred or holistic education is often associated with a romantic and

▶

radical tradition that tends to reject reason, dismiss knowledge, and disregard teaching and pedagogy. We will show how human-centred education does not need to be wedded to these assumptions.

Our aim in this part of the book is to build a theoretical framework for the recommendations about practice in the second part.

1
The aims of education

Introduction

This chapter is divided into two parts: the first will be devoted to a discussion about the aims of education. We draw on existing claims that education should have three aims: the social, the academic and the personal, and argue that only the development of the human being should have priority and the other two aims ultimately serve the flourishing of the person. Then we move on to explore why the social and academic ends are so powerfully influential in determining the aims of education. To investigate this question, in the second part, we discuss instrumental rationality, and point out the danger of it instrumentalising and dehumanising human beings when it confuses ends with intrinsic values and means with instrumental values. We propose that for education to move away from an instrumentalised view, it is necessary to perceive properly means and ends and their relationships with what is valuable. The clarification of such relationships can enable education to become a process for human flourishing.

The aims of education

What aims ought educational activities have? This is a core issue that parents, teachers and governments need to address systematically because many important questions regarding the nature of the curriculum, pedagogy, assessment and the structure of schooling depend on it. We cannot make progress in these other areas without first addressing the aims.

Fundamentally, there are two approaches to defining the aims of education: one that regards education as a means to an end; and one that sees education as an end in itself. We will examine these separately.

First, education as a means to an end. At the most general level, educational activities have three types of aims: the first regards education as a means to various social ends; the second as a means to academic goals, or initiation into 'ways of knowing and understanding'; and the third as a means to the development of the individual (Standish, 1999: 35).

Education as a means to social ends

According to this view, the main aim of education is to enable individuals to serve some of the needs of the society in which they will live as adults. Broadly, education enables society to function. This general view is expressed in many forms. Of recent prominence is the idea that we must train the next generation to help the country compete well in the global marketplace. Tony Blair called education 'the best economic policy we have' (Beck, 2003: 24). This is a perennial view that has weathered many changes in the political climate. Education also serves other current economic needs. For example, through schooling, it serves as a giant child-minding institution that enables both parents to join the workforce.

This general social objective can also include more noble political aims such as promoting equality in society, which has been an important consideration for past Labour governments in providing equal access to education. The issue at hand now, however, is not whether good education should be available for all the people in a country irrespective of their class, race, sex or income levels. Instead the claim is that education itself is a way of promoting social equality – or, in other words, this is part of the social function of educational activities.[1]

This broad category also encompasses the aim of fostering democracy (see, for example, Dewey, 1916; Neill, 1960; Giroux, 1989; Fielding and Moss, 2010). Many educational thinkers have noted that a democratic society needs to invest in its educational system because the quality of a democratic system depends crucially on who is elected and for what reasons (Barro and Lee, 2000; Glaeser *et al.*, 2007; Castello-Climent, 2008). It depends on the majority of voters

---

[1] For more discussion on the notion of equality and how to understand equality in education, see Chapter II in Wilson (1975).

making the appropriate choices and so democracy requires an education that fosters, for example, critical thinking and a willingness to participate in social debate in a public spirited way.

The category of social objectives does not need to be confined to mainstream political aims, however. Education is often seen as integral to a long-term programme of social reform (Dewey, 1916; 1938; Freire, 1970; 1973). For instance, insofar as progressive education is concerned with nurturing good citizens, it comes into this category, and whereas a radical reading of this aim would indicate that educational activities should challenge and help overthrow the status quo, the neo-conservative view insists that education should promote cultural restoration, such as the values associated with one's nationality or community and of family life (Beck, 2003: 21).

How this broad category of social aims ought to be made specific depends very much on the social and historical context. For example, in some countries, the education system arguably needs to foster multiculturalism and cultural integration; education should enable people to live and participate in a culturally diverse society (OECD, 1997).

Despite the wide variety of conflicting views that come under this umbrella, nevertheless, what they have is a very important common core, namely that educational activities should primarily serve certain ends of society. One might argue for this general claim as follows: education is a socio-political activity that is carried out by a society to ensure its continuation and to further its development. Society has a legitimate interest in such ends, and education is a *sine qua non* of these goals. Therefore, the primary aim of education ought to be to serve these objectives.

Education as a means to academic advancement

According to this claim, education is primarily about learning, which is narrowly defined as the acquisition of knowledge and the relevant academic skills. This view tends to be associated with the claim that there is a certain common cultural heritage that all students should study. However, the view does not need to be wedded to a particular programme of study or to a specific conception of the common heritage or even to the assertion that there is a clearly identifiable common heritage in any cultural tradition.

More generally, the idea is that education is a series of activities whose ultimate goal is learning. 'Learning' in this context is an achievement word; one has to succeed in order to be said to have learned; it is not sufficient to try. Therefore, the activities of learning inherently involve certain norms or standards that define what actually counts as learning, as opposed to failing to learn (Hirst, 1971). In other words, education involves norms that are defined primarily by the activity itself rather than by the external needs of the society or those of the student. These norms are broadly intellectual or academic, and vary from subject to subject.

Each subject area is defined by the knowledge that comprises it, and by the methods of investigation and research that are employed to gain such knowledge. Student learning should be directed towards this body of knowledge (or parts of it) and should be in line with the methodology specific to the subject area. As a consequence, the types of skills that students need to acquire are defined broadly by this knowledge. The skills needed are those dictated by the academic subject. Likewise, the structure of the curriculum is, to some extent, determined by the logical progressions of the subject matter. Calculus, for instance, requires prior understanding of gradients and algebra.

Education as a means to the development of the individual

Educational activities should be aimed at the development and needs of the individual – in our case, the young person. This view has its roots in the work of Rousseau, who has inspired a host of educators, such as Pestalozzi, Maria Montessori, Rudolf Steiner and Parker Palmer, to mention just a few, who interpret this third aim holistically.

As with the first category, however, this third category clearly cuts across traditions. For example, in the liberal tradition, this aim is regarded in terms of the development of individual autonomy (Hirst and Peters, 1970; Bailey, 1984). According to this view, by definition, a person has the capacity to make free choices, which is called 'autonomy'. Therefore, as a defining feature of what it is to be a person and as the necessary condition for any choice, autonomy is the primary quality of individuals that education needs to promote. From this, it is claimed, much follows: for example, a person needs to be able to have rational thinking skills and good epistemological attitudes in order to be able to make informed choices for him- or herself.

In contrast, insofar as progressive education is concerned primarily with the development of individual persons, as opposed to that of democracy, then it also belongs to this third category. If the idea of progressive education is not so much to promote and enable a democratic society but, rather, to develop individuals who have the knowledge and critical skills for living within a democratic society, then progressive education belongs to this third camp. In a similar vein, insofar as radical educational philosophies are concerned primarily with the emancipation of individuals, rather than the transformation of society, they do too.

From the point of view of educational aims, there is a world of difference between 'we need to educate young people to improve society' and 'we need to prepare individuals for living in society'. The difference is who or what has primacy and this has huge pedagogical and curricular implications. The former statement, which might come from a government agency, belongs to the first category, and the latter, which might be the statement of a teacher, belongs to the third. The basic idea of the third category is that education ought to be aimed primarily at the development of individuals – children and young people.

Priorities

Teachers and students daily experience the conflicts between these three aims. While much time in the classroom is spent on academic studies, schools themselves as institutions can often be seen as serving social ends, rather like a business which has economic goals but also serves social ends. Furthermore, many students need practical or vocational training in order to meet the demand from workplaces, but at the same time, schools want to maintain high academic standards. Whereas a pragmatic and economic-minded school principal might scorn the attitudes that once made students learn Latin and Euclid's geometry, one can imagine an English teacher lamenting how writing business letters tends to replace the love of literature and the appreciation of poetry, or a physics teacher bemoaning how the applied sciences tend to water-down pure theory. One can sympathise with both sides. The tensions are manifest as a shortage of time: there is not enough time to comply with the academic rigours of the curriculum, prepare students for adult life in a complex society, as well as look after them as individuals.

Of course, we need, and can have, both a pragmatic education for the sake of the future society and an academic one focused on knowledge. However, the idea of finding a balance between these two makes little sense unless there is a third principle that enables these two views to be reconciled. This third principle, we shall argue, is the development of the individual in a humane way.

In policy and practice, in reality, the three types of aim are mixed up. Different educational institutions will have each in varying degrees of priority. So, for example, whereas early primary school education, especially one that is open to a child-centred approach, might emphasise the third, academic institutions of higher learning will stress the second. Furthermore, government policy typically includes all three kinds of aims (see the National Curriculum rationale). One might be tempted to characterise the policy position of the English National Curriculum as the view that the first aim is paramount, and that the other two aims are subsidiary. The government makes many statements that imply this.

Nevertheless, this is perhaps not a fair description of the view. For instance, the UK government also has the development of children as human beings explicitly as part of its vision for education, despite the fact that it often stresses the socio-economic role of education. Here we summaries the aims of the new National Curriculum (released in 2008):

The curriculum should enable all young people to become:

- successful learners who enjoy learning, make progress and achieve;
- confident individuals who are able to live safe, healthy and fulfilling lives;
- responsible citizens who make a positive contribution to society.

(QCA)

This shows that the UK government does indeed have individual development as an aim. For this reason, it might be more accurate to portray orthodox positions as claiming that educational activities will have all three kinds of aim. To that one might add: governments and institutions may put different emphasis on the three elements according to the needs of the country. It is apparently a question of balance, culture and choice.

We challenge this position by arguing that putting the human being or person at the centre of the education process cannot be an issue of emphasis, balance and choice. Instead of balancing these aims, it is a question of correctly understanding the value relationships between them. We will argue that the development of the individual is, or ought to be, the primary aim; the others have a subsidiary relationship to it, which is not merely a question of balance. To claim otherwise would be to misplace the values in the relationship, as if one said, for example: 'It's a question of balancing the needs of the house and the car, with my own well-being.' Cars and houses are instruments for human well-being, and do not compete with it, so the comparison is not between like and like.

Furthermore, although the third category takes many specific forms, we shall argue for a particular understanding of what 'the development of the person' means in the context of secondary education. What we call the 'human-centred' approach involves three core considerations. The first is Kant's claim that the individual should not be treated merely as a means but should be respected as a person. This claim helps delimit the instrumentalisation of the education processes. The second is a broadly Aristotelian conception of human flourishing. Third, education should be addressed to the person as a whole rather than one aspect, such as the intellect. We shall argue that, together, these principles amount to the idea that secondary school education (at least between the ages of 14 and 16) ought to be a process of enabling young people to find the meanings in their lives. Although this may seem like a radical departure from government policy, and in many ways it is, it nevertheless emphasises elements that are already present in current education policy. It takes very seriously the idea that education is a process of enabling young people to live fully developed human lives in contemporary society, and makes this aim central to determining the appropriate pedagogy, designing the curriculum, formulating assessment and developing school life around this content (within a Kantian constraint) rather than trying to add in additional social and academic ingredients, which can end up distorting and diluting the process. Another part of the difference between existing policies and our conclusions is that 'preparing a person for adult life' is an anodyne phrase, which becomes translated in practice largely as providing young people with general knowledge, basic skills and, for some, a rudimentary specialisation. In contrast, 'finding the meanings of one's life' is rich and strongly value-laden, and what it means in practice might seem like an impossible and even incomprehensible metaphysical task. We will try to make this comprehensible, practically possible and a welcome activity.

The first consideration for the priority

There are two reasons for thinking that the development of the individual person ought to be paramount. The first, which relates to the Kantian thread in our discussion, is a rather abstract consideration, and it attempts to show that, in general, people necessarily have primary value among all other things of value, such as novels, factories, companies and toys. This is because all value claims function to guide self-conscious choice. If we say that something or some activity is valuable, the point of that claim is to guide some potential choice. Thus, the very meaning of value claims is dependent on choosers, or beings that can make choices, and by definition, beings that can make choices are sentient, and in terms of formal education, this means persons. This can be put simply but roughly: values exist only because of persons (Kant, 1998).

This point provides a good preliminary perspective on some of the ways in which things can be valuable. Beings that can make choices have a primary value in themselves, but those beings, or rather, persons, are not separate from the lives they are living. Your life is you in time. However, a person's living is made up of a complex web of activities and experiences, such as going out with friends, painting, eating and taking an interest in nature. These activities and experiences are non-instrumentally valuable as part of a person's life. They are part of or aspects of the process of living. Some material things such as books, toys and ski-shoes are valuable primarily by their enabling relationship to these activities and experiences. Many other material things have a secondary or instrumental value by making the production and working of the primary material things possible or more efficient. This is the value of electrical generators, accounting programmes and cargo trucks.

Of course, the ways in which life's activities, experiences and processes can be non-instrumentally valuable varies, as does what counts as an appropriate appreciation of the relevant valuable characteristics. For example, the chess was challenging, the music was moving and the skiing was exhilarating. In order for playing chess to be non-instrumentally valuable for the player, he/she has to be able to appreciate this feature of the game (among other characteristics). This appreciation requires perceiving or attending to the game in a particular way, and in turn, this requires, for instance, a particular attitude – feeling a desire to win that is not overwhelming as opposed to an apathy that is underwhelming. Another point that will emerge as crucial later is that the value of some activities involves connecting to the valuable nature of things and people outside oneself.

The second consideration for the priority

There is a second kind of consideration that shows us that the development of the individual person ought to be paramount among the three general aims of education. It is that the other two kinds of ends are subsidiary. In general terms, human development and well-being ought to take priority over academic standards and the needs of social institutions. However, this is a delicate point. It does not mean that the development of the individual always takes priority over the other two in all specific circumstances. Nor does it mean that the other two are valuable merely as a means to the development of the individual. Academic standards and political beliefs cannot be reduced to aspects of the development of the individual, but they have value only in relation to the value of the life of the individual.

Academic values

Let us explore this point in relation to academic notions. There are academic values, such as truthfulness, carefulness in research and being imaginative and open to other points of view. These general values translate into more specific standards within different areas of knowledge. So, for example, a good piece of work in the natural sciences would involve a carefully framed hypothesis and a controlled experiment designed to try to falsify the hypothesis. The written work would have to systematically lay out the procedure used to test the hypothesis. There are other kinds of standards specific to the interpretation and writing of poetry or to the understanding of a culture. These general academic values, and the various specific standards that they give rise to, are not reducible to the well-being of people. They are not valuable merely as instruments for people's well-being.

Nevertheless, these values are related to and serve human well-being in a less direct manner. The norms depend on the activities in question: they are the criteria for what counts as good research, or as a good interpretation of a play or as a good argument. They are supposed to guide these activities, even if indeterminately. This is why, although there are similar underlying general values, activities in different areas of knowledge, interpretation, communication and creativity typically will involve quite different specific standards. However, the main point is that these are all human activities. There may be norms or evaluative criteria that guide what counts as a good painting, but this issue matters only because painting as an activity is an important part of life. Likewise, doing scientific research is an important part of life. Therefore, the related norms matter. The norms of tiddlywinks matter less.

To say that painting is an important aspect of human life means that it is the kind of activity that can contribute to a life of well-being and meaning for humans – artists and spectators alike. Of course, not everyone is interested in painting. However, perhaps we can say this: everyone would benefit from having some activities in his or her life that are *like* or akin to painting. A person who does not enjoy the visual aesthetic experience of, for example, forms and colours, or someone who does not have the opportunity to create visually attractive things, or to create artistically at all, will have significantly valuable aspects of their life missing. The standards that pertain to painting cannot be reduced to well-being, but the activity of painting is valuable as part of well-being.

Similar kinds of considerations are relevant to scientific research and the host of values that pertain to truth. In such investigations, we have to be honest about the facts. This means that we must try to avoid error or ignorance. This may not be easy because, on the one hand, carrying out research can require guesswork and supposition, which may lead us into error, while on the other hand, the need to ward off false beliefs can lead to a caution that prevents exploration and creativity and keeps us ignorant. This value tension is encapsulated in the academic standards of various areas of knowledge (whether they count as disciplines or not), some more strict, others more lenient. The point is that these standards cannot be reduced to the value of human well-being and yet, nevertheless, the practices of investigating are activities that have value as part of human well-being. Finding out is part of human life.

We are not discussing here the hugely important instrumental value of scientific and other knowledge for society, or human life in general, but we are arguing that, as an educational goal in secondary schools, the development of the individual person has a general priority over academic aims. We should not think that education is solely about knowledge for its own sake. Knowledge is not a living entity with interests that human lives ought to serve. The very content of academic standards is defined by the investigative, interpretative, communicative and creative practices that form part of human life. Academic standards do not stand alone. They exist for people to have the right kind of relationship to truths and with each other in their investigations and interpretations.

As we will see in Chapter 2 where we discuss learning, there is a distinctive approach to knowledge and learning that embodies a human-centred approach and can be broadly called a virtue or quality-based epistemology.

Social and political values

Although education is unavoidably political, and has a social end, this is not an excuse for making it into a tool for social engineering. We should not try to design children so that they fit into a particular vision of society. One might be tempted to say: 'For the sake of social order, society needs compliant people; for the sake of economic competitiveness, society needs obedient workers who are happy to produce and consume; for the sake of its identity, society needs children to become adults who carry on its cultural traditions.' But can one be tempted to say 'For the sake of its security, society needs children who, as adults, are willing to lay down their lives for their country; for the sake of the revolution, society needs children to grow into class-conscious adults'? No! Instead of any of this, education should help young people to develop on their own terms, not society's. The child is not, first and foremost, a future citizen and worker; she is a person. Of course, she is and will be a member of and a contributor to a community and a society, but that is because she is a person with a human nature, and this comes first, as being social is part of being human.

The young person is not a cog in a machine, and because of this the classroom is not a political playground. However, while it constitutes a lack of respect to train a child to be part of the global economic mechanism, it would be cruel to not prepare him or her for the economic realities of working life. This might seem like splitting hairs. However, there is a world of difference between educating people in order to better society, and educating people to better themselves who thus can contribute to a better society. In the first, people are merely a means; in the second each individual is a socially contextualised end.

Dewey tried to explain that society ought to serve its people and education ought to foster certain virtues that enable the individual to become socially oriented towards a good life within a democratic society:

> A society which makes provision for participation in its good of all its members on equal terms and which secures flexible readjustment of its institutions through the interaction of the different forms of associated life is in so far democratic. Such a society must have a type of education which gives individuals a personal interest in social relationships and control, and the habits of the mind which secure social changes . . .
>
> (Dewey, 1916: 99)

It might be objected that the human-centred emphasis on individual development is too individualistic. The objection is that it embodies an atomistic, as opposed to a social, conception of the person. In reply, contrast the idea that the education of individuals is merely an instrumental means for increasing social capital with the individualism of the modern social contract theories of Locke and others, which render society a pact for mutual self-advantage. Both theories instrumentalise the relationship between the community and the individual, albeit in opposing directions, without giving any indication of any underlying value. It cannot make sense to picture mere instruments serving mere instruments ad infinitum. We need to transcend purely instrumental relationships.

In ancient Greek and Chinese cultures, the individual and the community were viewed as mutually constituted. People did not live in those societies merely for the sake of gaining benefit, but rather because humans are social and, by their nature, tend to live in relationships with others. Moreover, late twentieth century Western thinking has emphasised that the content of individual mental states is public, and requires social meaning. The psychological is social (Wittgenstein, 1953).

Yet, at the same time, this does not warrant embracing strong forms of cultural relativism that make the critique of a society's culture impossible (Thomson, 2002). Such a position would render it impossible to criticise the tendency of modern post-industrial societies to shape individuals so that they conform easily and instrumentally to the demands of society and production. (We might call it 'brain-washing', but it concerns our whole being, and it is not a cleaning process!)

The basis of the community as a common social space needs to allow individuals to be themselves. The idea of training young persons in order to fit into society is justifiable only when such training would allow them to be themselves. Beyond that point, we ought not try to force individuals to fit into society, but rather shape the ways of society so that individuals can grow freely within it. This is, in very rough terms, the principle that education needs to follow to be more human-centred, which is an alternative perspective to the instrumental principle prevalent in education today.

This has significant practical ramifications, especially in terms of the development of talent, direction of work and what might be called citizenship education. Purging the instrumental transforms these aspects of education, and, in their new transformed state, they are able to assume a more central role in secondary education. It is unacceptable that every year hundreds of thousands of young people leave school with very little idea of what kind of work they want to do, what their life might be and what kind of person they are. They are encouraged implicitly to become passive members of what is called 'the workforce'. It is important for a person to fit into a society well, but in a way that does not compromise the integrity of that person by, for example, turning him or her into simply a member of the workforce who contributes to a country's competitiveness and to an increase in GNP, and who obeys the laws and uses his/her critical faculties to choose who to vote for (not which party to vote for).

Conclusion

There are three broad types of educational aim: social, academic and personal. Of these, the third when properly conceived should have priority. So, when the academic and social conceptions of educational aim conflict, it is the third, the personal, that should be used to take a leading role and balance the requirements and recommendations of the other two.

Back to the bigger picture: we are advocating an education that takes the individual person most seriously, and this (for the moment) has two requirements. The first is that education processes should treat the person as a human being, with appropriate respect and care, and the second is that the processes should enable individual human development. Both of these needs adopt the word 'human' explicitly as a value term. They are vague and broad. They need explaining as ideas before we can even think of their application in practice. This is what we will accomplish in the second part of this chapter.

De-instrumentalising education

This sounds horrible! Perhaps a better heading might have been: 'humanising education', except that there is more to humanising education than de-instrumentalising it. To be more accurate, we could have called the section 'anti-dehumanising education', but this sounds just as bad. Whatever the phrase, we shall argue that a misapplication of instrumental rationality to educational activities is a misunderstanding of the nature of value. It dehumanises us as human beings.

The theory of instrumental rationality

The tendency to instrumentalise is strong in orthodox educational thinking, and 'intensified instrumentalism' is apparent in the policies of governments of all colours (Beck, 2003: 24). This instrumentalisation is seen, for example, in the policy of making decisions purely on the basis of cost–benefit analyses. Since 'costs' and 'benefits' refer to resources spent and saved, they are implicitly financial and can be converted into monetary terms. Because of this, such cost–benefit analyses are purely instrumental.

Many thinkers critique education policies for being too instrumental. However, it is not clear when and why this is a mistake. After all, we need good rational instrumental thinking to avoid inefficiency, and since education is a preparation for the future, it is bound to be instrumental. We cannot criticise education for being instrumental! The objection might be that it is inappropriately instrumental – so when is instrumental reasoning in education appropriate and why?

Before we answer this question, there are three clarifications. The first is to do with terminology: when we refer to an activity as valuable or having value, this means roughly that there are reasons for performing the action. These reasons can be overridden; they are not conclusive; it might be better to do something else in the particular context. These reasons are also a feature of the action or activity, such as it being enjoyable or useful, which are supposed to guide or be relevant to choosing/making a decision. To justify an action is simply to cite some guiding reason for performing it. A value claim is the assertion that something is valuable.

Second, we need to distinguish being valuable instrumentally and non-instrumentally. When something is valuable only instrumentally, it is good because of what it leads to, enables, facilitates or prevents. When something is valuable non-instrumentally, then it is valuable for what it is. Typically, money is valuable only instrumentally, and happiness is valuable non-instrumentally. Many things, such as good health, are both. Note that sometimes the phrase 'intrinsically valuable' is used to signify being valuable non-instrumentally. This usage is misleading because 'intrinsic' is also usually opposed to 'relational' and so it suggests that when something is valuable non-instrumentally, it has to be so non-relationally, or without relation to other things such as context and human nature. This suggestion makes non-instrumental value absolute, mysterious and problematic.

Third, we need to clarify a point that is related but not central to our discussion. In many societies there is a strong tendency to justify all value-claims instrumentally by citing some aim or purpose. Of course, this is not a problem when the value claim is instrumental. However, it is a mistake to justify non-instrumental values instrumentally. For example, we don't want to explain why schools have playtime only by citing the fact that it helps children concentrate better in their studies. The tendency to justify all value claims instrumentally is problematic because it cannot be true that all values are purely instrumental. Means require ends, or things have instrumental value only because something else has non-instrumental value. The problem is that many kinds of activities, such as work and study, are valuable in both kinds of way. The tendency to explain or justify value-claims only instrumentally ignores the intrinsic value of the activity. This is an important point, but it is not the main issue that we shall pursue here.

Most orthodox views of education depend on the theory of instrumental rationality. The theory claims that, given that a person wants X, and that in order to obtain or achieve X he/she will have to perform certain actions, which are means to X, then according to instrumental rationality the following theses will be true:

1. As means, these actions have only instrumental value.
2. The goal or end, X itself, has intrinsic value as such.
3. Thus, the person ought rationally to always choose the most efficient means to this given end.

The theory equates intrinsic value with goals, and instrumental value with means. It assumes that only goals or ends have intrinsic value, and means as such must have instrumental value. In other words, according to the theory, only the goals of an activity can make the activity worthwhile and, consequently, the activity itself has only instrumental value in relation to those goals (Thomson, 2003).

This way of understanding the value of our actions is so prevalent that it may be difficult to notice it or even see the huge ramifications of denying it. For example, such rationality underlies much economic thinking about, as well as the popular conception of, work. According to this conception, work is only an instrumentally valuable means to certain ends; the value of our work is only in the results. For a company, this means the contribution of the work to profits or institutional goals, and for the individual, his or her earnings and livelihood. This way of thinking puts results before the experience of working; indeed it rejects work as a (non-instrumentally) worthwhile activity. Given this conception of work, we ought to expect the theory of instrumental rationality to provide a similar view of education and to undermine human values in educational processes. In this manner, orthodox views of education reflect some of the basic assumptions of our society, and a critique of those views must be – at the same time – an evaluation of those aspects of modern society.

The theory of instrumental rationality finds its most abstract expression in a simplified version of some standard economic theories, which assume that the value of any activity is the utility that it produces. Utility can be explained in terms of pleasure and the absence of pain, or alternatively in terms of individuals' preference functions. It is a very neat theory. If all actions are valuable merely instrumentally as means to utility, then it is theoretically possible to weigh or quantify the value of any action and compare it to any alternative action under the circumstances. While, of course, the contingencies of the future place a practical limitation on rationality defined in these terms, the theory nevertheless provides, in principle, a theoretical decision-making procedure, a rudimentary form of cost–benefit analysis to help identify the best decision or course of action in any situation. While it is true that no economist would accept such an undeveloped theory without adding many caveats and conditions, the outlined theory captures the essence of a way of thinking that is prevalent in our society, even in education. This simplistic economic theory has three elements: the value of any action lies in its results; there is one underlying good, namely utility; and this good can be measured quantitatively. For the moment, we will refute only the first element of the economic view of rationality, which is the theory of instrumental rationality.

To repeat, the theory of instrumental rationality assumes that means have only instrumental value and the only things that have intrinsic value are ends. It identifies means with instrumental value, and ends with intrinsic value. It fails to separate instrumental from intrinsic value, and means from ends.

This theory cannot be true because of two simple but fundamental points. The first is that, insofar as something is valuable only instrumentally, it is dispensable and replaceable. Its use is a cost only, and it is always rational to reduce costs. If one could achieve the goal effortlessly without costs then that would be the rational thing to do. Since most, and possibly all, of our activities are means to goals, the theory of instrumental rationality implies that all those activities are costs that we must pay and endure for the sake of the ends. In other words, instrumental rationality is bound to portray human activities as only instrumentally valuable.

The second point is that, if we can identify a person with his or her life and with the many activities that comprise it, then the theory of instrumental rationality implies that we should treat ourselves purely as instrumentally valuable means to goals. It means that we should regard ourselves, and our lives, as dispensable tools, whose use constitutes a cost that should be minimised for the sake of greater efficiency.

In value terms, it turns us into machines whose sole value is to produce results and, in economic terms, into assets or capital whose entire value is their use. Weber (1958) points out that

This order is now bound to the technical and economic conditions of machine production which today determine the lives of all the individuals who are born into this mechanism . . .

(p. 181)

In this sense, the theory places the relevant value relationships completely back to front. Machines and assets are meant to serve persons rather than the other way round (and vice versa). The theory attempts to turn us into assets.

There is no escape from this point, for example, by claiming that it is sometimes expedient and brings the best overall consequences to regard persons temporarily as machines and assets. The claim that if we sometimes regard ourselves as machines, then this will make us wealthier, and consequently happier, does not constitute a good reply to our objection against the theory of instrumental rationality. Our original argument against the theory was *not* that it had bad results! That would have been a self-defeating argument. The claim was that the theory is, in principle, erroneous; it constitutes a value-category mistake. Therefore, the counter reply has to try to undermine that assertion about principle, and the claim that the theory of instrumental rationality sometimes has beneficial results is *not* a good counter-argument.

The rejection of the theory of instrumental rationality does not imply that we should abandon goals and results. It does not entail that they are valueless or that we ought not to work to achieve them efficiently. However, it does require us to reconceptualise their significance, and this is a really important point for education. Putting the human first requires not putting the goals first, and not treating a person merely as an instrument to achieve those goals. In this way, the denial of the theory of instrumental rationality, first, opens up new territory in which such vital concepts as 'purpose' and 'work' need to be reframed because the value relationship between activities and goals is reversed; and second, the denial frees us from equating intrinsic value with goals or ends, and means with instrumental value. The point of this principle is that ends or goals are no longer identified with non-instrumental value; rather, their significance is how they define or contribute to or improve the agent's life, processes and activities. It is the person's life and activities that have intrinsic value.

Application in education

We can see that the rejection of instrumental rationality constitutes a whole world of difference in education. Let's look at it from the point of view of the child or young person. If the culture of education is steeped in instrumental rationality, then the child or young person is being given the message that he/she *is* a student and the *raison d'être* of a student is to accomplish certain goals. He/she is identified with her role, which is defined instrumentally. This is equivalent to denying his or her personhood. To avoid this, we must overcome the tendency to identify persons (including ourselves) with their roles, and this requires a new conception of educational and school culture.

In more enlightened schools, the individual may be regarded as an instrument to his or her own better future; in less enlightened ones, merely as an instrument to better institutional performance and academic attainment scores. The young person perceives that, from the point of view of the teachers and the system, his or her time at school is only instrumentally valuable. In this way, he/she is encouraged to regard most of his/her activities at the school in the same way: merely as means to certain goals, such as to please teachers, avoid trouble, gain good grades, come top in the class, or even to 'invest' in his/her own future.

In effect, schooling is conceived only as a means in two ways: institutionally, in relation to the kinds of goals mentioned earlier, and by the students, in relation to their personal goals such as pleasing the teacher, or becoming a skilled professional. Given the theory of instrumental rationality, insofar as an activity is a means, then it is, *ipso facto*, only instrumentally valuable. Therefore, given this theory, what takes place in schools is basically only a cost: something that must be reduced or cut in order that the aim can be achieved more efficiently. Of course, this is a very good training for a life of work in a society that tends to instrumentalise all things of value, but that is not a recommendation!

Childhood and adolescence are not just a preparation for adulthood. They are part of a life. We have observed that secondary schooling (in the UK) in particular is often an unpleasant process for most young people, who feel passive as they are taught, confined to desks in the classroom, and who often find the subjects taught to them dry, remote and uninteresting. (See Chapter 10 for more views of the young people who were interviewed for our research.) We are tempted to say that such schooling is not relevant – but relevant to what? And if one answers 'to the concerns of young people', then the following question arises: 'Must everything be relevant to those concerns? Can schooling also include expanding those interests?'

In contrast, secondary schooling has the potential to be a wonderful time of life for young people. Imagine time for oneself, being more independent, to be together with other young people one's own age, and people of different ages, and to find out more about life and explore a million different things. During adolescence, one is not a child anymore and so has some of the pleasures of being treated as an adult, and yet has fewer burdens (such as bank loans). Moreover, it is a time when one is newly oneself and becoming more oneself, and finding out what this means. Everything is fresh and free, and one can be open to infinite possibilities. In short, it could be wonderful – and yet it is often far from that. Why? Of course, to answer this question we have to ask the young people themselves – as we report in Chapters 4 and 10. In part, the answer is the system itself, which is built upon material insecurity. Perhaps, the fear of insufficiency, reinforced by habit, makes us forget that goals serve life processes rather than the other way around.

Good work and 'we' consciousness

An instrumentalised vision of education implicitly regards children and young people as having purely instrumental value to certain goals. The positive value is to treat children and young people as having intrinsic value and, as A.S. Neill proposed, 'adapting the educational system to fit the child rather than the other way around'.

For a quick glance at what a less instrumentalised vision of education might look like, we might examine some of the principles of good work. The purely instrumental conception of the value of work regards it as merely the meeting of supply and demand, as defined economically. From the demand side, work is a factor of production that can be substituted by other factors. For a company, it is a cost that should be minimised as far as possible in order to maximise profitable returns. Its value is its contribution to production. From the supply side, the value of work is the income earned. We exchange leisure for income. In working, we forfeit leisure for financial gain for the sake of consumption and hence increased utility. In other words, we exchange our leisure time for the benefits of consumption through the medium of money. According to this concept, leisure time is non-instrumentally good; work is only instrumentally so.

For people who hate their work, or for people who turn off life because their work is so dreary, unfortunately, the purely instrumental work/leisure distinction may resonate with their experience. However, for people who love their work, this way of drawing the leisure/work distinction makes no sense. A goat farmer in the Pyrenees loves his work, which comprises spending a great deal of time looking after the animals, making cheese and taking the cheese to the local markets to sell. He seldom takes time off work because he never distinguishes between what he does for a living and what he does for pleasure. The non-instrumental conception of the value of work makes the distinction between work and leisure less radical. In leisure time, we perform many activities, such as gardening, reading or playing with the children, the value of which is largely non-instrumental. Some of these activities can be work. If one is fortunate enough to really love one's job, as the goat farmer does, then the activities are much the same. Work is paid leisure.

Another example. A decorator who has spent a week painting a house might admire his finished work with a great sense of satisfaction. He has created a light and warm ambience in the house, and has thus contributed to improving the environment and well-being of its inhabitants. This is what he does best, and he takes ownership of every piece of his work in a way similar to an artist who owns their work. When the house owners praise the quality and craftsmanship of the painting, the decorator feels a sense of pride. The fact that the decorator is paid a sum of money does not alter the quality of his craftsmanship. His craftsmanship depends on his sensitivity to value beyond himself.

For work to be meaningful in this way, it must satisfy at least five criteria:

1. We must work in collaboration and meaningfully with others.
2. It must connect to something of value beyond oneself.
3. The person must own his/her work in the way that one owns one's hobby.
4. It must fit the person's talents and temperament.
5. Work must present opportunities for personal learning and development.

Whether these principles are exhaustive depends on how generously one defines them. For example, variety is an important facet of meaningful work, but this could be included in condition (4). For work to be good, the doer has to be generally happy with it, but this point ought to be read in light of all the conditions.

Let us expand point (1). The majority of adults spend most of their waking time at work. It is an important form of relationship and a way of being with others. People work in teams or in cooperation with others. Through their collaborative efforts and shared experience, they develop a collective consciousness of 'us'. It is crucial to have a working environment that allows one to care for and form friendships with one's colleagues. We share a huge part of our lives and effort. Jobs that do not permit full working relationships and a sense of being part of a group are less valuable for this reason. Likewise, for most young people, the most important aspect of school is their friends, and perhaps, to a lesser extent, their teachers. Through studying and developing together, young people grow a 'we' consciousness. These relationships are valuable as a part of living and the school has to be structured in such a way as to facilitate them. In sharp contrast, large schools are often impersonal and students sometimes have different classmates for each lesson. Teachers certainly work with many different students throughout the day and may see each student infrequently. There are few opportunities for closeness.

Let us move to (2). Work contributes to a greater good. In order for work to be good and meaningful, one needs to understand how it does this – what is the value and point of what one is doing? It is vital to see how one's work contributes to the production of a good or the provision of a service, and how it fits into the collective effort of the company or organisation, or society at large. Also, it is important to understand how the good or service is itself valuable. No job is so menial that the person who does it deserves disrespect. Respect requires enabling the person to appreciate his or her own contribution. Moreover, some people have work that is interesting, and the work conditions need to facilitate this way of connecting to the value of one's work. Meaningful activities connect to something of value beyond us. To find work meaningful, one has to be able to appreciate and discover that connection (both instrumentally and non-instrumentally).

The same applies to learning. Institutions and teachers need to help young people to understand why they are studying the matter in hand and why the curriculum is as it is. In addition, the learning process has to allow the student to connect to the material in a way that reveals, maintains and deepens its interesting facets for him or her.

(3) Work as a hobby: hobbies are entirely self-motivated. They are activities that one generates and does for pleasure and the love of them. Work can be like that too. Getting paid can only make it better. There is a lot that can be done in a workplace to facilitate that kind of relationship to one's work. Likewise, the same applies to school learning. Young people need to have an active input into how and what they learn. The curriculum needs to be designed in order to make learning a hobby. Of course, there can be a significant difference between hobbies on the one hand and work on the other – one's responsibility to others, for instance. In this sense, work is more like a team sport than a hobby and in this sense, too, school learning is often more like a hobby than a team sport: one has fewer obligations to others.

(4) Talents and temperament: most people have (and perhaps everyone has) a more or less distinctive set of abilities that might be considered a talent. These would be something that comes easily to the person, which she enjoys doing and which he/she can do exceptionally well. The talent does not have to be a readily identifiable and marketable set of skills. It might be much more related to their temperament or quite idiosyncratic. For example, some people have the ability to make others feel at ease very quickly or have the ability to form certain kinds of relationships. Talent easily merges into temperament. Such endowments, however, are capacities and will remain dormant unless the person has the opportunities to exercise, develop and feed them. As well as developing and

identifying one's talents, one also needs to shape them so that they can be used in productive useful work. The idea that a talent comes easily, therefore, does not mean that fostering it does not require effort!

(5) Good work allows one to develop. As a form of self-expression, work is also a way for us to become more self-aware. This awareness in turn provides feedback for the ways we need to foster our own unique qualities in order to make our work better. 'Betterment' means improving the quality of our work, and enhancing the way our work contributes to the greater good. In this way, work motivates a person to continue to learn, and develop.

As Dewey put it, when one's work is what one is suited to do, it becomes an occupation, and when what one does as an occupation contributes to the greater good, one is in a state of happiness:

> An occupation is the only thing which balances the distinctive capacity of an individual with this social service. To find out what one is fitted to do and to secure an opportunity to do it is the key to happiness.
>
> (Dewey, 1916)

Claiming the dignity and nobility of work does not mean that we care little about the responsibilities of institutions and society to provide the appropriate conditions and environment within which one works. The ennobling of work has to go hand-in-hand with dignifying and humanising the place where one works (Kliebard, 1999).

The educational critique

In the above section, we examined some of the principles underlying a non-instrumental conception of the value of work. We did so in order to illuminate briefly the kinds of characteristics that such an education might have; these are points that we will return to in Chapter 6. Now it is time to return to the main discussion of this chapter – the aims of education.

It is unfortunate that schooling involves a series of activities whose value tends to be defined solely by the ends or goals of both the individual and the institutions. The problem with this is that something of purely instrumental value is replaceable and dispensable, and its use is a cost that should be – rationally – reduced as much as possible in the attaining of the goal. Human lives, and parts of those lives, do not fit into such a category. Thus, it is not a question of balancing the three kinds of aims that we mentioned at the outset. Such a balancing act would imply that, sometimes, we are forced to treat ourselves and others as less than we are (i.e. as less than human) for the sake of increasing wealth or completing a task. Rather, the issue is to re-conceive the relationship between the three aims so that we respect the sharp difference between what is intrinsically valuable and what is instrumentally valuable(rather than trying to balance or juggle them).

As the work of John Holt testifies, insofar as schooling is purely instrumental, it requires coercion (Holt, 1964). Because distant goals may seem psychologically remote to a child or young person, it seems reasonable to apply carrots and sticks to add further inducements. By its very nature, coercion is motivation that is purely instrumental. This constitutes a reinforcing cycle or feedback loop (we will not use the word 'positive' here). Indeed, this is a bit of a chicken and egg situation because coercing children works precisely by instrumentalising their motivation. We argued that such coercion is wrong in itself, as well as damaging to the development of the autonomy of the child.

Another major problem with this is much less frequently mentioned, and it is pedagogical. Such coercion deprives the child of the opportunity to appreciate and connect to the real values involved in the process or activity. Instrumental motivation bypasses content. Insofar as a student responds to instrumental considerations, he/she is not connecting to the content and to the intrinsically valuable nature of the activities and materials in question. In this sense, because learning must be appreciation, instrumentalism contradicts the very nature of learning. Indeed, this is a central point about learning, which we will stress in the next chapter. Moreover, such connecting is vital to living a happy life in a human way. It is the key to being in the present moment. We live happily by appreciating the value of what we are currently doing, and a recipe for 'living at half-mast' is to be always thinking of something else. Therefore, insofar as schooling habituates us to respond primarily to instrumental motivations, it thereby teaches us a bad lesson, one that ultimately defeats the overall purpose of education.

Of course, we could include the human qualities of the learning process as one of the pedagogical aims in our lesson plan. This would be a huge improvement on not including them at all, but the main critical point would still remain. It is one thing to improve the process because it is one of the goals that one has to accomplish, and it is quite another to improve the process because one is responding to the children or students as humans. The first remains within instrumental rationality; the second goes beyond it. We shall address specific goals and their measurement in Chapter 9.

Putting the human first requires not putting the goals first, and not treating the person and his/her activities merely as an instrument to achieving those goals. While we will explore in later chapters what this implies in practice, we can already see that this underlies a practical dilemma that many teachers wrestle with. Many recognise that the system tends to instrumentalise children (even if it is putatively for their own future benefit) and struggle to make the culture of the classroom freer and less task-driven. At the same time, they feel squashed within a system that sets relatively rigid goals, which are not easy for many children to attain. There is not enough time for both work and play when these are defined as mutually exclusive opposites. Many young people actively dislike school, and insofar as we are willing to accept this as a given, unfortunately, this indicates that we are willing to treat those young people as an instrument to larger aims.

To regard a young person *as a person* implies treating him or her with respect. As we shall see, this respect requires us to reconsider many aspects of current educational practice. For example, it requires us to rethink the size of schools: big schools are impersonal institutions where young people cannot easily form stable and long-lasting relationships with teachers and other adults. They are institutions in which teachers and mentors cannot easily have deep knowledge of any individual student, and in which it is harder to build relationships of trust. In these ways, putting students in a big school is a way of valuing less these aspects of the educational process. And to devalue these aspects is to pay less respect to the student as a person.

Responding to objections

Let us consider the major objections to what we are saying. First, young people themselves often see their education in instrumental terms and this may seem justifiable: without the right qualifications or exam certificates, one cannot easily make material progress in life, and one's future quickly becomes more limited. According to this view, students regard their learning as a means to an improved future life, and this perception helps them to be more focused on their studies; it is the most direct motivation for teachers to appeal to, and it gives a point and structure to their studies.

Let us be clear. The point of the above objection is *not* to try to justify exams and certification per se but rather to challenge the critique of instrumental rationality that we have given in this chapter (we will return to the specific point about exams in Chapter 9). The challenge is that education is a means to self-improvement. The challenge misses the mark because the critique is *not* that goals do not matter. It is to reframe how they matter so that goals are not the main source of value, but the living of life is. As we said earlier, goals matter primarily insofar as they define, improve and enable life processes. The value of running in a competitive race is not in the winning, but in the running-to-win.

Of course, winning also enables more running later on too, but this also reinforces the main point. This does not mean that all running should be competitive! It means that we usually misconceive the value of even competitive races by instrumentalising them (i.e. running them only for the sake of winning). Furthermore, this conception of the role of the goal does not imply that one should try less hard.

Let us translate this abstract point into educational ethos. School is a place where young people live most of their daily lives. The living processes that one undergoes in school should be understood as intrinsically valuable, to be enjoyed, savoured and appreciated. Otherwise, schooling does not treat the young people as persons. Those processes also have a direction that one might define with a handful of goals (or, if one is the Government, a lorry-load). But life-in-school is not for the sake of the goals.

The second objection might be that it is crucial for young people to form their own educational goals, and develop a strong sense of purpose. Indeed, one might argue that the main obstacle to excellence in education is apathy. Again, this objection to our critique misses the point. We shall be arguing later for the need to help students cultivate a strong sense of purpose. However, a strong sense of purpose is needed because this is a part of living better: not primarily because the results matter but, rather, because the person matters. For instance, young people need to be given the space to grow entrepreneurial qualities because this makes for a wider, more active and creative life, and not because it is good for the GNP. This is not to say that GNP is unimportant, but rather to assert that it is important precisely because people are valuable.

In addition, the idea that people need a strong sense of purpose does not justify the claim that they should treat themselves purely as a means to those purposes. A strong sense of purpose is needed to improve the quality of one's life, not for the sake of achievement per se.

A process has to have a direction and, in this sense, a point or purpose. One might call this 'a goal', but this does not justify encouraging student targets, especially 'performance targets' that are imposed from outside. It is important to weigh one's words to avoid language that implies support of the theory of instrumental rationality. In general, in the last two decades, educational language has become increasingly management-oriented in tone and content, and often (but not always) management discourse instrumentalises. It often implies that the value of any action resides in achieving a goal, and that the performance of the action is merely of instrumental value. As we have seen, this cannot be true.

Conclusion

If the critique of instrumental rationality is correct and relevant, then it transforms how the aims of education – the social, academic and human – should be conceived. Education should not be regarded as merely instrumentally valuable to certain ends or goals – whether these are the ends of society or of the individual herself – because this makes the result rather than the processes and activities of humans the font of value.

Indeed, even spiritual theories make this error: they tend to regard the individual and his or her life purely as an instrument to perfection (see, for example, Forbes, 2003). Perhaps this is not surprising since, insofar as religious views tend to treat all value as heavenly, then they must deny the value of living an earthly life except as a prelude or preparation for perfection. Spiritual traditions often reserve value for heaven. They tend to regard other values as a means to perfection.

Rejecting the theory of instrumental rationality liberates us to think of goals as instrumentally valuable and of means as intrinsically valuable. Goals are valuable insofar as they define and improve the quality of lived-through processes. The race makes running better. Goals improve the process of working.

However, we must also avoid instrumentalising all academic and other learning as part of the development of the individual. In part, what Bertrand Russell famously said about happiness also applies to individual development. To paraphrase, Russell affirmed that to pursue happiness is to lose it (see *The Conquest of Happiness* by Bertrand Russell, 1930). One finds happiness by engaging in activities and friendships and by concentrating on things of value other than one's own happiness. Likewise, a person who pursues directly his or her own development will become stuck. One develops not by focusing on oneself and one's growth rate, but in large part by appreciating more deeply the valuable aspects of life around one. Critical and appreciative self-reflection is still an important part of this process, but one has to have a life to reflect upon, and that life consists largely of one's relationships and interactions with other people.

Therefore, to have an informal or hidden curriculum or an institutional culture that is focused entirely on self-development is like cutting away the branch one sits on. To develop is (in part) to expand one's horizons. In essence, this is why the value of learning for its own sake cannot contradict the idea that individual development is *the* fundamental aim of educational processes. Here is one way in which the rejection of the theory of instrumental rationality helps us: regarding learning as a means to individual development does not require us to instrumentalise the value of learning. Learning can be a valuable process in and of itself (non-instrumentally), and yet also still be a means. In this way, we can preserve the autonomy of the second kind of aim whilst still asserting the primacy of the third. This means new thinking in order not to short-change either in our theory.

Further reading

Aristotle (1976) *The Nicomachean Ethics*. London: Penguin.

Elster, J. (1986) Self-realization in work and politics: the Marxist conception of the good life. *Social Philosophy and Policy*, 3, 97–126.

Marples, R. (ed.) (1999) *The Aims of Education*. London: Routledge.

Noddings, N. (2003) *Happiness and Education*. New York: Cambridge University Press.

Pring, R. (2004) *Philosophy of Education: Aims, Theory, Common Sense and Research*, London: Continuum.

Raz, J. (2005) The myth of instrumental rationality. *Journal of Ethics and Social Philosophy*, 1(1), 2–28.

Schroeder, M. (2004) The scope of instrumental reason. *Philosophical Perspectives*, 18, 337–64.

White, J. (1982) *The Aims of Education Restated*. London: Routledge and Kegan Paul.

White, J. (1997) *Education and the End of Work – A New Philosophy of Work and Learning*. London: Cassell.

Winch, C. (2002) The economic aims of education. *Journal of Philosophy of Education*, 36(1), 101–17.

2
The nature of learning

Introduction

Human-centred education is based on three main principles: first, that education should treat the person in a human way, humanely; second, that education should be directed towards the development of the human person; third, that it should be concerned with the person as a whole human being. Paulo Freire (1992) advanced a similar view: he coined the term 'conscientization' to refer to an educational process that enables people to become more fully human (see also Rogers, 1979). In his book, however, Freire does not explain what it means to be 'fully human', so in this chapter we will start to remedy this defect by examining the nature of learning.

In Chapter 1, we argued the case for the first two principles. We will now examine the third principle from two angles: with reference to the nature of learning (in this chapter), and in relation to motivation and emotion (which we will cover in Chapter 3). The aim of this chapter is not to provide a comprehensive theory of learning.[1] It is, rather, to articulate a human-centred approach to learning, and to show how this helps us to better understand learning and teaching. What is human-centred learning?

We shall discuss two ways in which the principles of human-centred education define a distinctive approach to learning. First, in very general

▶

---

[1] A theory of learning ought to tell us what learning is and how it occurs; it should encompass all learning in a general theoretical framework, such as Mezirow's transformative learning theory. Our aim is much less ambitious: we will highlight aspects of learning that are human-centred.

terms, the principles highlight the errors of treating people as objects. As we have seen, there is a perennial tendency to do this (i.e. treating people as objects or as tools) when formulating educational aims and goals, a tendency that the human-centred approach rejects. There is also an allied predisposition to treat the mind as an object, or a vessel, and hence learning as the acquisition of mental objects (Freire, 1992, Chapter 2). Learning becomes seen as a question of putting the correct mental objects (information, ideas, concepts, beliefs, etc.) in the correct part of the mind-vessel (or in contemporary cognitive science, in the brain). We shall show why this is an erroneous way of regarding learning.

Second, the human-centred approach has to be concerned with the development of the whole person, and this requires a view of learning that includes what can be broadly or roughly called a 'quality-based' or 'virtue-based' epistemology. This requires rewriting the traditional understanding of learning to allow the use of some relatively innovative pedagogical practices. The virtue-based approach also integrates academic learning into the development of the whole person, thereby avoiding some false dichotomies between the cognitive and non-cognitive, and between academic learning and vocational training. In short, it can help avoid a fragmented approach to learning, which divides the vocational from the academic, religious education from citizenship, and so on. If learning includes the development of certain qualities, then the personal development of the student and his/her academic path may coincide in some important ways. Likewise, despite the differences between vocational and academic training, they share the development of overlapping personal qualities or virtues.

In the second part of the chapter we will bring these two strands together to explore the concept of literacy and the distinction between understanding and knowing. How is it possible for someone to not really understand what he/she knows? This discussion will explore and explain the idea of the quality of a person's knowing. What does it mean to claim that someone knows well? How can learning have quality?

The questions that we will try to answer in both parts of this chapter are particularly relevant today. Internet and electronic technology make (and will continue to make) the acquisition of information easier for a significant segment of the world's population. We can imagine a perhaps not too distant future in which doctors can access diagnostic information about symptoms simply by thinking about them, in which lawyers can look up cases simply by connecting cerebrally to a database, and so on. Such future developments require us to challenge the idea that access to information is the key to expertise. They require us to ask: 'Can the acquisition of information constitute learning?', 'When does such access amount to knowledge?' and 'When can a person be said to understand what he/she knows?'

Conception of learning

The common and dictionary definition of learning is that it is acquisition, and that there are two broad categories of 'things' that one might acquire: knowledge and skills. We shall challenge this dictionary definition in three ways that we think are vital to understanding education.

Learning as acquisition – hiding intentionality

Learning is commonly defined as the acquisition of knowledge and skills; learning consists of *acquiring* some *thing*. This converts knowledge into a mental object, which is placed in the appropriate box in the mind (or brain) when learning occurs. We argue that learning cannot be the *acquisition* of some *thing*.

In technical terms, the argument is that reifying knowledge as an object is incompatible with the intentionality of cognition.[2] This is a much more important point than it may sound. Let us explain the term 'intentionality'. Whenever one perceives something, one does so within a certain range of descriptions as opposed to others (Searle, 1983). For instance, one can see a tree as a source of revenue, or in terms of its shape, or as a tree, or as part of a local ecosystem. Perception and cognition, in general, are always aspectual. As a result, a person can *believe* that she drinks water and that water is H_2O, and yet not *believe* that she is drinking H_2O if she does not make the link between the relevant assertions.

---

[2] Reifying is incompatible with intentionality. To reify is to treat something as an object. Objects have properties that do not depend on how one describes them. In sharp contrast, the subjectivity or intentionality of our experience is such that the content of our experience depends on how one describes what one experiences. In other words, the subjectivity of experience cannot be made into an object without betraying its nature.

The third statement ('she believes that she is drinking H_2O') just does not logically follow from the other two. In other words, the following argument is not logically valid:

1. person A believes that she is drinking water;
2. person A believes that water is H_2O;
3. therefore, person A believes that she is drinking H_2O.

The conclusion does not follow from the premises. People have contradictory beliefs. The person may not have made the relevant connection and not realise that she is drinking H_2O. This illustrates how cognition is aspectual. A child aged 5 who is asked 'Which weighs more: a pound of stones or a pound of feathers?' will not attend to the connection between 'weighs' and 'a pound' and will be distracted by the greater relative density of the stones or by the greater amount of feathers (see Piaget, 1950). This is to say that much learning consists of, and all learning requires, attending to the relevant features of the situation. This means ignoring the irrelevant features or not getting caught up in them. It also requires not ignoring the relevant characteristics.

In these respects, the idea of acquiring an object is a very poor metaphor for learning and cognition in general. If I hand over an object to you, then you have acquired it and you have possession of it as a complete thing. Getting someone to see, believe or understand something is not at all like that. They will inevitably understand or know a phenomenon under some descriptions or circumstances but not others. Understanding is always partial, description-dependent and, in this sense, subjective.[3] The portrayal of cognition as the acquisition of mental objects, such as lumps of information, hides the aspectual nature of cognition, and in doing this conceals the very subjectivity of knowing, perceiving and learning.

Learning must be conceived as intentional; this point is important in three ways. First, the tendency to think of learning in terms of the acquisition of knowledge as a mental object reinforces the instrumentalist assumption that the only real issue is simply how to acquire knowledge in the most efficient manner. Whilst, of course, this tendency has a real point, i.e. 'we do not want to be inefficient', it also hides issues that are especially crucial to the understanding of learning. In the final analysis, these concerns relate to the idea that knowing can be of higher or lower quality, which we discuss in the second part of the chapter, and which challenge the instrumentalist assumption that the only relevant goal is to acquire knowledge and skills efficiently.

---

[3] This does not mean that it is subjective in the sense that the truth of the descriptions depends on the beliefs or wants of the person or subject. Wanting and believing something do not make it so. Nevertheless, understanding is intentional and, in this sense, subjective.

Second, the aspectual nature of learning is necessary for understanding phenomena such as paying attention and concentrating (Winch, 1998:134). Attention is doubly selective. Not only do we select what we focus on, but also how we focus on it. We always attend to something under a certain description. For example, we see a planet as red, or as round in shape, or as a cold, empty place, or as the potential home of imaginary aliens. (Note: in none of these examples are we attending to the planet *as* a planet or *as* part of a solar system.) This is a vital point in the learning of concepts, as we shall see, because such learning consists of being able to pick out relevant similarities, and ignore the irrelevant ones.

This is an important part of a teacher's role because he or she needs to able to anticipate students' errors and gaps, and have a sense of how students attend to things. Such a sense would help in making implicit connections explicit, and directing the students' attention to the aspects under consideration in many different contexts so that students know how to carry on and practise in a similar way.

Third, the aspectual and selective nature of attention is also important to better understand motivation. What we attend to most is what interests us. To concentrate is to pay attention to the relevant features of something apart from oneself (except in the case of introspection). In this way, to concentrate is to find something else interesting. Thus, to be concentrating on a lesson on the life cycle of bees is to find bees interesting and to want to learn more about them (Winch, 1998). This point underscores a point that will be important later regarding learning as a connection with the intrinsic value of the subject matter, which we shall return to in Chapter 3.

Being interested in a topic is largely a question of how one perceives it (and under what descriptions one sees it), which depends – in part – on how one connects it to other things of interest. As a consequence, teachers not only have to communicate their own passion for a subject, but also reveal or make apparent the interesting aspects and connections of the subject matter at hand.

So, despite the fact that language contains many such metaphors, learning is not like the acquisition of a mental object that one either has or does not have. It is much more of a shaded affair. Furthermore, the acquisition of a mental object model portrays cognition as passive as opposed to active. Indeed, the more we use descriptive nouns, rather than verbs (e.g. 'I have a belief' as opposed to 'I believe that') to describe cognitive processes, the more we tend to overlook the intentional or aspectual nature of learning and cognition.

In summary, 'acquisition' is a word suitable for referring to the transfer of objects but not for human cognition, which is aspectual and subjective. The idea of acquiring lumps of information, like cold custard, conceals the intentionality of cognition and therefore instrumentalises learning. In so doing, it lends a hand to an impoverished understanding of learning. A better understanding of cognition will enable us to facilitate more effective learning processes.

To learn is not to absorb or acquire mental objects such as pieces of information; this false view is presupposed within the incorrect and pernicious idea that it does not matter how the mental object gets in, so long as it does enter the mind and does so efficiently (i.e. without costing too much time). Rather, to learn involves perceiving in the appropriate manner. In the wider context of a person's development, what counts as an 'appropriate manner' must include the interesting facets of the subject matter, which cannot be constituted solely by a description of the 'interesting only for the sake of getting a reward'.

Some critiques of mainstream schooling misstate the point. For example, one hears the complaint that orthodox education *too often* involves learning as the transmission of information (see, for example, the social constructivist critique of learning from authors such as Piaget, 1926, and Lave and Wenger, 1991; or from humanistic learning theorists such as Rogers and Freiberg, 1993). However, the point really is that there is no learning that consists of transmitting chunks of information, and no remembering that consists of simply absorbing facts, putting them into the memory box and spitting them out later. This is not a question of *bad* learning, which is to be replaced by *good* learning. The point is rather that this is a thoroughly mistaken view of what *any* learning is.

In general, we tend to use nouns, such as 'thoughts', 'ideas', 'concepts' and 'feelings', to describe feeling and thinking, which is an understandable, but misleading, shorthand. It reinforces the tendency to model the mind (sic) on our everyday understanding of material objects. For normal everyday purposes, this is not problematic, but it creates many obstacles to the deeper understanding of learning that we require as educational theorists and psychologists, some of which we have explored in this section. It leads us to ask questions of the very general form 'Do you have it now?' as opposed to 'Can you do it now?' For instance, whereas the first question suggests that learning Spanish requires possessing something, the second indicates that it is a question of being able to do something (i.e. speak Spanish).

In this way, philosophically, the verb forms (such as 'A thinks', 'A feels' and 'A understands') are less misleading than the noun forms. The verbs also highlight the intentional and hence aspectual nature of thinking, feeling and seeing. (To say that perceiving is intentional implies that to perceive is to perceive that p, and the content of one's perceiving is articulated by the meaning of 'p' rather than what 'p' refers to or picks out.)

Knowledge and skills

The definition of learning as the acquisition of knowledge and skills faces another challenge. As we dig deeper into the nature of knowing, we find that knowledge and skills are not as distinct as we might have first thought. The standard definition seems to provide us with a hard and fast dichotomy between knowledge and skills, but this dichotomy is a false one because knowing can consist of complex sets of skills. The understanding of these issues can help us as educationalists. There are two important points here.

First, for much of the time that students are supposedly acquiring knowledge, they are actually building concepts. When we learn the fact that all living things are made of cells, this is actually part of the process of understanding the concept of a cell. Much classroom time is spent helping students understand and apply key concepts in a subject or topic. For example, in a biology class, the teacher may ask the students to observe the shapes of plants' leaves in different climates to illustrate the concept of adaptation. Of course, such concepts are not objects or ideas to be placed into the mind and so, strictly speaking, they are neither built nor acquired. Rather, to have a concept is broadly to be able to classify objects appropriately. It is a set of practices (Wittgenstein, 1953), central to which is the ability to recognise (paradigm) instances of the concept. To have a concept is to be able to recognise relevant similarities and differences. This point reinforces our earlier discussion of the importance of the aspectual nature of perception. For the student, the lesson is to be able to pick out the relevant similarities and ignore the irrelevant ones; this is a practice that requires seeing the relevance in different types of contexts. This immediately implies that such learning requires presenting similarities and differences under the right descriptions, and that one or two contexts would be insufficient to practise this skill.

The more abstract the concept, the more the relevant abilities are essentially about using language appropriately. For instance, to 'have' the concept of a dictator is to be able to say appropriate things about dictators, and especially to be able to pick out defining characteristics in relevant ways. It is more like mastering the appropriate use of vocabulary. All of this implies that learning concepts is a set of skills that require practice in diverse circumstances rather than an exposition of meaning (Stones, 1992: 22).

Returning to the example, the concept of a political dictator is abstract and actually difficult to define. A dictator is not just a bossy political leader, because a dictator could be benevolent. Hitler was a dictator despite the fact that he was elected into office. To explain what a dictator is requires grasping concepts such as 'election' and some understanding of the work of political leaders and the nature of power. To learn the concept, one has to have his/her attention directed to the relevant features in many different kinds of contexts. If learning concepts is a question of having classification skills over a range of contexts, and this requires seeing relevant similarities, then knowing this helps us design processes that facilitate the learning of concepts.

Classifying is an activity similar to continuing a series (Wittgenstein, 1953; McDowell, 2001). When one uses a word in a new context appropriately, one is continuing with past usage. For example, to understand the word 'vehicle' consists of – at least in part – knowing how to correctly and appropriately apply the term to instances of vehicles in many different kinds of contexts. It is not the contemplation of a mental object. It does not consist of knowing a rule, because the rule itself needs to be applied appropriately. It is a question of seeing the relevant similarities and carrying on in the same way – where 'same' and 'relevant' are essentially open-ended but not purely subjective. A person learning the concept of vehicle, then, not only has to be able to see the relevant similarities between cars, trains, buses, aeroplanes, carriages, trams, bicycles, boats, submarines, helicopters and airships but also know how to apply the word to new instances of vehicles. He/she would need to know what to say about skateboards and parachutes. Are they vehicles?

The point that is important here pedagogically is the idea that teachers should help students understand and apply key concepts rather than just acquire pieces of knowledge. With a full knowledge-based curriculum to munch on, students have a lot of details to digest without those details being adequately distinguished from overriding principles or central key concepts. In such a case, everything seemingly becomes reduced to the single levelled idea of information. It is the fate of many students to spend time learning detailed facts without having command of the overarching ideas and, much worse, without even knowing that areas of knowledge usually have general umbrella principles that make help one to make more sense of the bits (for more on this, see, for example, the International Baccalaureate Organisation's 'Theory of knowledge' http://www.ibo.org/diploma/curriculum/core/knowledge). Having knowledge does not make one at home in a subject area. Understanding the organising principles does.

In conclusion, much of so-called 'knowledge-learning' is in fact concept building, which consists of developing classificatory abilities, as well as the perceptual skills related to seeing relevant similarities and differences. This point questions the hard and fast 'knowledge–skill' dichotomy that forms part of the standard definition of 'learning'.

This dichotomy is put under pressure by another point. The British philosopher Gilbert Ryle established a new orthodoxy by distinguishing between 'knowing-that' and 'knowing-how', between propositional and practical knowledge (Ryle,

1949). Propositional knowledge, or knowing-that, is knowledge that some proposition is true. For instance, I know that force equals mass times acceleration or that Mercury is a planet. I know that the proposition expressed by a relevant sentence is true or false. In contrast, practical knowledge is constituted by knowing how to do something, such as ride a bike or perform a calculation. Such knowledge does not consist of knowing that a proposition is true or false; it consists of knowing how to perform some set of actions. Ryle's distinction is relevant to our discussion because it apparently supports the standard definition of 'learning', insofar as that definition requires a difference in kind between knowledge and skills.

However, Ryle's distinction has been challenged in at least two ways. First, one could argue that knowing-how is reducible to knowing-that (see, for example, Stanley and Williamson, 2001, on 'knowing how').

Second, one could claim that all knowing-that is at the root of practical knowing-how. According to this second idea, knowing-that is always a form of knowing-how: all propositional knowledge can be converted into (and ultimately is a form of) knowing-how. For instance, to know that Paris is the capital of France, it is necessary and sufficient to know how to answer a set of relevant questions about France, its capital and Paris.

There are reasons for thinking that knowing-how has some priority over knowing-that, although these points are contentious. First, if to know-that is to grasp the relevant propositions and know that they are true, then the standard account of knowing-that may imply that there exist Platonic ideal entities or non-physical propositions, which we grasp when we know-that.[4] In this case, it seems committed to an extravagant ontology.[5] Second, the best way to avoid this excessive ontological commitment is to adopt a broadly functionalist view of mental contents. According to this functional view, the content of our mental states does not consist in our being in a relationship to non-physical propositions. Rather the content is behavioural or action-based. According to this view, to affirm that a person believes that p (where 'p' is the content of his or her belief) is to assert that the person has various dispositions to behave in certain ways given his or her desires.[6] In summary, knowing-that requires grasping of

---

[4] Propositions are roughly the sense or meaning of a statement, independent of context. These are supposedly Platonic entities in that they do not exist as physical objects in space and time. The view that such Platonic entities exist is problematic.

[5] An ontology is a view about what kinds of things exist. The Platonic view is extravagant because it would be better if we could account for knowledge-that without invoking strange non-physical entities.

[6] According to a functionalist view, mental states are to be identified by their causal role, which means their typical causes and effects, including their potential effect on other mental states and behaviour (see Crane, 2001).

the relevant propositions, but this grasping is constituted by various know-hows because cognitive accessibility to the world must be understood in action-terms, according to a general functionalist theory of mind. To have the relevant knowledge is to have a range of know-hows.

As we said, this argument is contentious, especially because it relies on a functionalist theory of mind. However, if the argument is sound then it implies that there is no hard and fast distinction of kind between knowing-that and knowing-how, and this means that the traditional definition of learning is mistaken insofar as it relies on a dichotomy between knowledge and skills.

This is important pedagogically because the main way of learning skills is by doing, by guided practice and with feedback. To see the importance of this point, let us return to the first theme of this section. One significant set of know-hows is how to organise what one knows around the relevant principles and concepts (Brandsford *et al.*, 1999). For instance, a student learns the periodic table and the concepts of an element and atomic number as a set of principles around which to organise other knowledge. This means that the student has to know some of the relevant facts that can be organised around such principles; without such knowledge, the principles would have no personal meaning for the pupil. It also means that he/she has to pay attention to the relevant aspects of this knowledge. Thus, it is not a question of 'having' knowledge but attending to the salient features of the world, such as what things are composed of. Recognising the intentionality of cognition enables to us appreciate better the importance of 'seeing as' in learning (Wittgenstein, 1953) and of perceiving relevant similarities and dissimilarities appropriately. The point that we can now make is that this perception/conceiving of relevance must be understood as a set of practices in a variety of contexts.

This aspect of learning (the organising principle) is very important. Often the most interesting part of a subject is its core, these principles. Understanding them enables one to have an overview of the subject field, and the art in a subject involves knowing how to apply those principles in a contextually appropriate manner. Without these core principles, the subject becomes a list of facts disconnected from anything else, and which have little or no further significance.

In summary, in this section, we have challenged an orthodox view of learning in order to gain new insights relevant to human-centred education. The definition of learning as the acquisition of knowledge and skills is problematic because 'knowledge and skills' are not mutually exclusive categories. There is no sharp and clear-cut distinction, as we might have originally imagined. So-called 'knowledge' consists of complex sets of skills. For instance, the learning of concepts consists of the perceiving of relevant similarities, which may be regarded as sets of classificatory practices.

Qualities

In this first part of the chapter, we are offering three challenges to the definition of learning as the acquisition of knowledge and skills. The third challenge is that the categories 'knowledge' and 'skills' are not exhaustive. The acquisition of knowledge and skills does not provide a complete view of learning, even if we were to include 'concepts' and 'organising principles' within this duality. There is here in the standard definition a huge gap, which is central to the attempt to articulate the meaning of human-centred education: virtues or qualities. Consider the following examples. A lawyer requires a complex set of skills, for instance, for dealing with clients, presenting cases, constructing arguments and writing briefs. However, these skills are not sufficient to make a person a good lawyer, and there are other qualities or character-traits that a good lawyer must also have. We need not assume that such qualities will be the same for all lawyers in all contexts, but there may be some common factors. For example, a good lawyer should have a certain respect for the truth, which typically will manifest itself in a love for detail, and in carefulness. A good lawyer also needs to have the desire to win cases.

A constructor or builder needs another set of qualities or virtues. For example, as a contractor, a builder has to deal with a wide range of people, each with their own agendas. This requires a set of personal virtues, such as patience and perseverance, in addition to building and general management skills. The main point is that these personal qualities are more than skills because they involve caring in appropriate ways. In general, a person can know how to do something without having the appropriate care that would motivate him or her to do it well. A technical ability in drawing does not amount to a love of art and beauty. The mere ability to reason and argue well is not the same as a concern for truth. Nursing know-how does not amount to a caring attitude or compassion.

We have argued that a vision of learning must include the possible development of personal qualities, a process that is distinct from the acquiring of knowledge and skills. So far, we have examined only professional training. Nevertheless, the same argument can be extended to academic subjects, such as astronomy, mathematics, literature and history. A central part of being a good historian is having certain qualities, even if those qualities are not the same for all historians. The same point can be applied more generally to the liberal ideal of being an educated person, or to the more radical idea of being politically and ecologically aware and active, or to the ideal of being a person who lives in accordance with his or her own nature.

Academic training always involves more than just learning knowledge and skills. It also requires the development of appropriate personal qualities and epistemic virtues. This aspect of academic training tends to be ignored because it is harder to define and measure than 'knowledge acquisition' and technical skills, which tend to be specific, detachable and atomistic (as opposed to holistic). To be at home in a subject area, it is not enough and not always necessary to have a detailed knowledge of facts. It is, however, necessary to understand in depth the overarching principles and core basic concepts, and also to have certain personal attributes. For example, natural scientists need to have developed a particular attitude towards the need for evidence.

In conclusion, at the end of an educational process, the proposed outcome should not always merely consist of pieces of knowledge that the person has acquired (which might also be significant to extend our cultural heritage), and a set of actions that the person can perform which he/she couldn't do before. More importantly, the person him- or herself might have changed in the sense of having acquired different character traits and in the sense of being in a different state or having a different orientation. For example, he/she might be more confident, more caring of others, more careful, more willing to explore, more proactive, and so on. We might call these qualities 'virtues' or 'aspects of being', although in this context we should not understand 'virtue' as a moral term. Of course, this does not automatically imply that every educational process should involve deep transformation or change. For example, this might not be appropriate for a one-day course on the workings of transistors or for a lecture on the life cycle of bees.

In the last thirty or so years, virtue theory has become an important force in ethics partly because it tries to answer the broad question 'What virtues ought a person to have?' rather than the more atomistic 'What actions should a person perform?' (see, for instance, Aristotle, *Nicomachean Ethics*, and more recently an essay by Anscombe, 1997). The wider question seems to capture an aspect of ethics because actions are valuable in part as expressions of character traits or ways of being. Traditional virtue theory in ethics and epistemology contain insights of importance for our endeavour. Strictly speaking, however, such theories are designed to answer theoretical questions that are not our concern. For example, ethical theories are concerned with defining what makes an action right or wrong, and virtue theory, in this sense, tries to redefine and answer this question. In epistemology, virtue theory tries to reframe and answer the traditional question: 'What counts as good justification for a knowledge claim?' (Sosa, 2007).

Education involves developing appropriate non-moral virtues or ways of being. This idea has important broad consequences. First, it deepens our understanding of ordinary academic learning. Much of the educational process involves students becoming different, acquiring epistemological virtues such as inquisitiveness, independence of thought and respect for evidence. Students who lack these virtues may find it hard to develop skills and acquire knowledge because their character traits may prevent them from seeing the overarching point. Their way of being may impede them if, for instance, they are inattentive and passive, and lack a caring or questioning attitude. Because such qualities are more a question of attitude or character than skill, they concern the development of the whole person, not just the intellect.

Often the situation is like this: if a student is motivated to learn then he/she will learn for him- or herself and will not necessarily need much teaching in the traditional sense (but the student may need other kinds of support, such as direction and mentoring). If, by contrast, a student is not motivated to learn, then traditional teaching will not help him or her learn either. Of course, that is not an argument for the irrelevance of teaching, but rather for a new conception of it. It suggests that when a person has the appropriate virtues then he/she can generally learn the required skills, concepts and knowledge more easily.

At this point, we need to be careful. Let us suppose that there is plenty of systematically garnered empirical evidence to support the specific claims that having the appropriate qualities or virtues will increase the efficiency at which students 'acquire information' (sic) (say in the case of different subjects). We might be tempted then to argue in favour of a more virtue-based pedagogical approach based on this empirical evidence. The problem or danger in this is that it completely ignores the argumentation of the previous chapter. In the case of business theory, one would not want to fall into the contradiction of arguing that treating one's customers as humans is good practice because it increases profits. The slogan 'Don't instrumentalise the customer because it is bad for business' contains a contradiction. A more general version of this subterfuge is to argue that one can do things more efficiently if one rejects the theory of instrumental rationality. 'Don't instrumentalise; it is inefficient' is a self-contradictory motto. Let us apply this lesson to the case at hand. We are trying to argue for a consistent view of education that includes the development of the whole person, and to this end, we have pointed out some of the flaws in the traditional definition of learning. It would be absurd to argue that treating a student as a whole person is a more efficient way to get him or her to learn the facts or to become part of the political and societal machine. Consequently, the main point is *not* that acquiring virtues or qualities is a more efficient way to learn information in order to pass tests. The main point is rather that the development of the whole person is one that involves changing the profile of one's character and acquiring new qualities.

Second, in a way, virtues or qualities take priority over skills and knowledge. We can appreciate this by considering two points. We can see that learning knowledge without the appropriate skills is very much less fruitful than the learning that includes skills (this assumes that we can make sense of the separation). For example, teaching history is not merely about telling students when and how events took place in the past; it is more about helping them to develop the capacity to think historically.

Indeed, one could argue that learning knowledge ought to support the skills rather than the other way around. In other words, a curriculum that took certain pieces of knowledge as its starting point and that envisaged students' learning skills for the sake of acquiring that knowledge would be less valuable than one that took the relevant skills as the starting point and saw certain pieces of knowledge as necessary support for that process of skill learning and development. This is especially obvious if one regards key concepts as constituted by skills, as we argued earlier. Understanding central concepts organises the knowledge. It is a point of emphasis, but in general, it is better to have the relevant skills rather than the relevant knowledge (insofar as one makes that dichotomy), because without the former, the latter cannot be used.

The same point also applies to qualities or virtues. An education based on the learning of skills and knowledge without the appropriate virtues would be much less valuable (even if it were possible) than one that includes those qualities. This is because virtues or qualities include the appreciation of the appropriate values, and in this sense, they include care, emotion and motivation, which are excluded from the conventional definition of 'learning'. If one has the appropriate qualities then one will be motivated to acquire the relevant skills and knowledge and apply them appropriately. Becoming a self-motivated learner is not a question of acquiring a skill but rather of developing an attitude that permits and guides sensitive perception and action. This is a reason why one might reserve the term 'understanding' for a state that is both cognitive and non-cognitive. We will return to this in the following chapter.

From the point of view of much mainstream thinking, qualities are often ignored because they are vague and cannot be easily measured. Also, because their value is so general and varies from context to context, it may be assumed that their value is purely a matter of subjective opinion, which again cannot be measured. This assumes a questionable theory of measurement, which we will argue against in Chapter 9.

Furthermore, concentrating only on measurable skills cannot be the way forward. There are many so-called 'skills' that require qualities. In other words, what we think of as skills are sometimes much more than that and involve the exercise of non-moral virtues. For example, learning to read well and in depth is much more than a skill. It is an art. One has to know how to enter into the mind and hear the voice of someone else and bring that voice into oneself. One has to interrogate the text, but in a way that does not destroy the value of the book before one has had the chance to appreciate it. One has to know when to skip and try to get an overview, and when to concentrate meticulously on details. In this case, because the skill is really an art, it cannot be separated from the personal qualities that one develops in learning how to read better. In this sense, it is a misnomer to call it 'a skill', or even 'a set of skills', because it has features akin to the personal development of qualities.

In a similar vein, much the same can be said of many other academic subjects, in which central to the discipline is an art that cannot be reduced to a set of skills because the art requires appropriate appreciation and judgment. In this sense, mathematics is an art. Of course, so are the various forms of writing. Indeed any form of activity is an art insofar as it involves more than just exercising a set of skills but rather involves also having certain qualities or character traits or virtues that allow the person to make the appropriate value-sensitive perceptions and judgements or decisions.

Anyone would be totally dismayed on hearing that many young people do not know the capital of France or think that the Second World War was two hundred years ago. The shock is not the lack of this specific knowledge per se but rather the fact that it is taken to be expressive or indicative of a more general state of deep-seated ignorance, a set of qualities such as lack of interest in what is around one, apathy and low self-expectation. If one imagined instead a young person expressing interest in learning that Paris was the capital of France, and who then went on to ask lots of questions about the city and what a capital is, then in this case, one would not feel shock or horror, but rather surprise. The point is that the knowledge in itself is less important than the state of mind that it illustrates.

In this sense, being ignorant is not merely a lack of knowledge. It is more akin to ignoring one's lack of knowledge. The ignorant person is hardly aware that he/she lacks the relevant knowledge and/or does not care. In this sense, ignorance is a negative *quality* (or a non-moral vice) rather than a shortage of information. Its antidote is to take ownership of questions. The person who questions has taken the first step towards understanding. The process of education must nurture the qualities of inquisitiveness, of inquiry and investigation. Of course, good questions require a framework to be intelligible and interesting, and therefore part of the process of cultivating curiosity is to build appropriate frameworks so that younger people can ask better questions that have more significance for them. Indeed, insofar as education does involve learning knowledge, it might be best considered as responding to questions. This is because answers without questions are like food without hunger. Learning knowledge requires stimulating the appetite.

While society tends to conceive of learning academic subjects simply as the acquisition of knowledge, we can see that, implicit in this process, students are actually learning to use concepts, refine perceptions and develop appropriate academic skills. Likewise, in the course of developing these skills, there is an implicit process of fostering qualities such as questioning and inquiring. A deeper conception of the curriculum would make these implicit processes more explicit and create spaces for their development (see Chapter 9). This has huge pedagogical implications that we will explore in Part 2 of the book.

Third, the virtue/quality approach widens our understanding of the aims of education. If we follow a broadly Aristotelian view of these matters, then we would expect education, especially education at secondary level, to involve facilitating the processes whereby young people become more mature in a fully human sense. The aims of education would then have to be spelt out in terms of the qualities to be developed rather than just skills and knowledge. We will take this idea seriously when we discuss the design of the curriculum in Chapter 7.

This third critique of the dictionary definition does not imply that all learning necessarily involves the nurturing of qualities. Rote learning doesn't. However, a definition that excludes the possibility of nurturing qualities is defective.

Summary

To summarise: 'learning' is typically defined as the acquisition of knowledge and skills. This is a mistake in three important ways. First, 'acquisition' is a word that is apt for objects or possessions, but *not* for aspectual sensitivities and active cognition. Second, the definition disregards that knowing is doing, and thereby tends to ignore conceptual abilities and organising principles. Third, and most importantly, it overlooks qualities or non-moral virtues, which contain the only adequate principle for organising the other two (i.e. knowledge and skills).

The quality of cognition

As caring educators, we need to know that our students are developing or building themselves up as learners. We can believe and hope that their learning the skills and knowledge of various disciplines or subjects in a school setting facilitates this process of their development, but this does not guarantee success. In order to deliberately aim at such development, and construct curricula and institutional spaces to allow it, we need to know what it consists of.

To this end, in this second part of the chapter, we will examine the idea that one can know more or less well, where this phrase 'knowing well' does not refer simply to what or how much the person knows. Perhaps, readers will not be so familiar with the idea that knowing can be better or worse when these qualitative words are not explained quantitatively, in terms of how much a person knows. To introduce this unfamiliar idea, we shall first look at the concept of literacy in order to show how this complex notion consists of more than a set of linguistic skills. Second, we shall examine the distinction between knowing and understanding to show how this distinction requires the idea of the quality of knowing or of cognition.

Literacy

One of the interesting features of a human-centred approach is that it prompts us to re-conceive core cognitive and academic notions such as literacy. The term 'literacy' is usually associated with a complex set of skills related to reading and writing. Contemporary definitions of literacy aim to broaden the conception beyond elementary writing and reading skills, as we shall do too (see UNESCO, 2005; Bynner and Parsons, 2006). Modern discussions also attempt to show how literacy thus defined is embedded in a set of cultural practices and so therefore exists in a value system. However, these contemporary points do not challenge sufficiently the idea of literacy as a set of skills.

This aspect of the traditional conception can be challenged. The traditional conception of literacy is associated with the theory that language is a tool for communicating ideas, a view first articulated by John Locke[7] 1690 (also see Yates, 2003). Locke's theory has been criticised for instrumentalising language (Hacking, 1975). It underestimates the role of language. It assumes that we already have ideas to communicate and that these are non-linguistic. In opposition to Locke, however, these ideas are constituted by thoughts and concepts that are already linguistic. Thus, language is not merely a tool for communication; it is

---

[7] See John Locke's *Essay Concerning Human Understanding*, Book III (Locke, 1979).

more like the architecture of our minds or an essential aspect of our mode of being. In other words, our language defines in part what we can think, feel and perceive, and because of this, it constitutes the framework of our phenomenal 'world' or of the world as we experience it.[8] Our relationship to it is much more intimate than just a tool for expressing ideas. It constitutes the ideas. As a result, the traditional conception of literacy as a set of skills pertaining to reading and writing can be challenged because our literary capacities have a much closer relationship to the kind of life-world that we forge for ourselves.

As most contemporary writers in the field already understand, to be literate, it is not enough to be able to read and write. One has to be able to do those things *well*. One has to be able to understand what one reads, and have an understanding that makes te text worthy of being written. Reading is an art as much as writing is. Understanding what one reads is an active process of appreciating things from another person's point of view, seeing the connections between elements within a story and making connections to elements beyond the text in question.

So, our first point is that literacy is not simply a set of skills. It is also includes what we have called virtues or qualities. For example, literacy requires a fine but secure sensitivity to words. Suppose that a person was not at all attentive to words and their meanings. We would not want to say that such a person merely lacked a set of skills. We would indicate that the person lacked some intellectual virtues. Perhaps unkindly, we might call such a person 'dull' or 'unreflective'. Likewise, a literate person can see the points of a story quite naturally even when that involves adopting the point of view of a character in the story who is quite different from oneself. The capabilities that are often grouped together under the category 'literacy' are more than skills. They also include virtues or personal qualities, and as such, they are more integral to the development of the person than the title 'literacy' suggests.

The second main point is that the idea of literacy involves the concept of sensitivity to appropriate values. As we saw earlier in this chapter, there is a fundamental difference between the capacities that constitute skills and those that comprise virtues. The former lacks, but the latter includes, the idea of having the appropriate value-sensitivities. For example, a scientist with the relevant virtues will know when to question some data and when not to. Underlying such a judgement there is an attitude of care: he/she cares that the results are accurate but also does not want to distract the endeavour with insignificant queries. Virtues include knowing which skills to use and when. Being a literate person involves knowing when to read for detail and when to attend to the

---

[8] We are not claiming that the experiential is literally a world in addition to the real physical public world. It is our way of experiencing the real physical and public world.

landscape of a text. It involves connection to the appropriate values: in this case, caring about the content of the text.

Among other things, literacy requires implicit sensitivity to the relevant epistemological values. The word 'epistemology' refers to the philosophical principles regarding knowledge. These principles express the ideals that should guide what one believes. Here are some simple examples: one should not believe a claim that has no evidence to support it and has evidence against it; if a claim has no evidence in favour or against it then one should suspend judgement as to its truth. Since such principles guide choices regarding beliefs, they express epistemological values.

These traditional epistemological values derive from the claim that it is better to avoid error or false beliefs. In this way, literacy has familial connections to critical thinking. Usually, a person who cannot read, listen, write and speak well also cannot think well. To be a good thinker is constituted in part by a wide range of skills, sensitivities and virtues, which include sensitivity to epistemological values. For example, a person has to have a healthy degree of scepticism; this requires for instance asking if there is evidence in favour or against some point, and determining whether the evidence is adequate to support the conclusion. To think, one has to be able to apply such standards to the statements of other people and, moreover, self-reflectively to one's own thinking. Of course, this is far from a complete picture of what constitutes good thinking. For example, thinking also involves being able to make more relevant and fruitful connections.

Indeed, although traditional epistemological values tend to pertain to avoiding error or false beliefs, there are other epistemological values and virtues that relate to escaping ignorance, such as inquisitiveness and creativity. One of these virtues pertains to the capacity to make creative connections between different areas of knowledge, which can generate new understanding for the person concerned. For example, a young person might make connections between the history of the Tudors and elements in the work of Shakespeare, or between the study of optics in physics and features of artistic design. Put in a different way, it is good to create new ideas or hypotheses.

However, this point is subject to an important qualification. To generate new ideas is to risk having false beliefs. It is to open oneself to misunderstandings. In other words, the epistemological values that pertain to being careful and avoiding mistakes conflict with those that relate to being creative and escaping ignorance. Consider our beliefs about those around us. Some people form ideas quite quickly about what motivates their acquaintances; they are willing to draw conclusions about people's characters based on slender evidence. In contrast, other people may hardly consider the character traits of others. In a similar fashion, some people can imagine what it was like in different periods of history without having detailed knowledge. They can creatively fill in the gaps. In contrast, others stick to what they have read or been taught, and don't try to imagine what it was like, for instance, to be a Crusader or live in Victorian times. In these cases, we can see the conflict between avoiding error and avoiding ignorance. Such conflicts are inevitable, but to resolve them needs a kind of wisdom. It requires appreciation of the relevant values.

The third point is that because the idea of literacy involves the concept of virtues, and hence sensitivity to values, it also requires the qualitative notion of knowing well. The more that a person masters an area of knowledge and the more that person becomes self-aware as a learner, the more their understanding of the field cannot be adequately conceived of as simply a collection of known facts or even as a set of skills. A person's expertise has to be thought of not only in terms of his or her knowledge and skills, but also in his or her capacities to make sound judgements, to value the right kinds of things. This point will be explained more fully in the next section.

These ideas suggest that literacy or linguistic capacities should not be just another component of the curriculum; they are right at the core of, and weave their threads through, nearly all learning. A little reflection shows us that what one might call 'the language skills' of students can affect their ability to learn in a multitude of disciplines and contexts. Although there are exceptions, students with strong linguistic capabilities can more easily master the vocabulary of (and hence concepts and claims of) diverse areas such as biology, physics and the social sciences, as well the humanities. This centrality of language abilities is hardly a surprise because these diverse subject areas require in common the capacity to read and listen with good comprehension, and the capability to talk and write using fluent sentences. (Of course, these diverse fields involve many other abilities too, but that is not the point.)[9]

Although the above encapsulates much of the position from which the English government stresses literacy (DfEE, 1998), these capacities, and the epistemological values that underpin them, need more explicit attention in the curriculum. It is almost a platitude that these general linguistic abilities depend very much on how a child is treated at home. Children who are less often encouraged to

---

[9] This claim about the centrality of language does not necessarily apply to young people who have special needs in language development. Our discussion here by no means suggests that they do not have intelligence. On the contrary, these young people may be capable of developing thinking-architecture in other ways. However, we do not have the scope to address the development of children and young people with special needs in this book.

have long conversations at home, who read little and who have few opportunities to write will tend not to have strong language abilities. (Often it is children who are from socially deprived backgrounds who are less equipped with the language sensitivities described above; see Benton and Fox, 1985; Yates, 1997. If this is correct, we would expect schools to invest a great deal of energy and attention into providing young people with plenty of opportunities for practice guided by feedback. Furthermore, students with poor speaking skills sometimes have consequently diminished writing capabilities (Corden, 2000). Their restricted ability to talk is often to do with self-confidence and lack of practice (Bearne *et al.*, 2003). So, again, we would expect schools to provide many opportunities for young people to practise discourse and gain confidence.

Nevertheless, the standard practical (or in-practice) understanding of literacy does not encourage such provisions. Usually, once they can translate marks into sounds, students are not trained systematically in intelligent reading, except for the special reading skills and sensitivities required for understanding literature (see Dixon *et al.*, 1993). Often, young people do not receive personal training in active reading (Schoenbach *et al.*, 1999). In a similar fashion, young people are not given tuition in speaking, even though it is clear that the more articulate students often tend to understand more (*ibid.*). As we argued earlier, such shortcomings are symptomatic of placing the acquisition of knowledge at the centre of the stage, and of building the curriculum and learning process around that. Much school-time is devoted to the delivery of the national curriculum conceived in terms of imparting knowledge of academic subjects.

In contrast, the curriculum and learning processes are best conceived first in terms of the development of persons and their qualities. From this, it will follow that certain skills need to be learned and certain abilities enhanced. From that, the knowledge menu will follow. In other words, the qualities dictate the skills, and the skills define the knowledge. This is not a question of enhancing qualities without building knowledge-content. We need knowledge learning and skill training. The issue is rather that the standard definition of learning focuses exclusively on knowledge and skills, thereby ignoring qualities and what is distinctive about them. More positively, it is a question of what comes first in the designing process. According to writers such as Hirst and Peters, policy-makers should start from a conception of what children need to know, and construct from that an idea of the skills and qualities that young people need, and from this general picture shape a curriculum. We are advocating the opposite approach by focusing on the question: 'What are the qualities that young people need to have both in general and in relation to their learning?' By answering this, one can try to better understand the kinds of skills and knowledge that young people need. From there, we can try to construct a curriculum. Therefore, it is not a question of eradicating the need for knowledge, but rather recognising that it is secondary. As we argued in Chapter 1, what is primary is the person. Academic and social educative aims must be evaluated from the point of view of the development and well-being of the person. As we shall see in later chapters, this means that motivation and emotion play an important role in the curriculum and that, as part of the learning process, young people themselves need to be involved in the construction of their curriculum. Better to be the student who has the will and ability to find out than the student who already knows but has no such will or ability. It is better still to know because one has will *and* ability.

The kind of cognitive training implicit in what we are saying lies at the intersection of what are thought of as different types of education, such as academic, personal development and vocational. For example, the thinking abilities and understanding of epistemological values discussed above form in many respects the core of much academic training. Some academic formation consists of appreciating what counts as relevant evidence, and what does not. In this sense, at its core, academic training can be human-centred because it involves developing these capacities of human beings.

Furthermore, a human-centred conception of learning includes the development of the person through the cultivation of virtues or qualities. This inclusion can help harmonise the kinds of interests students have in vocational and academic learning; many of the qualities needed for both overlap, and both should be judged in terms of their potential relevance for the development of the individual. This is the criterion that might enable a reconciliation of academic and vocational concerns. How such decisions might be made, we will examine in Chapter 7 on curriculum construction.

Understanding

One reason for thinking that we need the concept of the quality of knowing is that there is an important difference between knowing and understanding. According to this distinction, a person can know something (propositionally) without understanding what he/she knows. We shall show that the best explanation of this distinction relies on the notion of the quality of our cognition or knowing, the idea that we can know more or less well.

First, let us establish the distinction. The words 'know' and 'understand' serve different purposes and mark different kinds of evaluation. They have different roots. For instance, knowing (knowledge-that) requires some kind of warrant or evidence or reliability. One cannot claim to *know* 'p' unless one has some strong reason or evidence for thinking that p is true. In contrast, understanding requires that one 'stands under' an idea or that one lives within it. So, for example, if someone understands something well, he/she is not easily swayed by other people's confusions. If he/she understands it then he/she knows it solidly and stands his/her ground.

Second, the explanation: how is it possible to know something without understanding properly what one knows? Knowledge without understanding is possible because one can know superficially, so to speak, with the tip of one's mind, when for instance the knowledge has no or little impact on one's actions and feelings. For this reason, understanding admits of degrees in a way that knowledge does not: understanding can be deep or shallow in ways that knowledge cannot. This is because we can know all the relevant facts, and still not live in this knowledge; it can be remote or disconnected. In a nutshell, a person's understanding depends on the quality of his/her knowing, and not simply on the quantity of facts he/she knows. Understanding pertains to the way in which one knows. For example, one's knowledge can be solid and well integrated. If a person is consequent with his or her knowledge then he/she may be said to understand well what he/she knows. Hence, the explanation of the difference between knowledge and understanding requires the idea of the quality of the person's knowing. Understanding is deep when a person is consequent with or in tune with his/her knowledge, and superficial when he/she is not. We will explain this in a moment.

It might be objected that we can refer to a person's knowledge as profound and that, therefore, there is no significant difference on this score between knowledge and understanding. In reply, this objection fails to take into account that when we refer to a person's knowledge as superficial or deep, this concerns the content of *what* he/she knows (rather than *how* he/she knows it). For example, a person has a profound knowledge of earthquakes when he/she knows the underlying principles about their generation and effects under different conditions. This relates to the content of his/her knowledge rather than the way in which he/she knows it. To claim that a person knows all the relevant facts does not necessarily indicate how this knowledge affects him or her. It might or might not be well integrated into the person and with the other things he/she knows. We could put the point like this: if we think of knowledge as a relationship between a person and some set of facts, then the content of the knowledge concerns only the right-hand side of the relationship: the facts known. On the other hand, the quality of understanding concerns the left-hand side of the relation: the person and the way in which he/she knows.

Full understanding requires that a person's thoughts, feelings and interests be unified in a way that is consequent or in harmony with the knowledge. In very broad terms, we might distinguish different degrees or levels of understanding in three ways. These correspond to different kinds of psychological integration.

First, if a person makes the appropriate cognition–verbal connections, then he/she has one level of understanding. In such a case, there is no dissonance between what the person believes and what he/she says. A greater degree of understanding would require the appropriate connections between cognition, words and feelings. If I understand the plight of my friend, then not only will I know what to say and how to say it, but I will also feel what the words express (presuming I am sincere). Deeper understanding would result in the appropriate feelings expressing themselves in action and behaviour. In which case, the cognition, words, thoughts, feelings and actions will be of a piece or in tune with each other. This lack of dissonance is one kind of integration.

Second, a person understands something well to the extent that this knowledge appropriately affects other things that he/she knows. Failure to make appropriate connections would count towards someone not understanding something. For example, one may know that Muslims attend the mosque on Fridays but still be curious why many shops are closed on a Friday in a Muslim country.

Third, sometimes, the connections that we make between cognition, words, actions and feelings can be very context-dependent or circumstantial. For example, if the teacher asks a question of a student in a particular way in the classroom, he/she might know the answer. However, if the teacher changes the context or asks the question in a slightly different way, then the student may no longer be able to answer. Outside the classroom or the academic context, the student will not know. One might say that his/her knowledge was fragile or not deeply rooted.

The difference between degrees of understanding lies in how much a person is integrated. If a person's beliefs, feelings, desires and actions are out of harmony, then we might say that he/she doesn't understand well some of the things that he/she knows. Consequently, a lack of understanding can be regarded as a cognitive/non-cognitive/behavioural dissonance. In contrast, the behavioural sign of good understanding is that one's words, actions and feelings are all congruent with one's knowledge. In this sense, understanding expresses unity.

We can bring these strands together by claiming that a lack of understanding is a failure to come to grips with the reality of something. To understand well is to be appropriately and fully connected to some set of facts. Therefore, for instance, a person does not understand fully the horrors of war if he/she is emotionally disengaged from the facts. Thus, failure to care can count as failure of understanding. In a similar way, one can fail to fully understand simple and known facts, such as that one will die or that other people have feelings, by not being fully connected to them. Not understanding what one already knows is made possible by not being appropriately and fully connected to what one knows.

This idea of being more or less connected to the facts supports the claim, made at the start of this chapter, that learning is not a question of acquiring mental objects or items, such as ideas, information and beliefs.

Earlier we also distinguished between cognitive and non-cognitive mental states. The cognitive concerns how we learn about and represent the world. Belief, thought and perception are cognitive states. The non-cognitive states, such as desires and emotions, do not represent the world, insofar as the distinction makes sense at all; whereas 'knowledge' is a cognitive notion and 'understanding' is both cognitive and non-cognitive. Understanding can be from the heart (and even the body) as well as the mind. It lies at the intersection of the cognitive and non-cognitive, where the one spills over into the other.

Relevance to education

There are many instances in which a person may have the necessary knowledge; the problem is the way in which he/she knows. For example, many people know that 100,000,000 times 100 equals ten billion, but few of us understand the number ten billion. For instance, few people have the kind of intuitive feel for the difference between say a billion and 10 billion that they have for the difference between 4 and 5. Likewise, many people know what x^2 means and can perform the relevant calculations, but it is often the case that people are surprised at the exponential growth rate associated with the iteration of x^2. Exponential growth is surprisingly fast, like breeding rabbits. In a similar vein, a person can know Newton's laws of motion, explain them and work out problems with the formulae, yet still may have expectations of the physical world that predate Galileo (McCloskey, 1983).

In these cases, the problem pertains to the narrowness of cognition. For instance, I can know intellectually that one kilogram is 1000 grams and that this is roughly 2.2 pounds or 35.2 ounces, without being able to estimate accurately the weight of the suitcase I am lugging upstairs. The intellect may know the weights; the body may not.

This is one of the problems that some young people have with history. They might learn the relevant dates of the Norman Conquest of England without really realising that this happened nearly one thousand years ago quite nearby. They may not have an inkling of what this meant for the English people of the time. It seems too remote. Increasing their knowledge of history does not necessarily address that problem, although it may do. As we have seen, additional knowledge is not always the answer to the problem of not appreciating or understanding the knowledge one already has. The difficulty is more concerned with the quality and depth of cognition: is the cognition fully integrated with the person's feelings, imagination, expectations and actions?

As we saw earlier, a lack of understanding is often a failure to grasp fully the reality of something. A person for whom the reality of the past has not really sunk in will not be able to fully appreciate historical knowledge. In a similar vein, a person for whom the reality of distant countries is remote will have a weak socio-geographical understanding. Places that are far away may not feel real, and the reality of the fact that, say, the majority of the population in Egypt is Muslim may not have sunk home.

We might compare this to the person who is not able to relate in an integrated way to his/her own future. Such a person knows many things about his/her future, but if it does not seem real, then this knowledge will be impotent. For example, most people know that a bad diet may cause serious health problems later in life; fewer really understand this fully.

Finally, a person may have similar limitations in his/her relationships with other people. One might know that one's behaviour causes suffering to others without really taking in what this means – in other words, without having one's feelings, imagination and expectations in line with this knowledge. In this sense, one may not really understand commonplace knowledge about other people. This counts as a moral failing, and our explanation of it indicates why having learnt purely cognitive lessons in morality or ethics may do little to address the problem. Better to exercise the imagination and the feelings.

The distinction between knowledge and understanding underscores the inadequacy of the acquisition model of learning, which cannot account for the quality of our knowing. It also underlines the need for a conception of learning that includes qualities. Understanding requires appropriate qualities. This is why even the most academic study is a preparation rather than a cramming. It also shows why these qualities need to be holistically conceived. Trying to feed the intellect alone will not help grow the person. Understanding is necessarily both cognitive and non-cognitive. This means, as we shall see in the next chapter, that emotional development and learning must go hand-in-hand with cognitive learning and development.

Further reading

Bennett, H. (2007) *Emotional Reason: Deliberation, Motivation and the Nature of Value*. Cambridge: Cambridge University Press.

Friere, P. (1990) *The Pedagogy of the Oppressed*. London: Continuum (Chapters 1 and 2).

Ryle, G. (1949) *The Concept of Mind*. London: Hutchinson (Chapter 2).

Searle, J. (1983) *Intentionality*. Cambridge: Cambridge University Press.

Sosa, E. (2010) *Knowing Full Well*. Princeton, NJ: Princeton University Press.

Winch, C. (1998) *The Philosophy of Human Learning*. London: Routledge.

3
Motivation and emotion

Introduction

A major thread of the human-centred approach stresses the importance of the whole person. Although we started to elucidate this point in the previous chapter by widening the conception of learning, there is a lot more to say about the educational development of the whole person. We still need to address questions such as 'what does it mean in educational terms for the whole person to develop?' and 'What are the implications of the whole-person approach for teaching and learning in secondary education?'

In this chapter, in answering these questions, we will continue to elaborate the importance of this idea of the whole person from new angles; in particular, we wish to show how cognitive and non-cognitive states are intertwined, as well as examine the educational implications of this for motivation and emotion. We also aim to explain how this approach will shed new light on student motivation – and the lack of it.

An educational emphasis on the person as a whole precludes stressing the cognitive at the expense of the whole person. One might be tempted to claim that much current education is mistaken because it concentrates almost exclusively on cognitive capacities, and virtually ignores the experience and development of emotions, feelings or the non-cognitive in general. However, this way of making the point dichotomises the cognitive and non-cognitive in a manner that may be educationally misleading. Furthermore, insofar as alternative approaches to education try to correct the current overemphasis on intellectual development by stressing the non-cognitive, they too fall into the same trap of dichotomising the two, and become vulnerable to the charge of neglecting intellectual growth.

In contrast to this dichotomy, to form educational principles that respect the wholeness of the person requires us to avoid any sharp division between the cognitive and non-cognitive. There cannot be one versus the other because they are both aspects of the same person. The difference between the cognitive and non-cognitive cannot be a division. Consequently, in principle, education should be development that includes both as one. Thus we will set out to address questions such as: 'What does this abstract recommendation really mean?' and 'What are its implications in terms of principles for practice?'

In order to do so, we need a couple of points of clarification. First, debates often put intellect and emotion in opposite corners (James, 1950). However, this is too simplistic because not all cognitive states are intellectual, and not all non-cognitive states are emotions. To elaborate, let us look at how 'cognitive' and 'non-cognitive' are usually defined. Cognitive mental states are those, such as belief, perception and thought, which aim to represent some aspect of the world. Because of this aim, they can usually be evaluated as true or false, or as accurate or misleading. The supposition is that one will try to make cognitive mental states conform to the way the world is (however one understands that phrase). Suppose I believe that Mozart composed 104 symphonies. However, if I am then presented with evidence that Mozart wrote 41 symphonies, the supposition is that I will or ought to change my belief accordingly. In contrast, non-cognitive states, such as wanting and liking, do not have the aim of representing anything, and in this way cannot be accurate or misleading, or true or false. With wants, one does not try to make one's mental states agree with the way the world is, but rather, one tries to make the world conform to the state, by changing things to satisfy the want. This is the usual way of drawing the cognitive vs. non-cognitive distinction (see, for example, McNaughton, 1988). It may need some metaphysical surgery or refinements (for example, regarding the concept 'the way the world is'), but this is not pertinent to our purposes here.[1]

In practice, it is very difficult to separate the cognitive and non-cognitive aspects of a person's psychological states because the two are tightly intermingled. For example, suppose I see a situation as sad and feel sadness. As perceptions, the first is a cognitive state, and the second, as a feeling, is non-cognitive. However, it seems that the perception can be part of the emotion, and vice versa, and while such a claim would not contest the cognitive/non-cognitive distinction itself, it would challenge the assumption that mental states can be assigned simply to one box rather than another. In other words, the psychological reality of our everyday experience confirms that our mental states are a mixture and blending of the cognitive and non-cognitive. Even when reasoning, one's attention is drawn to different facets of what one is thinking about and these subtle shifts in attention are affected by one's likes and dislikes, and by one's mood.

The second point of clarification concerns a major argument of this book, which is that education should be focused on the person as a whole. One way to unwittingly sabotage this idea is to use a psychological carving knife to slice the whole person into parts (which is a misleading spatial analogy), such as the intellect, feelings, senses and desire. For example, Plato presents a three-fold division between appetite, emotion and reason (see *The Republic*). Such divisions might lead to the concept that each part has its own educational programme, such as education for the intellect, for the emotions and for the will. This box-by-box set-up misses the huge educational opportunities that a truly integrated approach has to offer, which we will describe below.

However, the distinction between, for example, desire, emotion and intellect must make some sense even within a holistic approach. To make sense, the distinction cannot be treated as a division. In other words, these are not parts of a person. They are abstractions of the person as a whole; they are aspects of the functioning of a person. The difference between aspects and parts is relevant because one can talk

---

[1] For example, value realism, which is roughly the claim that there are evaluative facts, may need to disown or distance itself from the concept of absolute reality (see McDowell, 2001; McNaughton, 1988).

about aspects without the implication that there is such a thing as a finite total of aspects. In contrast, there has to be such a thing as a whole made up of all the (finite) parts, because that is what the whole is, the sum of the parts.

Several writers have drawn attention to the significance of the non-cognitive in learning (for example, Macmurray, 1962; Heron, 1992; Winch, 1998). According to this view, the process of learning can include the development of feelings and emotions, not merely as an accompaniment or as an external aid, but rather as an integral part of the process. This latter clarification is important: the point is *not* that feelings can help us to learn cognitively in a more effective way, true though that is. The point is rather that the process of learning itself ought to include the non-cognitive (instead of being facilitated externally by it).

Motivation

Good motivation makes a world of difference to learning. With guidance and the right opportunities, self-motivated students can develop independently, both in a group and alone. In contrast, students who apparently lack educational motivation may seem to be totally closed; they appear deaf to guidance, blind to opportunities and unwilling to change. Secondary school students have legendary levels of disenchantment with their schooling. Many complain that school is boring (Riley and Docking, 2004). The standard response to this lack of motivation is four-fold: to increase the punishments for being lazy and the rewards for being diligent; to help the teachers become more enthusiastic; to make the taught content more relevant to students; and, more radically, to help make students become more self-motivated. None of these moves can be bad for student motivation, except perhaps the first. However, whether they get to the heart of the issue is another matter. Certainly, the core issues concerning student motivation need to be addressed.

Traditional theories of motivation (see Maslow, 1954; Herzberg, 1959) tend to fall into one of three traps. First, they can be descendants of behavioural stimulus–response approaches, which ultimately try to use a minimal amount of psychological language, replacing it with behavioural-outcome language in an effort to be more scientific. Such theories usually end up making all motivation instrumental and, in the long run, this can be fatal to understanding the education process (Holt, 1964/1982). The second pitfall makes motivation hydraulic. According to this view, drives *push* us to act. They cause *pressure* or change the internal *balance*. These metaphors tend to understand motivation as analogous to an inner Newtonian system of forces. This treats psychological states as physical objects. The main problem with this is that motivation is inherently intentional, and these kinds of theory ignore that or are inconsistent with it. Third, theories can fail by being reductionist. The idea here is that all motivation can be reduced to three or four basic needs or drives, and perhaps even just one, such as pleasure. However, it is a mistake to ignore the variety of motivation that people have, even though it is important to distinguish between more fundamental and less basic motivation.

Our aim in this section is not to produce a new theory of motivation that avoids these pitfalls. However, we do need to make some observations about the nature of motivation, especially insofar as it may help us to understand how to overcome the disengagement, disenchantment and/or school fatigue syndrome suffered by many young people. We will draw attention to four features of motivational states that traditional theories tend to overlook and which have educational importance.

Intentional motivation

First, motivational states are intentional. As we saw in our earlier discussion on cognition, this means that they have a content, and as a result, an aspectual nature. One may desire something under one set of descriptions, but not under another. I very much want to visit a tropical country with regard to one group of characterisations, i.e. friendly people and beautiful beaches, but not with regard to another group, i.e. very hot and full of mosquitoes. The same applies to likes and dislikes. Oscar Wilde said that there are two tragedies in life: to not get what one wants and to get it. This alludes to the aspectual nature of wanting. Indeed, this is part of the problem of being human; one may like something intensely under some descriptions, and dislike it vehemently under another. This can cause feelings of confusion, especially perhaps when one is young. Liking and wanting are aspectual (see, for example, Chapters 6–8 in Crane, 2001).

One of the educational implications of this intentionality is that it is not enough to know what individuals find boring or interesting in school or what they love and hate. We also need to know under what descriptions these motivational states apply. Unfortunately, this may not be a simple matter of asking, or filling in questionnaires or making surveys. Because of the intentionality of perception and motivation, mental states are not always transparent even to the person who has them. One may not be able to articulate what one finds interesting or why one is engaged. Furthermore, it is possible to be mistaken.

That motivational states are intentional also means that the very same activities or material can be seen as dull in one light, and as fascinating in another. Since such perceptions are highly sensitive to contextualisation, we need to understand what makes a young person perceive a lesson as dull or a subject as uninteresting or a school as monotonous or irrelevant. For instance, under what descriptions does a student interested in mathematics perceive the activities that constitute a class in mathematics? For example, the challenge of solving problems can be attractive. Some people appreciate the wide applicability and usefulness of mathematics as a language. Others are attracted to its austere aesthetic appeal. Some are attracted to the fact that mathematics has definitive answers. Others like its abstractness. When a child dislikes mathematics, under what descriptions does he/she perceive the relevant attributes?

Cognition motivates

This introduces an important idea, which sheds new light on motivation, namely the idea that evaluative perception can motivate action. Although the initial steps in this argument may seem a little abstract and remote, by the time we discuss love later in the chapter, we hope that the reader will *see* fully the force of these points for education.

Evaluative cognition is the idea that we can perceive something as valuable (McDowell, 2001; McNaughton, 1988). The main point is that, contrary to some scientific and empiricist accounts of perception, cognition can motivate. Empiricist theories tend to think of perception as merely the passive reception of concept-free or raw sense data, such as coloured dots. According to an empiricist view, perceiving is distinct from the conceptual interpretation one places on the perceptions. According to traditional empiricism, perception itself is concept-free and motivationally inert. It is dead (see Hume's *An Enquiry Concerning Human Understanding*).

In contrast, more phenomenologically oriented theories regard perception as fully conceptual. Perceiving the world always already involves concepts, and there is no concept-free passive perception of raw sense-data. One always perceives something *as* something. In this sense, perception is conceptual and intentional (or aspectual). To describe how someone perceives something, it is necessary to use all the concepts that pick out relevant aspects of what the person saw (Searle, 1983). One has to enter into the point of view or the subjectivity of the person. According to this phenomenological view, I can directly perceive a face *as* a face. Concepts are an integral part of the perception rather than an interpretative add-on (Merleau-Ponty, 1962).

The conceptual nature of perception allows for the idea that perceiving can be value-laden or evaluative, and hence motivating (McDowell, 1994; Marples, 1999: 138). I can see something as disgusting or charming, attractive or dull. This idea makes sense when one considers one's perception of the character traits of people. If I perceive a person as joyful and bright then I may be attracted to him. If I perceive someone as angry and aggressive then I will avoid her. These cognitive states can motivate directly. They are not inert. Because of this, our wants can sometimes be explained in terms of our perception or cognition of the evaluative properties of the things that we want (McDowell, 2001). For example, I want a holiday because I think that it will be relaxing.

The idea that actions, feelings and wants can be explained in terms of cognition provides us with a framework for understanding motivation that is quite different from both the internal motivations and drives postulated by Rousseau and other Romantic thinkers, and also from the 'reward–punishment' extrinsic model advanced by behaviouristic psychologists such as Pavlov and Skinner. This alternative model should be of special interest to educators because it connects motivation directly to attention by stressing the point that how one perceives or attends can in itself motivate. Motivation can be a sensibility. Sensibility can be trained (see essay 3, 'Virtue and reason', in McDowell, 2001).

This means that it can be motivationally important for students to form the appropriate perceptual contexts for their activities at school. It matters dramatically how students contextualise their activities (Gladwell, 2006). In practice, this means, for example, that teachers need to explain the point of the courses or programmes they run; institutions need to explain what the school in general is about so that students are not thrown into programmes of study without knowing why. However, explanations need to avoid being overly authoritarian and instrumental because these tend to make student ownership of the process difficult. Instead, it is necessary to have guided group discussions of the following kinds of points: 'What do we need to understand in history and why?', 'What makes a person a good historian?', 'Why are we studying chemistry?' and 'What is interesting in the study?'

Let us explore one example of evaluative perception. Given the primary point of education and given the nature of learning, students need opportunities to conceptualise learning processes in terms of their own development, i.e. the abilities and qualities that he/she needs. Because of such opportunities, one might expect that young people feel pampered at school, even when it is tough, because education is a time dedicated to their own growth and well-being. Of course, the reality is sharply different: students often feel that they are forced to engage in activities that have little meaning for them. Students in large schools, in particular, often end up feeling part of an impersonal and uncaring system (Wallace, 2009). These negative perceptions reveal an institutional failure to help students conceptualise and perceive what they are doing in sufficiently personalised terms. Such perceptions cause horrible feelings of alienation. So, for the individual student, the opportunity to understand the personal meanings of the activities in school is vital to the motivation to perform them (Harvard and Hodkinson, 1995).

This opportunity is bound up with the young person's perception of him/herself. Educational activities are part of a process of understanding oneself, forming an identity and finding meanings in one's life. It is not enough for the students to understand why such and such course of study is important; it needs to be connected to their own development and their own sense of that development. It has to make connections outside to life beyond the classroom and inside to the person's awareness of him/herself.

The sense of oneself is always related to time. By selecting aspects of his/her past and ignoring others, a person forms an awareness of his/her identity and character. By projecting forward in some ways and not in others, one forms a feeling for one's future. Both are precarious exercises. I can damn myself in the selection of my past, and I can condemn myself to a limited imprisoned future. In terms of the past, it is easy for young people to see their own limitations, and not appreciate their own strengths. A lack of confidence can be overcome by building a new past either by doing new things or by reframing past actions and events. In terms of the future, people can have very limited horizons or perceptions of what their future could contain. Being youthful, it may be difficult for young people to have a solid appreciation of the extraordinary opportunities that life contains. It is deeply ironic that the young, who have so many possibilities, need more of a past in order to really see the fullness of their future possibilities. To have a big future, one needs a long past. *Why?* For many young people, the sense of their personal future is often limited to what they think it is likely to be rather than being expanded by the good that it could become.

In adolescence, a person usually has an increased sense of him/herself. This kind of self-perception, the awareness of oneself as a person who is in the process of becoming, can be a very strong source of motivation. Given this and given that education is a process of development, it is important that young people have opportunities to conceptualise their learning in terms of their own development (Rogers, 1969; Mezirow, 1991). In other words, if a young person can be shown how the study of a subject is an integral part of his/her own self-development, then this may help motivate the study. It is the perception of purpose that links to self-awareness, which in turn can motivate (Wentzel and Wigfield, 2009).

However, this approach does have important limitations. If the teacher explained all activities in such terms, it would cast a shadow of boredom ('Oh no! Not self-development again! Can't we do something different for a change?'). Moreover, such an explanation of the point of learning instrument-alises the activity; it treats it as valuable merely as a means to something else. Remember the theme of Chapter 1: 'If only we could have self-development without the chore of having to learn!' In other words, unfortunately, 'learning for the sake of self-development' treats learning as something that should not be done for its own sake but only for the sake of some other end. Furthermore, self-development renders the value of learning as purely self-regarding. It focuses the attention of the young person on him- or herself. It does not connect the attention to the content of what is learned. To overcome these limitations, let us now look at another example of evaluative perception, one that reaches outwards.

Connecting to what is valuable beyond oneself

As we have seen, the learning of facts is a much more multifaceted process than some learning theories would seem to imply. For example, when I am learning about the periodic table, I am not acquiring chunks of information. I am con-necting points to an overarching principle, seeing new kinds of similarities, differences and relevancies, learning new vocabulary or concepts, and adding new dimensions and connections to an already existing vocabulary. These involve new behavioural dispositions and new know-hows. In the process of learning, I may be changing my attitudes and adapting my character – as I learn more chemistry, I become more scientific in my outlook. This learning involves a systematic paying of attention under the appropriate descriptions. For instance, in the study of the periodic table, there are layers of relevance.

This illustrates how we can connect to the content of what we study. By per-ceiving the relevant connections, one begins to understand why the periodic table is *important*. Consequently, one begins to perceive it evaluatively or under evaluative attributes such as 'important'. In this manner, learning is a way of connecting to what is valuable outside of oneself. As I learn about the lives and history of other peoples, this can be an experience of connecting to something of value beyond myself. For example, once I begin to understand the historical significance of the Sumerians, I can then start to appreciate their historical value and relevance. Learning involves appreciation, which is a connection to a valu-able aspect of what one studies in an appreciative way, i.e. under the appropriate kinds of characterisations. In this way, learning has content. It is often a process of pointing one's appreciative attention towards things other than oneself, such as the natural world, the history of a region or the life of other societies.

This idea reverses the normal conception of motivation. Usually, it is conceived as an inner force pushing us outwards. Here, we stress the opposite; motivation is often like drawing in the valuable aspects of what is around one. It can be a pulling in rather than a pushing out. Think of love. When one loves, one is intensely aware of the beautiful characteristics of another person. This brings a feeling, which leads to the person becoming even more aware of those features and which gives birth to wants. Love is not simply a projection of a feeling inside of oneself onto the other person; the person one loves had beautiful characteristics all along. One tunes into them with increased intensity to the exclusion of other things. In love, one becomes especially keenly aware of the reality of the other person. Love is perception with feeling (Thomson, 2003).

This way of looking at love has interesting consequences. Rather than inhabiting a stone-like, value-neutral universe, we live in a rich world, full of value-possibilities (Thomson, 2003). All of the people whom one does not fall in love with have qualities that one could perceive in a loving way. One could connect to them but usually one doesn't. Much of the time, we hardly see others as real. We have other preoccupations, and pass on by. Likewise, there are students who fall in love with biology as a study, and there are those who don't. Lovers of biology connect to the reality of the living world; others pass on by with hardly a glance. The difference is how they relate to the lives of plants and animals.

The ethos of the curriculum and of many textbooks seems to be to provide the young person with what he/she needs to know about biology in order to take the next step and become a student of biology (Keeffe, 1989). The curriculum is purely academic in its implicit goals, and it simply assumes that students will fall in love with biology. In its wish to be efficient and businesslike, the curriculum seems to ignore that we need to become lovers of biology. However, we could affirm that the need to fall in love with biology is primary; once a person begins to fall in love with the subject matter then, with guidance and the right opportunities, he/she will be able to understand much on his/her own without force-feeding.

How can appreciation lead to love? With people, this often happens in three phases (Gladwell, 2006). First, there is the initial perception of another, which might be superficial, insubstantial or quirky. One sees a person's smile as honest or his gait as elegant or her voice as soothing. This initial perception is highly contextual. It is dependent on one's own mood and state, among many other factors. Second, there must be no events that disconfirm that initial impression. For a while, a person may be open to revising or reconsidering his/her very first impressions of another. If they are not rejected quickly, the first impressions usually set the tone for later perceptions. Having started off with a positive idea of another, if one perceives other attractive qualities in that same person then one will retain that initial impression; it will survive disconfirmation. Third, the time frame or window of opportunity for later changes of perception is usually limited. If first impressions are not quickly defeated, then they tend to remain. Once a first impression has been formed, and has survived a few subsequent encounters, it is then likely to become more fixed. Having survived disconfirmation, early impressions often provide the framing context for later perceptions and therefore, after this period, reframing can be very difficult.

One finds parallel phases in the appreciation of what one is learning. Students are quick to form a first impression of an area of study, which is highly dependent on the context and on their mood and state. Nevertheless, despite their quirkiness, these initial impressions can constitute a preliminary hypothesis about the subject-matter, such as 'maths is dry' or 'history is old-fashioned'. For a limited time-period, however, later interactions can rebut this first impression. If the hypothesis survives and is not rejected then the initial perceptions will tend to create a fixed framework, which will tend to contextualise, and be reinforced by, all later perceptions.

Earlier we stressed the psychological aspect of finding one's passions in life. However, this is a slightly misleading way to put the point because motivated learning is not merely a question of discovering oneself inwardly, so to speak. In the first instance, it is rather a question of looking outward appreciatively in the way described above and then making a commitment, which becomes reinforced in the process of learning. In short, the education process has two elements. On the one hand, it points inwards: the process is one of increased self-awareness, of forming oneself and growing. On the other hand, it points outwards beyond the self to other people and to things of interest and of value, such as the life of society and the natural world. Both directions constitute perceptual sources of motivation. This is roughly the difference between confidence and conviction. Whereas self-confidence is more inward pointing and pertains to how one perceives oneself, conviction points outward; it is about the certainty of one's evaluation of a perception. One has conviction when one feels sure that something is important or good or right. This is a precondition for commitment.

There is a dilemma here. On the one hand, traditional approaches to education that stress cognition in a narrow way are liable to be focused outwardly on the subject-matter to be studied, sometimes to the exclusion of the person who is doing the studying (see research by Riley and Docking, 2004). On the other hand, approaches to education that are more open to the non-cognitive are inclined to over-emphasise the psychological. They tend to be more inward looking, stressing self-confidence and the formation of identity, sometimes to the detriment of external connections. Neither of these two options is entirely satisfactory. The alternative that we are advocating takes a quite different tack. It emphasises the non-cognitive aspects of cognition and the cognitive aspects of non-cognition, such as motivation and feeling. Education should, first and foremost, connect appropriately to things of value outside oneself, which is the primary path of self-development. Self-development is the opening of the self to the valuable aspects of life beyond oneself (Rogers, 1961). These aspects need not only be areas of formal study, but include connecting to other people, to the life of society and to social causes and moral issues, for instance.

Teachers usually conceptualise what young people do at school as learning. This is probably a good way for teachers to think of the processes, because the point of education is that young people *learn*, in the broadest sense of the word. However, from the point of view of the young person, this is not necessarily helpful. If young people perceived all activities at school as learning then all those activities might be perceived as having the same flavour. There are so many reasons for reading, so many good things about reading, and many different other things one can do by reading. To label the broad variety of these activities simply as *learning* (or indeed reading) is to cast the curse of sameness over all with one damning spell: 'let it all be *learning*'. In the eyes of the student, all school activities can easily become either studying for exams or learning to be an adult. When all activities are conceived in terms of learning, even self-development can become tedious. Imagine that you fracture your spine. Your physiotherapist is very worried for your recuperation. Under these conditions, it is easy for all physical activities to turn into therapy. You cannot walk in the park, go for a swim, catch a ball, or even lie on your bed without it being therapy. You may soon long for the day when you are better just so that you can walk in the park without it being a form of rehabilitation. The young person needs tastes that are new and fresh, as well as good solid fare. Not all school activities should be painted the colour of learning. Indeed, as we have already seen, the learning of biology needs to be coloured by the interesting features of the natural world – in other words, by what one is connecting to. Likewise, history isn't just a school topic, but is the past of humanity. To always portray what we do in school as learning may deprive the student of the opportunity of connecting directly to what he/she studies and conceptualising its value on his/her own terms.

Furthermore, if activities are always framed as learning, then they can easily become seen as valuable merely instrumentally, rather than as something worth doing for their own sake. Thus the young person would no longer be connected directly to the valuable (interesting) features of what he/she is studying.

In a similar vein, if schools as institutions have a strong culture that permeates all activities then this will affect the perception of the students; no matter how much variety the curriculum has, everything will have the flavour of the school (also see Hargreaves, 1982; Hoy, 2003; Stoll, 2009). This may be why a person can enjoy an activity performed outside school, when the very same activity during school time is a chore. If everything tastes of the institution itself then nothing has a special savour of its own. The institutionality of school can make it dreary (Illich, 1971). It colours everything. Somehow, school can make most areas of knowledge rather dull (even calling them 'subjects' makes them seem uninspiring). For some students, going to school can be like being transported every day into a foreign country that they don't really understand and don't really like (Klein, 1999). There is evidence to show that most pupils are bored at school, and that school actually makes subjects boring that are not intrinsically boring (Keys, W. and Fernandes, C., 2004). For example, the natural world is incredibly interesting. In sharp contrast, for many students, 'science' means a musty classroom with test tubes and burners, and posters on the wall with formulas. It is a world of people in white coats, who seem to dream in mathematical symbols (Schuck and Pereira, 2011). How do bored kids perceive the learning of chemistry? It just does not speak to them. The same applies to many other subjects. Once again this indicates the need for radical reframing.

The feeling that school is not cool may be in part a reaction to this. When some students are not appropriately motivated, schooling often feels like force-feeding, and this affects the culture of the school as a whole (Nardia and Steward, 2003). If the institutional culture of a school breeds dreariness, then it will incite discontent and rebellion. Young people can be very sensitive to how other people perceive them, and this exacerbates the anti-school reaction. Furthermore, if a young person feels judged or condemned or put into a box by his/her teachers, then he/she may have little option but to rebel, and to disown the institution that has apparently rejected him/her (Boaler et al., 2000). Since most young people care about how they are perceived by their peers, it is easy for such disowning to spread.

Partly because of this, the whole classroom exercise can be remarkably slow. For example, someone who really wanted to know about the functioning of cells could learn in 10 minutes the material that it often takes a whole 50-minute class to cover. The class time passes slowly and the content is minimal. This reinforces, as well as being caused by, the first problem (i.e. weak motivation), so there is a positive feedback loop reinforcing the syndrome.

Doing one's own thing

For many, school is the experience of coercion and being told what to do in nearly every activity (Noddings, 2000). Furthermore, one is not the owner of one's own time. Perhaps because of this, some students experience drudgery. Unfortunately, this is similar to many people's experience of work. Like work, the school as an institution seems to expect students to be passive. Students are seldom encouraged to become co-constructors of the learning processes they undergo. The whole experience occurs within a fixed framework with regard to aims, the curriculum, timetabling, and the objectives and activities of a session or class. Of course, a good understanding of what one is doing and why is necessary for the possibility of being able to shape what one does. The more young people understand, the more they can participate in shaping the educational process they are supposed to benefit from, and the more they can have ownership of the process (Fielding, 2007a; Fielding and Moss, 2010). However, there are limits to this involvement because it is very difficult to know what one doesn't know: without good background knowledge, one may have very little idea of what there is to be known. More importantly, students may have little idea of the skills and qualities they need to cultivate. They need guidance, some framework and the right opportunities for practice.

Nevertheless, despite these caveats, it is educationally counterproductive to inculcate and expect passivity in students. There are three points here. First, this practice does not treat the student as a person. It regards him/her as someone who should only do what he is told. This is not how we should behave towards people, as we stressed in the first chapter. It shows disrespect for the person.

Second, the expected passivity negates the development that is supposed to be the very point of education. A big part of one's growth as a person is the development of initiative. A person needs to have an entrepreneurial view of his/her own life, even if he/she is not going into business; an entrepreneur creates and initiates projects and endeavours, gathers resources and organises things so that people can work together (UNESCO, 2006). Children often do this when they play. A person without these qualities, and the well-developed abilities that result from them, will lead a more passive life, exercising his/her decision-making within a rigid and assumed framework. As we said before, many people do live within a reduced sense of their own possibilities (i.e. of what is possible for them).

In many ways, school can encourage young people to be like that. It is already a highly hierarchically structured environment, but the student is not privileged to know this structure and how it works. However, he/she is aware of the fact that school life is planned and decided elsewhere. He/she knows that education is highly planned and that he/she is not in a position to change the structure or plan. It is handed down from above. Therefore, as a student, he/she is passive. School could support the student to be more proactive in the shaping of his/her own education. Planning one's own education, with guidance and within a framework of process guidelines, would itself be a very significant element of the education one would like to have (Fielding, 2007b).

Third, a young person needs to have every encouragement to not be indifferent to his/her own education. He or she needs to own the process as if it were his/her own hobby in order to blur the distinction between work and leisure, as discussed in Chapter 1. This requires the kind of co-construction that we will outline in Chapters 7 and 11.

In order for a person to own the educative processes, it is necessary for the young person to commit to what he/she is doing on his/her own terms. For example, some students can commit to their own self-interested future, to the idea of a particular kind of work, to some aspects of a particular area of knowledge, to oneself as an improved person, to helping others, and so on. These are examples of different terms of commitment, and as a little empirical reflection shows, they can be quite idiosyncratic, varying from person to person. However, if a person cannot engage in a process that accords with his/her own terms (or descriptions under which he/she is willing to commit) then engagement becomes psychologically impossible. Commitment is a decision to engage, which changes the student from a passive spectator, who occasionally and reluctantly participates, into an active agent. A little non-empirical reflection shows us that a person cannot be forced to commit.

This is why we sometimes need the idea of learning without teaching. Typically, people tend to rebel against being told things if they contextualise the telling as authoritarian or paternalistic. Sometimes, rebelling takes the form of switching oneself off or hiding in a corner. However, this is not necessarily a rebellion against learning. It might be an aversion to being told in a particular manner, which may indicate a need for self-guided learning. The student needs the opportunity to learn for him/herself without perceived interference. This does not obviate the need for guidance and facilitation, but it means that *sometimes* the teacher needs to be close to invisible. Everybody has had the experience of guiding someone to an idea and the result is that the person thinks the idea is his/her own, something that he/she came up with by themselves. These points indicate why it is essentially self-refuting and counterproductive to tell young people to be responsible for their own learning. A sense of self-responsibility has to grow and be discovered by the young person themselves, by definition. They cannot be cajoled into having it.

As we shall see in later chapters, the practical solution to these problems is to reduce the time spent providing students with answers that have no corresponding questions. This means increasing the amount of energy focusing explicitly on cultivating questions.

Summary: one thing out of place

The everyday practical problems of facilitating student motivation are exacerbated because the list of possible blocks and obstacles seems open-ended as well as somewhat obscure. For example, a young person who feels lost within himself will not be able to concentrate easily on learning. A person who experiences self-loathing or no self-respect will find motivation difficult. Similarly, the young person who is subject to severe mood swings or who feels anxious cannot learn. Some students have short attention spans; others have emotional problems at home or difficulties with their boy/girlfriends. Some just dislike school. While the list is not endless, it seems to be imprecise. Furthermore, chronic boredom may be a symptom of another condition, in which case making lessons more interesting will not solve the underlying problem.

Nevertheless, the school has a duty to turn indifference into caring. It must nurture the process whereby the young person takes more responsibility for his/her own development by facilitating his/her active engagement with aspects of the world. A person cannot take responsibility for him/herself simply by deciding to. It requires preparation and the cultivation of caring (Noddings, 1984). As we have seen, caring has its roots in the connecting (as evaluative perception) to the valuable aspects of what is outside of oneself. The rebel who sees the faults in society *ipso facto* can also perceive possible social improvements and has begun to care. This caring can be nurtured. The young person who can see the stars and galaxies as mysterious can care about astronomy.

In practice, to nurture caring often means to help remove the obstacles that destroy it. For example, if a student gets stuck on details in his/her reading then he/she may become discouraged because he/she has failed to grasp the overall point. How does one avoid getting stuck on details? This involves a set of skills and qualities. For example, one has to be able to recognise that one is lost in details; one has to care enough to take corrective action without being discouraged. One has to have the confidence to be able to bracket the details, and return to the main point. All this requires experience, which only comes by doing. There are many ways that caring can become undermined and undernourished. Therefore, there are equally numerous corrective actions that the tutor needs to take to facilitate the student's progress.

The society that we live in can be indifferent and impersonal. This may be because many of the interactions one has with strangers are commercial, and commercial relations tend to be impersonal. School can avoid echoing this aspect of society. To foster caring attitudes, it must escape the depersonalised aspects of social life.

Emotions

If education involves the development of human qualities and preparation for a full human life, then emotions must be included in the process. Emotions are a vital aspect of life. However, emotions tend to be undervalued in some Western societies. They tend to get pushed out by time spent thinking, working and wanting, which often preclude the feeling of emotions. In a moment, we will examine what this means. We will use the terms 'feelings' and 'emotions' interchangeably.

Schools tend to shy away from direct involvement with the emotions of young people. There are several reasons for this. First, there is an underlying assumption that emotions are part of the purely private and personal realm and therefore do not warrant a full or direct place in schooling, which is public. This usually unvoiced assumption is increasingly under challenge, however. The boundaries between public and private spaces may vary in different cultures and societies. For example, in a Colombian school, Colegio Amor, the boundary between the private and the public is blurred in the school environment, and adults and children are directly involved with each other's emotions (more on this in Chapter 11). Such close involvement with emotions would be difficult to imagine in a normal English secondary school.

This is by no means to suggest that schools in England do nothing about emotions. Over recent years, personal social health education (PSHE) programmes and social and emotional aspects of learning (SEAL) programmes have been introduced in British state schools. These show that there is recognition of the importance of emotions in education. The limitation of these approaches is that they risk implicitly regarding emotions as of purely instrumental value. The general idea of these programmes is that if we know how to deal with our emotions more wisely, then we will be able to study and work better, and achieve better results (see, for example, Parker *et al.*, 2004). Emotional intelligence programmes sometimes take this one step further: we need to know how to express our feelings appropriately so that we do not hurt others and so that we can live more peacefully. Certainly, this is not false, but it is limited: it hardly acknowledges the emotions as lived-through experiences, and therefore as constitutive (in part) of one's life, as opposed to something to be controlled in order to perform better. It tends to make emotions into forces that either damage or enhance our ability to work and study, and, therefore, relegates them to a secondary position compared to study, which presumably means intellectual growth, and treats them as if they need to be managed. In contrast, we claim that the development of the feelings requires that they are experienced or felt. It is not enough to discuss emotions and try to understand them intellectually in the attempt to use them. They need to be experienced (Macmurray, 1962).

Another possible reason why schools shy away from emotional development is that feelings are unpredictable. We cannot set student performance targets in feelings – the idea of testing will then go out the window. Teachers can only have limited responsibility for the emotions of their students. It is not like studying for GCSE where the teacher is held (and is supposed to be) responsible for the students' performances. Furthermore, the expression of feelings can be dangerous. For example, anger and depression can breed violence and, with that, a host of legal issues. So, although the teacher's responsibility is more limited, it is more acute.

Despite their severity, however, these are practical problems that could be overcome. Counsellors and facilitators know how to manage the expression of feelings in groups. The assessment of student progress needs to be revisited, and with it the notion of what a teacher is responsible for. Some secondary schools in England have started integrating social and emotional aspects of learing in teaching, and have seen some positive outcome in students' overall experience of education. This is because SEAL encourages students to feel their emotions and discuss with peers how their feelings affect the way they are in relation to themselves, their peers, teachers and other adults, as well as the way they participate in learning.

Typically, our strongest feelings are about ourselves and other people. Young people value very highly their friendships at school. This can be a good starting point for education that includes the development of the emotions. There are two points here. First, if the school can cultivate an atmosphere of caring and happiness during any activities dedicated to learning then this will permeate the culture of the school or learning institution as a whole (Weare, 2000). The school will be and be felt as a caring institution. To do so, however, it needs to dissolve the societal expectations that interaction between people should be impersonal in a public setting (Noddings, 2002). It can also be a joyous space rather than a place of insecurity, anger and saddening seriousness. We will discuss this more fully in Chapter 11.

Second, during the normal course of the day, young people need to be together in groups. Kids usually form into groups by themselves, and often identify with the groupings that schools impose on them (such as forms) (McLellan and

Pugh, 1999). Large impersonal secondary schools in which young people hardly ever share class-time with the same individuals are antithetical to the formation of such groups. Nevertheless, a school can help create true group feelings among its members, through facilitated processes that we will describe in later chapters. A feeling of being close involves each member feeling part of the group, recognising that the others in the group feel the same way and knowing that they recognise this of oneself. It also involves the people caring about each other and having the opportunity as a group to exercise this care. To become such, the group needs to have an open and free space, a special time when people can express their feelings without fear, knowing that they will be listened to with care. This will be the opportunity for members to help and support each other and experience emotions together (see Fielding, 2009, for suggestions in terms of the use of spaces within the schools for creating a culture of care and listening).

What is the development of feelings? Emotions usually involve other people. Of course, we can become angry when the car doesn't work or sad when a favourite vase breaks. In such cases, however, other people are usually involved implicitly: the car breaks down when you are late for an appointment, and the vase was a special gift. We also have self-directed feelings, which are usually mingled with evaluative self-perception: I feel sad because I am not as good as everyone else; I am angry with myself because I did not do well. Often even self-directed feelings involve other people indirectly.

The development of the emotions has three aspects. The first is to really feel them. As we said earlier, in some Western societies, people are not encouraged to feel emotions. It becomes a routine to think, work and want in a way that precludes experiencing one's feelings directly. It should not be a surprise that one can have feelings without really experiencing them fully. The emotion will typically manifest itself in some other way: sadness can be a heartfelt feeling like a stab in the chest but it can be a relentless churning of thoughts around some topic. The development of the emotions requires that we actually feel them more fully.

The second is to feel appropriately. For example, it is appropriate to feel fear at something harmful, and anger when someone commits a serious injustice against oneself. It is usually not appropriate to feel fear when someone presents you with a gift, or anger when someone breathes near to you (Aristotle, *Nicomachean Ethics*). Some adolescents are infamously prone to mood swings that make this aspect of emotional development difficult (see Chapter 5). Although often one may not be able to immediately control what one feels, nevertheless, feelings can change over time through healing, therapeutic and cathartic processes, or through a process of maturation (Be-Ze'ev, 2000), so that, for instance, underlying anger, insecurity or sadness can change.

The third is to open one's feelings more towards other people. The emotions of the young child tend to be self-centred and self-directed. As moral psychologists have noted, as the child becomes older, he/she is able to better understand the feelings of other people and feel appropriately (see Chapter 5). He/she then becomes less self-centred. As this happens, he/she will tend to feel less anger, fear and sadness, insofar as these are self-centred sentiments. Being open to others requires that one is relatively free of the anxieties, insecurities, resentments, antagonisms and sorrows that constitute and cause unhappiness. Such feelings tend to close one off from others. To be more open requires that one has a general feeling of happiness as well as emotional stability and strength. The development of the emotions is towards caring and feeling love for other people and therefore towards a greater sensitivity for the feelings and interests of other people.

The development of the emotions relates to education directly as well as indirectly. Directly, education includes the development of the emotions as part of the growth of the whole person. Indirectly, it is relevant because having closed and undeveloped feelings is a root cause of three educational malaises: indifference, lack of confidence and lack of appreciation (Schutz and Lanehart, 2002).

Earlier we discussed indifference and ended on the inconclusive point that some students' apathy may be a symptom of some other chronic condition. If this is so, then the underlying condition in question pertains to the feelings. Indifference can be the result, for example, of insecurity and anxiety, which a person may not be fully aware of feelings. It can be born of hemmed in resentments or of the pressure of built-up sadness. These spatial metaphors would need to be explained in terms of the perception of the person who is under the sway of an emotion that is not fully recognised. Resentment will manifest itself, for instance, in seeing the behaviour of the teacher as insulting, arrogant or snobbish. Resentment will then reinforce itself through the collection of grudges. A young person who has grudges at school will probably hide them and become stonily indifferent. (If not, he/she may be aggressive and rebellious.) Thus many young people could be at risk of becoming disaffected and disengaged from the school system (Lumby, 2011).

For a person to flourish, he/she needs to appreciate the value of the activities that he/she engages in (see Chapter 6). For instance, it is no use having a walk on the beach, if all the while one is worried about something else, or if he/she is hardly present in his/her own awareness. For the activity to be worthwhile in a way that has meaning for the individual, he/she has to appreciate it. Better appreciation of the value of experiences and activities requires alert awareness; the duller the awareness, the less appreciation. In effect, a person needs to have self-conscious awareness to be fully present and alert. Having one's awareness more awake is also a precondition for better learning. Students who are distracted by anxieties or are numbed by sadness cannot learn well. Freedom from the feelings of sadness, fear and anger will enable the person to have clearer awareness.

Conclusion

A human-centred approach rejects the dichotomy of the cognitive and the non-cognitive as if they were entirely separate and exclusive. Each is an aspect of one person. Exponents of alternative education often argue that the mainstream traditional approach emphasises the intellectual, ignoring the emotional. However, the unity of the person is a point that we can miss also by following too closely the spirit of Rousseau's romanticism and reaction against reason. It seems that non-traditional forms of education often emphasise the noncognitive (such as the emotional) at the expense of the cognitive (such as the intellectual), thereby committing the traditional error in reverse. However, the redress is not so much a question of balancing the two but rather recognising that they are two aspects of a person and thereby trying to articulate the way they can work together symbiotically. We don't want balance but rather unity.

In this chapter we have tried to examine the development of motivation and emotion from this whole-person perspective. A common theme has emerged. The development of both motivation and emotion involve going beyond oneself. Both consist in part of opening oneself to other people and to the world, by caring more. Such caring has preconditions, among which is appropriate evaluative cognition.

Further reading

Frankfurt, H. (2006) *The Reasons of Love*. Princeton, NJ: Princeton University Press.

Helm, B. (2007) *Emotional Reason: Deliberation, Motivation and the Nature of Value*. Cambridge: Cambridge University Press.

Kristjansson, K. (2010) *The Self and its Emotions*. Cambridge: Cambridge University Press.

McDowell, J. (2001) Virtue and Reason, in *Mind, Value and Reality*. Cambridge, MA: Harvard University Press.

McNaughton, D. (1991) *Moral Vision*. Oxford: Blackwell Publishing, Chapters 5 and 7.

Noddings, N. (1992) *The Challenge to Care in Schools: An Alternative Approach to Education*. New York: Teachers College Press.

4
The experience of being an adolescent

Introduction

In the first three chapters, we have introduced the concept of human-centred education and attempted to support the fundamental principles that are enshrined in such a concept. Our next task is to apply these abstract ideas to educational practices at secondary school level. This will be the focus of the second part of the book. However, before we delve into such discussions, it is important to first understand better the nature of adolescence and the young people who would be the recipients of and participants in human-centred education. We need to understand their ways of learning and growing, the challenges they face in their lives, and their wants, needs and aspirations in order to be able to apply the principles of the previous chapters. For example, in order for education to respect the person, it must care for the individual. What this means in practice depends on how that person lives his or her life.

To do this, we shall adopt a two-pronged approach. First, in this chapter, we shall present some insights into being an adolescent from our research, which consists of interviews with young people about aspects of their experience. Then, in the next chapter, we shall present some of the major findings in psychological and social research about the nature of adolescence. Given the input of these two chapters, we shall present a more complete description of the human-centred approach to education in Chapter 6.

▶

In gathering the young people's views, we used a methodological approach termed 'peer-to-peer' research, which was intended to empower the young people to reflect on their experience. Our peer-to-peer research generated a large amount of data. For the purpose of this chapter, we will select and present the results in three sections: first, the adolescents' relationships with friends, family and other adults; second, their perceptions of themselves; and finally, how they see their future direction after secondary schooling. We tried to select results from the interviews that are relatively clear and forceful without being repetitive. For this informal presentation, we have tried to be comprehensive. We also asked the young people about their experiences of schooling, but we will share these views in Chapter 10.

The overall aim of the peer-to-peer qualitative research is to provide empirical input into the reflection about the practical significance of human-centred education: what does it mean to help students learn? Such questions have more theoretical and more practice-orientated answers, and as we pass from the former to the latter, we need our answers to be informed by the nature of adolescence and experience of the young people who receive an education.

Introducing peer-to-peer research

Because we wanted the perspectives of the young people to be at the heart of our research, we decided to apply a methodology that is emerging out of the 'student voice' movement. Fielding (2004a, p. 199) points out that student voice can be conceptualised as:

> A range of activities that encourage reflection, discussion, dialogue and action on matters that primarily concern students, but also, by implication, school staff and the communities they serve.

The student voice movement aims to encourage these participatory activities in educational innovation, school improvement and community development. Fielding (2004a) reports that, over the last decade, there has been an increasing number of initiatives that engage student voices in education including research inquiry, policy feedback, teaching and learning development.

Table 4.1 Students as researchers – characteristic examples

Teacher role – listen in order to contribute.
Student role – initiator and director of research with teacher support.
Teacher engagement with students – dialogue (student-led).
Classroom – e.g. what makes a good lesson?
Team/department – e.g. gender issues in technology subjects.
School – e.g. evaluation of PSHE system, radical school council.

Source: Fielding, 2004a: 202

This has led Fielding and McGregor (2005) to suggest that students might act as researchers, participating in the design of research (see Table 4.1). The authors argue that, in this model,

> It is students who identify issues to be researched or investigated; students who undertake the research with the support of staff; students who have responsibility for making sense of the data, writing a report or presenting their findings; and it is students to whom the class teacher, team/department or school community are bound to respond in ways which are respectful, attentive and committed to positive change (Fielding and McGregor, 2005: 7).

One of the promising aspects of this approach is that it encourages student engagement and active reflection about their own learning and their own interests, so that it becomes a learning process as well as a research methodology.

We shared Fielding and colleagues' optimism for student-led research inquiry. As a methodology, we felt that having young people interview each other might foster more open and generous reflection on their experiences. It would enable us to reach more students. We also wanted the input of students in the design of the research.

In 2008, we approached a large number of schools in south-east England with an open invitation to participate in this research. Three schools responded positively and agreed to help identify volunteer students to act as researchers. All three schools are state schools: two secondary schools and one six-form college. School A is a community school located in a relatively deprived area with 99 per cent of the school's enrolments being children from white working-class families. The student researchers from School A are all British-born Caucasians, two male and one female. School B is situated at the centre of an affluent town. The student researchers from School B were two female students: one English Caucasian and one born to an immigrant family originally from the Far East. The young people interviewed in School B are of good mix of ethnicities. The

Table 4.2 Profiles of student researchers of the peer-to-peer research

Pseudonym of student researcher	Age in 2007	Gender	School
Nick	15	Male	Community school
Mick	15	Male	Community school
Jacquie	15	Female	Community school
Mimi	14	Female	Secondary school
Hannah	14/15	Female	Secondary school
Rowena	17	Female	Sixth-form college
Amelia	17	Female	Sixth-form college

student researchers from the sixth-form college are both British-born Caucasians, and they interviewed students from diverse ethnic and social backgrounds.

For reasons of privacy, the three schools, the young researchers, and the adolescents interviewed have all been kept anonymous. Table 4.2 summarises the profiles of our young researchers using pseudonyms.

The peer-to-peer research involved the participation of the young researchers in:

■ formulating the research questions;

■ working as researchers to find out their peers' experience of being an adolescent, learning and schooling;

■ analysing with the adult researchers all the interview data after it had been collected;

■ identifying further questions for follow-up inquiries;

■ helping with the reporting and concluding.

We explained to the student volunteers that our research was concerned with how young people perceived their experience of adolescence, including peer relationships, personal goals, experiences at the school and direction for the future. The volunteers from each school met, discussed and compiled a list of possible questions for the interview. We collected these questions and synthesised them. The following were agreed by all seven student researchers:

■ How does the young person perceive him/herself at this time?

■ What is it like to be a young person in secondary education?

■ What impact does school have on the young person's growth and development?

- What has the young person learned through education and schooling and how has he/she learned it?
- In what way does education help the young person to identify their future direction in adulthood?
- If there are changes they would like to make in their education, what would they be and how do they think changes could take place?

In 2008–9, each volunteer researcher interviewed between 5 and 7 other young people, and we interviewed the volunteer researchers. All interviews were recorded and transcribed. Unfortunately, only two young researchers (Rowena and Amelia) were able to participate in the debriefing meeting and to help interpret the data collected. The others didn't get permission from their schools to attend this meeting outside their school hours.

A total of 50 participants took part in the study.[1] During the interviews, they all chose pseudonyms for themselves. These names were common names (mostly Christian names), even though some of our young participants were from diverse ethnic backgrounds. Adult researchers interviewed 20 per sent of the participants.

Our young volunteer researchers reported that, because of the research, they were able to better understand the significant issues confronting themselves and other adolescents. All seven young researchers confirmed that, through taking on this research, they had learned more about themselves, and had become more mature. The recordings and transcripts indicate that their interaction with their peers became more sophisticated during the process.

The experience of being an adolescent

We shall report the research findings in two parts: the first, which is reported in this chapter, concerns the participants' perceptions of themselves as adolescents. The second part is reported in Chapter 10, where we focus on their experience of secondary education within their schools. In relation to the participants' experience of being an adolescent, we report the findings under three broad themes:

1. Being an adolescent
2. Self-description
3. Future direction

[1] In this book, all the adolescents interviewed will be referred to as participants.

Being an adolescent

In this section, we will examine some of the participants' accounts of being an adolescent through their perceptions of themselves. Our researchers asked the young people what they considered to be the most important thing for themselves at the time of the interview and also questioned the negative and positive experiences of being an adolescent.

In brief, most of the young people mentioned the need for friendship and the search for independence as central to their adolescence. Intertwined with this was their relationship with their families.

Several young people mentioned friendship as the most important aspect of their life during adolescence, even compared to family.

The words of Hannah (17 years old) are not atypical:

> I'd say my friends are most important in my life [at this age] because, I think I could, well, I really like my family as well, but friends [are] just on top because I am very conscious that I'm going to uni, so I've made them the most important thing in my life. And I know that without a circle of friends I'd be awful. I'd just be so depressed, honestly.

Charlotte (16 years old) said that she had changed schools twice during adolescence, and that, in between time, she was home educated. The home schooling turned out to be a difficult experience and she resented it due to not having other young people to socialise with.

At the same time, according to the participants, relationships with friends and peers at this age can be very problematic, especially in large secondary schools. For instance, when Charlotte finally ended her home education and attended a state school, she was intimidated by the different social groupings, and felt pressurised to belong. Similarly, many of the young people interviewed agreed that social groups and their subcultures could be threatening. They reported that they had felt forced to decide which rival crowd to belong to, at the risk of being excluded from all of them. The participants shared stories of how pressure from peer groups tempted some of them to sacrifice their integrity in order to feel included.

The interviewees also linked this peer pressure to a negative collective attitude towards learning and school, namely that to learn or work at school is 'uncool' and that to be cool requires being disengaged and disrespectful to teachers and other young people. For instance, Rowena recalled her experience at secondary school when she was 14:

To be 'cool' is to be popular and to be popular you can't appear to be hardworking or learning. I remember trying to become friends with this girl who was really obnoxious and really loud and quite rude and of course I wasn't at all, but I felt like I had to fit in so I remember, like, leaning back in my chair and talking back to the teacher, and feeling better about myself and noticing that she was then more responsive to me . . .

Indeed, in this research, students cited peer pressure and destructive subcultures as one of the most negative aspects of adolescence. David (16 years old) seemed to feel that some peer culture had tainted his view of life:

A bad experience was just meeting 90 per cent of other teenagers that attended the same school as I did. Just the way that people acted and how so immature – but not in a silly kind of way, like a scary kind of way – the way that everyone nods along and lets really bad things happen, like bullying, bad bullying. Like a lot of people would spray deodorant all over the tables and let them catch fire and everyone would crowd around and watch. You'd just think 'What the hell is going on? Why?' It's just horrible. And people are getting their faces kicked in and other students are just watching and asking everyone else 'Did you see it?' You just realise how bad the world is. You just appreciate all the fine people who aren't like that.

However, only the younger participants (14–16 years old) described youth subcultures in the present tense. The older students (16–18 year old) recalled these in the past tense as memories of their earlier secondary education experience. Perhaps, the reason for this is that, as adolescents become more mature, they are more capable of recognising the potentially destructive nature of social groups and subcultures. For example, Hannah used to be intimidated by the groups in the same secondary school as Charlotte. However, at the age of 15, Hannah started speaking to a few young people at the school who were from different social groupings. She crossed the boundaries. Because of this, she made an important discovery:

When I was in Year 10, I learnt something quite important. I learnt that everyone is the same fundamentally and that really helped me. There are a lot of groups and it's all a bit vicious. But then in Year 10, you get talking to different people [in these groups] and you just realise, like, hang on a second, you can talk to anyone because everyone is feeling the same sort of thing. You know, like, little things, like you get embarrassed about this sort of thing or you do this sort of thing and you realise that everyone is pretty much the same. You know, like, the differences [in attitudes towards the peer groups] are so small, they're negligible.

In a similar fashion, some time after Charlotte returned to school from home education, she decided to stay out of all of the rival groups, even though she felt intimidated and under pressure:

> There were so many more people [in peer groups] and kind of more definite groups – like that's the cool group and that's the sad group and it's like who you are depends on which group [you belong to]. Well I wasn't in the group [laughter] and I didn't really mind because even then I didn't have, I didn't really think, I didn't, I didn't really feel that I had to be in it.

The need for friendship prompted many young people interviewed in our research to discuss their dilemma of whether to belong to a peer group, or not to belong. However, many of the participants also said that this struggle was part of their search for better self-understanding, independence and autonomy.

Seventeen-year-old Grace described her search for independence as central to her experience of being an adolescent. She related independence as having a strong sense of herself. She said that what was most important was to remain true to herself:

> Well, probably the thing that stands out most [about being an adolescent] as I've grown older is to just be yourself, to just like regardless of, that sounds really cheesy, just regardless of what anyone says or anything, the most important thing is to stick to who you are – which might change as time develops and as you grow – but umm, my behaviour is always like true to me sort of thing.

Rowena interviewed Grace and, during the interview, they discussed the role of friends in their life and how important friendship is to their 'being oneself'. This suggests that an important aspect of development during adolescence is to form a better sense of oneself as a person, which is a theme we will return to throughout the book. In Chapter 5, we will discuss this aspect of adolescence from the viewpoint of the existing literature.

From our interviews, parents come across as ambivalent figures during a young person's search for independence. Many of the young people said that, as they grew older, they prefer to receive less help from their parents. Some found that parental involvement can 'constantly interfere' with their own plans, and that they wanted to have more independence from their parents. Rowena (17 years old) told us about her conflict with her mother:

> I think I must have been 13 when I really wanted to disassociate from my family, so I was not talking to my mum much at all about my life and therefore she wasn't trusting me. Because I wasn't confiding in her any more and

it was like such a sudden change for her and for me as well. So it kind of went to a crescendo – a peak, and I was just arguing with my whole family the whole time. I was just having such bad relationships with everybody. I was also like I would have such big mood swings. I would get so angry and blow up over nothing.

Obviously Rowena's needs for independence and disassociating herself from her family intertwined with her mood swings. She was in the minority of the young people interviewed who had such a strong desire to break free from the family's involvement in their life.

In general, however, many of the participants found themselves in a dilemma when it came to their relationships with parents. Their desire for independence and autonomy was very strong, but this desire was compounded with a simultaneous need for more support and care. Some explained that what they really wanted from their parents was encouragement and support towards their adolescent explorations without being 'overbearing'. When this balance is not there, the young person can appear to be rebellious or, as with Rowena, is always 'getting into trouble with the whole family'.

At the same time, many young people interviewed seemed to recognise that family was important in their life and that family can shape the way they think and the way they are. Many cited travels with families as a good experience. For example, Sarah (15 years old) recounted her family holidays:

> I really like going to Spain and seeing my cousins . . . They live on a mountainside with an orchard and me and my baby cousin sit on a window sill and eat yoghurts or something and look over the mountains . . .

Mary (15 years old) also mentioned a family holiday as a good experience:

> Once I went on holiday at Christmas and my Auntie was there, my Uncle, my Granny and we just spent a week together and there was like loads of dogs and people and it was really fun.

Grace shared similar experiences, although she recognised that she was very privileged to have had such encounters:

> The thing that sticks in my head is like travelling. And I think that is one of the best [experiences]. Well the best thing my parents have ever done is to take me and my brother and my big brother to all sorts of different places and experience lots of different cultures and environments. And that's probably the thing that's shaped me most, like it's really hard to describe. You can't just look in a book and understand [another place] – you've got to be there.

As Grace went on to say, learning to become oneself may be achieved through relationships with others, including meeting other people, and having friends. She also suggested that experiencing different places and cultures was important in developing her self-concept:

> And it's absolutely fascinating that there are so many different types of people in the world who all have a different view of things and I don't know [about them]. I find the whole thing astonishing, you know, really difficult to put into words. [. . .]

> But it's mainly through the people that I've benefited, like meeting different sorts of people and learning things not through a textbook but through people's experiences and through my friends and things like that. And that's probably one of the most important things I'd say [about learning during adolescence]. And of course, visit all sorts of different places and experience lots of different cultures and environments.

Many writers have confirmed that encounters with other people, including young people, is an important aspect of adolescence. The reason for this will be reviewed in the next chapter.

Self-description

To a large extent, the young people interviewed for the research seemed to have had some trouble answering this question in a straightforward manner. It was noticeable that especially those under 16 found it hard to describe themselves with just a few words. Some young people seemed to need the question explained. Others simply found it impossible to answer – they appeared to be uncertain as to what to say and their descriptions were often limited in scope.

Here are a few typical examples of some adolescents' responses to the question about themselves:

Q 'How would you describe yourself as a person?'
A 'Umm . . . I'm quite quiet . . .'

Q 'How would you describe yourself as a person?'
A 'I'd say I'm quite an enthusiastic person, err . . . quite loud, creative, musical in a way.'

Q 'How would you describe yourself as a person?'
A 'I'd describe myself as a lively character. I'm well behaved most of the time.'

Q 'How would you describe yourself as a person?'
A 'I'm quite funny . . . and . . . talkative and quite a happy chappy . . . yeah.'

Q 'How would you describe yourself as a person?'
A 'Umm . . . pretty kind. Sometimes a bit argumentative . . . yeah.'

Q 'How would you describe yourself as a person?'
A 'I'd say I'm quite an outgoing person who gets along with most people.'

Q 'How would you describe yourself as a person?'
A 'Bubbly . . . a bit hyper you know . . . I can be calm at times . . . but you know . . . I have my moments when I'm hyper.'

In the example below, the interview was conducted by 17-year-old Rowena; the interviewee, George, was 18. Feeling flummoxed, George repeated the question to himself again and again, which Rowena tried to explain in different ways:

Q 'OK, George, how would you describe yourself as a person?'
G 'Describing myself as a person? [pause] Bloody Hell, that's pretty hard, in terms of what, I don't know.'

Q 'It can be anything, anything that comes to mind, that is about you.'
G 'Umm . . . that's so hard. I can't [brief pause]. Describe myself as a person . . . umm . . .'

Q 'What makes you different from other people? Or what describes you?'
G 'What makes me different from other people?'

Q 'Not necessarily different, but just anything about yourself.'
G 'Ah, man, that's such a hard question. How would I describe myself?! I don't know. I'm an art student, but I don't know if I want to do art. Maybe I don't, maybe I do – I don't know. Umm, what else? I went to a Steiner school, which is slightly different [from other schools]. I also went to a prep school. Umm – I don't know, I can't think of anything else.'

The question also had to be explained several times for Charlotte (15 years old), as she didn't really know how to answer it at first. Again, our young researcher had to reformulate the question in several ways:

Q 'Let me rephrase this for you. What do you think defines you as a person? What makes you different from other people? It doesn't have to be about education, just generally, who do you think you are, or what kind of person are you?'
C 'Umm . . . well, I guess I like to be different from everyone else. I like to stand out from the crowd and I don't mind if people think I'm weird. And . . . umm . . . but at the same time, I like to like to . . . fit in. I don't know. That doesn't really make sense, does it?'

Q   'Well . . .'
C   'Umm . . . [laughter] . . . that's a really hard question . . .'

Some of the more mature students also found the simple question bemusing, but managed to articulate why. Katrina, who was very articulate throughout her interview, said that she wasn't clear about how to describe herself as a person. However, she then went on to portray herself from a number of aspects, including her age, location, family, education and hairstyle:

> I'm not really sure. I'd define myself as an 18-year old female who lives in B City. I'm in a single parent family. I guess educationally I do quite well. I have short hair. I don't know how else.

Although Katrina's self-portrayal seemed very brief, her entire interview portrayed a highly motivated young person with positive self-regard and a clear view of her own strengths and talents.

Likewise for 17-year-old Claire, the immediate response was 'I don't know', although she went on to try to explain why it could be difficult to spell out who we are straight away:

> I don't know [how to describe myself as a person]. I would say there are so many different things about every single person. It's the combinations of things that make people who they are. So . . . I don't know how to describe myself simply.

How did the young people describe themselves? Of course, this is a question of emphasis, because most of the interviewees mentioned many different aspects of themselves. Nevertheless, the answers fall into five categories.

First, physical features. Among the young people interviewed, only Katrina and Bob mentioned physical features as part of their response to the question, despite the fact that, according to the literature, early adolescents take their looks and how they appear to others extremely seriously.

Second, character traits. Many of the interviewees described themselves in terms of their character traits or personalities, such as being outgoing, chatty, sociable or friendly. This kind of response was more common amongst the younger participants. Sixteen-year-old Debbie, for example, turned to her character traits as an answer to the question:

> I'm quite bossy. I like people to do what I tell them to. I think I'm quite kind and I share things with people and I like looking after people and I . . . yeah . . . I like looking after my little sisters a lot and . . . yeah . . . and I think I'm quite sociable and I like to speak to lots of different people and yeah . . . I can't think of anything else. Umm . . . also and I am not very

brave, which is one of the things which I don't like about myself. I would like to be daring, but I'm not.

Then she described herself as a person of independent views, but at the same time, indecisive:

> I have completely different views on life, and I see things differently [from my peers]. I question everything. So maybe . . . probably . . . that would be what I would say [about myself]. Again, I really . . . I couldn't say. I'm very very indecisive. I enjoy creative things. Umm . . . and I love being around people. There are so many things that interest me, but I am far too lazy to actually work properly towards the things that interest me, which frustrates me quite a lot. That's all I can say really.

Seventeen-year-old Bob was unusual among the young participants in that he appeared to be assertive about himself – and, in particular, his character traits:

> I'm quite tall, yeah, I'm quite a confident person. I am quite confident in everyday life. I'm not afraid to say things if I want to say them. If I think something about somebody I will say it to their face normally . . . yeah.

Third, in terms of their family. A few of the participants also described themselves in relation to their family. For example, 15-year-old Ken attributes some of his character to his family:

> I'd say I'm a very outgoing person who gets along with most people well, and hopefully most people want to be friends with me. This is because I take after my Dad, have a good sense of humour and . . . umm . . . although I'm very sporty and the rest of family isn't.

Fourth, in terms of friendship group. A few young people also described themselves in terms of their friends, their social group and those around them. For example, 14-year-old Mimi illustrated that friendship group played a big part in a young person's idea of herself:

> What you are is always determined by your friendship group. It is impossible to be yourself because you can only be a particular type of person in order to be part of a particular group. Although we all think of ourselves as unique, if you look closer, all of us in the group are very similar – we listen to the same kind of music, read the same books, look at the same films, and all that. Otherwise, you would not have anything in common with the others in your group. So in a way, you are what your group are. If you are different, then you wouldn't be a part of your group.

Amy (15 years old) reflected on how her character traits depended on who she was with:

> I suppose I differ depending on how I'm feeling and maybe who I'm with. Generally I'm quite studious and I like reading and things like that . . . but I do go crazy sometimes as well especially when I am with people who are just wild. I'm fairly confident . . . and yeah . . .

Like Mimi and Amy, Bob also attempted to answer the question by explaining how identity depended on one's relationships and the people around one:

> Who you are around shapes who you are to a very large extent. Yes, people. As to how much time you spend on your work and how much time you spend socialising will shape you.

Fifth and finally, in terms of their interests. A few of the older participants described themselves mainly in terms of their interests, an approach which requires a good degree of self-knowledge. Here David (who had just turned 17) describes himself as a keen writer and musician:

> Well, I was born in 1991 and I like playing music. I wanted to do English but I never had a good English teacher. So my hopes weren't very high for college. And so I thought 'well how else can I have a creative output?' I thought 'oh wait, I can do music'. And then someone said 'oh look, there's a modern music college over there'. So I went to IMM [Institute of Modern Music] mainly just because it's the only thing I can picture myself doing other than writing and I felt IMM's a lot more . . . you can do what you want kind of thing rather than other [classical music] colleges.

Despite some ambiguity in defining and describing themselves, the young people interviewed seemed to have relatively clear ideas in terms of their physical features, personality traits, personal interests, and how they were connected with their friends and families. They also used these broad categories to portray themselves. We will explore this aspect of being an adolescent further in the next chapter when we stand back and review literature that discusses an adolescent's self-concept and identity.

Future directions

Academic studies

Many of the younger participants (14–16 years old) in our research, especially those who have come from less-privileged social backgrounds, tended to simplify their criteria for a good future life to 'being rich and famous', 'having a nice house', 'having a good job with good pay', 'a nice car', or 'having an amazing boyfriend'. The young people interviewed generally believed that they will achieve these future plans by obtaining good grades and going to university. For most of the younger students in our research, this seemed to be the main interest in pursuing their studies. Comments from some of the older students interviewed suggested that they were beginning to connect their choices of A level subjects to their personal interests and, in a couple of cases, what they valued. So for older students, their academic trajectories from A level through to university were somewhat integrated with their overall decision of who they were.

Two criteria for future jobs were common: income and job satisfaction. The view expressed by Cecil (14 years old) is representative in terms of an ideal adult life:

> I'd like to be quite well paid. Obviously, I want the money. And yeah, but a job that I really enjoy. It's not just about money; it's also about happiness. If you had a job that pays a hundred grand a year but you hate it, then you are not going to come back home to your family with a positive mind frame. You're going be grumpy and unhappy.

Lily, who was also 14, had a more specific idea in terms of what her ideal adult life might be and the kind of work she would like to do. Like many other young people interviewed, she seemed to view higher education as necessary to achieve that:

> Well . . . I'd like to live in New York, in the States, but that will be tough because of the green card and stuff. And I'd like to work in the film industry or something. I know I need to go through University and get the grades I need to qualify.

Some young people seemed to assume that school–college–university would be the natural progression to adult life, including work. For these young people, they took this trajectory for granted, due either to their families' influences and expectations, or to such a trajectory being seen as the 'normal' route for young people coming from a particular social background.

Here is how Kate (17 years old) described it in her conversation with the interviewer:

> Q 'What made you decide to stay on in the sixth form [college]?'
> K 'Ummm – well, I actually never considered the fact I wouldn't. It just always seemed like something that was going to happen . . . going from school to sixth form was what people did. I didn't really think about leaving.'
>
> Q 'So like a natural progression?'
> K 'Yes, just something you do.'

Q   'Right . . . why did you think that?'

K   'Oh, I don't know what made me think that. I don't know. I suppose it was just the fact that everyone I knew had always done it, just seemed to be normal to be honest, and I think I was enjoying school at the time, so it seemed natural to continue.'

Q   'Have you got any clear idea of what you want to do with your time in college and where you want to go with it after that?'

K   'Yes – I'm hoping to go to drama school, but we'll have to see what happens about that! If not, I'll definitely go on to university, to study drama of some kind. In college, I just want to get the grades that I want and sort of enjoy the subjects and learn as much as I can, but also meet new people.'

This conversation doesn't give a clear idea of what Kate would like to do after studying drama. She told us that she hadn't thought about work yet, because all she wanted to do at the time was to focus on studying.

In contrast, for some of the young people from less-privileged social and economic backgrounds, the future horizons for higher education were somewhat limited. Molly (14 years old) explained why she had never even thought about going to university:

University is all the . . . umm . . . university is just . . . you know . . . where the really smart people . . . and everyone goes to college . . . you don't have to be exceptionally smart to go to college [sixth-form college] but . . . you know you have to be quite clever to go to university.

The assumption that 'only smart people can go to universities' was not uncommon for the participants from School A – the community school in the deprived area. Fewer of them mentioned any plans to go to higher education than young people from School B – the other secondary school situated in a relatively affluent area. A few from School A did indicate that they might go to a sixth-form college to do A levels, in contrast with the participants from School B, who all expected to move on to study for A levels and then go to higher education.

Apart from the impact of social background on the young people's expectation to pursue further and higher education, several of the interviewees had experiences of having their futures limited by being labelled academically. Perhaps the most illuminating was Katrina's. She told the interviewer that in her first secondary school, she was labelled as 'thick' by her peers due to her dyslexia. Her teachers had low expectations of her. For instance, she said that she was put in the lowest set in most subjects and that she was not encouraged to take her SATs at GCSE level. In Katrina's view, this was due to the fact that she was not considered bright enough. Later, however, her family moved her to a different school, where the teachers treated her as if she was capable and intelligent. She learned to read and write more confidently, and also achieved good grades in her SATs. Katrina said that doing well in exams had boosted her confidence in studying. She had been able to break away completely from the image of being 'thick', had enjoyed her studies and done well in all of her GCSE subjects, and was confident that she would do well in her A levels. From her interview, Katrina seemed to have made some clear choices with regard to her future academic path:

K   I always assumed I wouldn't [carry on with education]. It wasn't some-
     thing I thought about that much initially, because it was something my
     family didn't expect. They didn't think I'd get through my GCSEs. But
     I guess as each step came I made the decision [to stay on in education].
     I did quite well in my GCSEs so I just carried on going, and then I'll go
     on to university . . .

Q   What are you going to study at university?

K   I'm applying to a few universities but I'm not sure which one
     I am going to go to. At the moment I want to go to Bristol, they do
     biochemistry, but I'm not sure what to do. I've applied for biochemis-
     try, human biology and bio-medicine at the moment, but I may reap-
     ply for just medicine. I'm not really sure, but at the moment it's Bristol
     for biochemistry.

Q   Why did you choose to study for biochemistry?

K   Well, chemistry and biology are what I did best in all my subjects. So
     my parents and teachers suggested that I should study biochemistry. I
     like these subjects, they don't bore me.

In general, the young people interviewed in this research confirmed that they do value education, although as we have seen, many view education from a purely instrumental perspective – they believe that they will be able to get a well-paid job if they have a degree, and the choice of their degree is also associated with the value that society places on a particular vocation or profession. These young people discussed this in light of their decision of whether to stay on in education after they complete their GCSEs. Obviously, since then, the school leaving age in England has changed, from 16 to 18. Therefore, the question of whether to continue with education would no longer be viable under the new policy.

Older adolescents interviewed seemed to place more emphasis on their own interest when deciding what to choose as their subjects of studying in further and higher education. They also showed that they were beginning to see the link between what they studied at sixth-form college and university, and their future adult life.

Work

Most of the young people in this research expressed the view that it was too early – at the age of 16–18 – for them to choose a career direction and the kind of work they would like to do when they are adults. It seemed that they wanted more time and experience in order to find out what vocation or profession they would like to pursue in adulthood and why. Furthermore, as we have seen, the interviews indicated that, in general, these young people were more capable of choosing the focus of their future studies as opposed to their future work or careers.

In this situation, some young participants said that in terms of their career direction, they would rely on the adults around them to offer inspiration, aspiration and, in some cases, help and suggestions to identify their own direction for work. For example, 15-year-old Samirah idealised the life of a teacher due to the influence of her own teacher:

> Hmm . . . [my ideal adult life is] teaching as an English teacher at a secondary school. Still having a brilliant social life, an amazing boyfriend and being able to drink a lot without having hangovers, and listening to lots of music.

In a similar vein, Ken, who was 15, told us that he was deeply inspired by his science teacher:

> I would like to be a successful scientist, a heart surgeon, and someone that everyone turns to if they ever need help, they can come to me, and I can put things right and sort their problems out.

There were a few similar cases where the young person regarded a teacher as a role model in the way that Samirah and Ken did. However, older adolescents were more capable of recognising that it was they who must take the responsibility for determining the direction of their future work. George said:

> Ultimately it's up to myself. Teachers, they are vehicles to our motivation, they can inspire me, or put me off, but I am the one who has to do the work. My parents, they can tell me their expectations, but I have to work out what is best for me, and my future . . .

Rowena's independence in taking the responsibility to finding out her own interest was due to her parents' careful nurturing:

> How did I find out about choice of work? Well, umm, I think, I am quite privileged because in my family, we are always being told that you can do whatever you want to do as long as you enjoy it, and that is the main thing that counts, apart from money really, but that comes second. So I've been really helped along knowing what I want to do and have a clear idea. Whereas a lot of people are just, you know, their parents say that medicine or accounting is a good area to go into to get money. So they just spend 10 years doing that and then when they are in their thirties, they then realise that actually, no, I don't really want to do this, I want to be a fashion designer.

All other replies that we received were non-committal. Many students expressed an attitude of wanting to leave their occupational or work choice open. Even when they knew what they were interested in, they felt unable to choose a specific area of work based on this interest. Bob's story illustrates this.

Bob has long been interested in and excelled at mathematics. At the time of the interview, Bob was studying further maths in a sixth-form college, and he expressed the wish to pursue mathematics at university. When talking about his future work plans, Bob was happy to leave his options open, but at the same time, he was very confident that it would be centred round mathematics:

> I have lots of plans. I am moving to Australia in the summer, or end of summer hopefully and umm . . . yeah then off to university to study Mathematics for 3 or 4 years and then I'll come out with a degree and see what happens then . . . I'm leaving my ends open . . . yeah, I'm leaving my options very open . . . as to what a maths degree is good for . . . umm ideally I would like to do something in the aviation industry . . .

Most of the adolescents interviewed agreed that out-of-school experience, such as work placements, could help them identify their personal interests in terms of work in adult life. Here Kate realised that she actually would love to work with young children:

> Because I have been doing child development [GCSE subject] and doing childcare as part of my work experience, it is making me want to do social work, and care for young children. I really enjoyed it . . . I can't say this is anything to do with my talent, but certainly it is something that stands out as what I really want to do . . . so now I want to go to M college and do heath & social care.

In general, the interviews showed that future work was a topic that was somewhat remote from current concerns for the younger participants (14–16) as well as the slightly older ones (16–18). Many acknowledged that they would need more time in order to make an informed decision about future work. Work placement, experience outside of school, meeting inspirational adults and learning about their work, including their teachers, and parent guidance and support were all considered helpful in enabling the adolescents to have more ideas about their future direction.

Conclusion

What conclusions can we draw from these young people's comments and reflections? Of course, any conclusions will be tentative, informal and selective. Our intention is to stress those points that may be less comprehensively covered in the literature on adolescence, which were nevertheless significant in our investigations.

First, we noted that there were substantial differences in the level of eloquence between the young people interviewed. On the one hand, some of the younger people had difficulty expressing themselves even to peers, which presumably removed some of the inhibitions of being interviewed by adult strangers. On the other hand, some of the older students were able to express sophisticated and nuanced ideas that involved articulating how they felt and thought about an issue. On the basis of the data we have, however, we cannot draw any conclusions about the social or psychological causes of this significant difference. Nevertheless, the point will become important later.

Second, we noted that, as the students developed, their sense of themselves became more independent of the judgements of their peers. The younger students were more willing to identify with their friendship group and to perceive this identification as central to their lives. This meant that they were less able to gain critical distance on the negative aspects of this identification. A few of the older students reported having struggled to gain freedom from this and seemed to have come away with more confidence and a broader outlook on their lives, both in the present and for the future.

Third, although the young people may have had a nascent sense of their own interests and abilities, they had very little idea of the possibilities that life had to offer. Their vision was limited by a lack of knowledge of the kinds of work that people engage in. Sometimes, they seemed to latch onto one particular experience or person as a guiding model for their future in an ad hoc manner. Their vision was also limited by the expectations that others, especially family, had placed on them. As we saw, for some of the young people going to university was a huge step. Thinking of one's future without the confines of such expectations is very difficult. To see beyond one's own horizons requires encounters with new possibilities. Many of the young people found it hard to articulate what was important for their future life: what would count as a good life? Such criteria were difficult for them to sort out. Most had a very instrumental view of the value of work, and of education. Many of them seemed to express implicitly a lack of hope. This whole area seemed to us to be one where the young need much guidance and positive feedback.

Finally, we would like to make some comments about the research methodology, which will be important in Chapter 10 when we discuss the young people's overall experience of secondary schooling. In contrast to the optimism of Fielding, the methodology raised some sceptical questions, such as 'Can students who have been brought up and "educated" within the dominant educational discourse and political agenda lead a dialogue that might impact on broader and more profound systematic reforms of education?' 'Can a young person who is struggling with his or her own future think beyond their immediate concerns to develop an educational vision?' This does not mean that we should question young people's ability to play an important part in determining their learning and education. The concern is rather how much help young people may need in order to think outside of the 'box' that constitutes their horizon.

Further reading

Fielding, M. (2007b) Beyond 'voice': new roles, relations, and contexts in researching with young people. *Discourse*, 28(3), 301–10.

Kincheloe, J. (2007) Clarifying the purpose of engaging students as researchers, in D. Thiessen and A. Cook-Sather (eds) *International Handbook of Student Experience in Elementary and Secondary School*. Dordrecht: Springer.

Robinson, C. and Taylor, C. (2007). Theorizing student voice: values and perspective. *Improving Schools*, 10(1), 5–17.

5
Understanding adolescence

Introduction

Adolescence is a period often considered to be the most complex developmental stage in a person's life. It involves the transition from being a child to an adult. The adolescent sometimes occupies a special space between the two worlds – a space that is neither and has its own characteristics. Sometimes the adolescent swings from a childish mode to a more sophisticated one. Many adolescents experience contradictory expectations from adults: sometimes they are treated like children, but are expected to behave like adults.

The adolescent's autonomy has been viewed by some as a consequence of the progressive developmental process or individuation in which the young person moves from a state of physical and emotional dependence to one of psychological autonomy (Erikson, 1968, 1980; Blos, 1967; Steinwand, 1984; Smollar and Youniss, 1989). This progression is often characterised by a transformation in parent–child relationships during adolescence and early adulthood.

In addition, adolescence can be the most exciting time in one's life: one becomes fully alive in one's mind, more autonomous and mature. One begins to experience the world as an independent individual rather than merely as a part of a family. Life is fresh and new, and full of possibilities. One has many of the benefits of being an adult without some of the drudgery.

At the same time, however, adolescence is also riddled with complexities and paradoxes. For instance, as adolescents become more fully self-aware, they are increasingly able to appreciate and think critically about others' perspectives (Rosenblum and Lewis, 2006). Yet some psychologists argue that adolescents are egocentric (see Geldard and Geldard, 1998). Some have suggested that adolescents may have the idea that everyone is watching them as if they were on stage or that they make up personal fables (Dacey and Kenny, 1997). Others have proposed that adolescents' acting out is part of attempts to develop a coherent identity (see Peter Blos, 1967, and his theory of a second individuation).

In order to develop a vision of education appropriate for adolescents, we wanted to understand better the general attributes of adolescence, and for this reason, we will review the current theories regarding the changes that occur in adolescence as well as major developmental features at this time. A good knowledge about adolescence can help us better understand the needs and wants of young persons at this crucial time in their life, and allow us to consolidate educational design and activities accordingly.

This chapter is divided into two parts. In the first, we will discuss some of the important changes that an adolescent experiences. In the second, we take a closer look at what is often considered the major focus of discussion about adolescence – the formation of a greater sense of oneself. Some psychologists term this aspect of development as identity formation. This is sometimes referred to as the internal transformation of the conception of oneself (see the reviews in Kroger, 2004). This conception of oneself points to the future because it includes the young person's perception of the possible parts or roles they could play in society and the relevant academic and vocational paths that they might undertake. Many researchers suggest that adolescence is the time when young people learn to make the decisions (academic studies, choices for work, social relations, etc.) that will affect their future. These decisions are often based on their current ideas about what they value and appreciate, and how they might live their life later in adulthood. Such future-oriented decisions are part of the young person's effort to consolidate their identity (Marcia *et al.*, 1993).

We are aware that it may be overly simplified and fragmented to examine literature on adolescence from just a few aspects. We will reaffirm, as most of the literature reviewed has suggested, the holism of these aspects throughout our discussion and try to show how the interconnections contribute synergistically to the young person's over-all development. Later, we will use these discussions to define the meaning of human-centred education in practice.

Changes in adolescence

We will examine three key aspects of the changes that adolescents undergo between the ages of 14 and 16. The first is the physical changes, which include the onset of puberty, other visible bodily changes, emerging secondary sexual characteristics and brain development. The second set of changes concern the young person's cognitive capacities. This is often marked by a major broadening of advanced thinking abilities, as well as by an increased capacity to comprehend abstract notions, such as higher mathematical concepts, abstract values and moral principles. The third aspect consists of the changes that young people undergo in their emotional and social lives. Adolescents become more emotionally mature; they have an increased capacity to empathise with and show concern for others; they develop the possibility of having intimate and loving relationships with other people.

Physical changes

The beginning of adolescence is marked by puberty and by dramatic changes in the body, including rapid gains in height and weight, and gender-specific changes such as increased facial hair and deeper voices in boys. It also includes the appearance of secondary sexual characteristics due to changing hormonal levels in both boys and girls. For our purpose, instead of detailing the changes as identified by the current literature on adolescence, we will explore the ways in which these radical physical changes may have a fundamental impact on the adolescent's psychological state. Understanding such impacts can provide a holistic picture of education appropriate for the adolescents.

First, for some adolescents, there might exist a gap between their pubertal development and the maturation of their brain function that facilitates regulatory competence, i.e. their ability to regulate behaviour (Steinberg, 2005). This discrepancy creates challenges for the young person to be able to regulate his/her behaviour, and therefore, increases the possibility of risk-taking and other emotional and behavioural problems. This imbalance between physical development and lack of mental and cognitive ability to facilitate the changes is described by Steinberg as a situation in which 'one is starting an engine, and without yet having a skilled driver behind the wheel' (*ibid.*). This could explain why some adolescents appear to be inconsistent in their ability to control emotions and impulses or make sensible judgements.

Second, young people often experience anxiety, fear, discomfort and embarrassment as a result of their physical changes. These feelings have been particularly noted in girls during puberty (Coleman, 1995; Moore, 1995). Although in some cultures, sex education and other preparations may be in place, puberty inevitably causes inner turbulence in many young people.

Third, marked physical changes may also have a considerable effect on the way that a young person sees him/herself (Coleman and Hendry, 1999). In early adolescence, young people rely on their physical characteristics as the basis for self-conception, as opposed to mid and late adolescence, when they tend to depend on cognitive, social and interpersonal aspects of their personality to describe themselves (*ibid.*). This may explain our observation in Chapter 4 that the younger people interviewed appeared to be less clear with regard to who they are, whereas the older adolescents seemed to be more articulate.

In addition, some adolescents may feel stressed and dissatisfied about their physique. This is often caused by their ready acceptance of norms for physical attractiveness based on images of beauty and success projected by the media, which in turn can have a negative impact on their conception of themselves (Durkin and Paxton, 2002).

Fourth, self-image and self-esteem connected to physical appearance also have a significant impact on a young person's relationship with individuals of the opposite sex (Kostanski and Gullone, 1998). Young people at this age also begin to have an increased sense of sexual orientation and gender identity, and he/she may start experiencing sexual attraction and erotic feelings towards others. The link between puberty and sexuality makes adolescence a significant time for a person's sexual development (Gaffney and Roye, 2003). A young person's sexual experience can be motivated by biological needs as well as being affected by social cultural influences, peer pressure and adult role models (*ibid.*). The possibility of pregnancy and disease also makes sexual experience a risky business for both boys and girls. Sexual development in some ways marks the adolescent's entry into adulthood as he/she is no longer a child, yet at the same time he/she is not completely ready to accept adult responsibilities, such as raising a family or maintaining a committed love relationship.

Our brief glance at the impact of physical changes and development during adolescence on the young person's cognition, emotions and social relationships indicates that this is a complex process involving more than just biological elements, such as hormones and bodily changes. It also includes psychological, emotional and socio-cultural influences, such as the changing patterns of family constitution in the twenty-first century, shifting attitudes towards sexual experience resulting from the feminist movement, and the increased availability of birth control to 'underage' teens as the result of the British government's attempt to reduce the number of teenage pregnancies.

Adolescence can be an exciting time of change and growth. However, the disjunctions between the biological processes and the development of the relevant cognitive and behavioural systems, together with the varying times that young people take to mature, may also mean that for some young people adolescence can be a period of frustration, vulnerability and risk. These teenagers may be more prone to confusion, depression, anxiety, fear, violence, substance abuse and other forms of social, emotional and behavioural disorders. Indeed, physical changes in adolescence must be understood in the light of cognition, emotion and self-conception. In fact, many 'behavioural disorders' in adolescents are closely connected to the developmental process within their cognitive capacities, such as risk-taking (Furbey and Beyth-Mariom, 1992, cited in Steinberg, 2008).

Changes in cognition

'Cognition' usually refers to thinking, linguistic and perceptual processes, but it also relates to a person's overall intelligence, including their capacities for problem solving, understanding concepts and processing information. An adolescent's cognitive development refers to 'the attainment of a more fully conscious, self-directed and self-regulating mind' (Steinberg, 2005: 70).

Adolescence is a period during which individuals experience enhanced self-awareness and increased concerns through encountering and coping with a series of life-changing issues. An adolescent's self-awareness goes beyond the proximal self-concerns about their bodies and primary family relations to include other concerns, such as one's relationship with others and the wider world. Along with enhanced self-consciousness comes adolescents' increased ability to think critically about other people and impersonal matters. During this transition, complex interdependencies emerge between biological growth, self-perceptions, relations with a wider social world, and the formation of new meaning systems (Chen *et al.*, 1998).

Starting at puberty, adolescents experience qualitative changes in their mental capacities. The changes in the brain at this time take place in the prefrontal cortex, which affects an individual's cognition and action. In general, adolescents become more capable of abstract, multidimensional, planned and hypothetical thinking as they enter from late childhood into middle adolescence. These major changes have been termed the 'executive suite' of capabilities (Keating, 2004), which allows the adolescent's thinking to be more deliberate and more controlled.

According to Piaget, at adolescence, a young person enters a formal-operational stage in their cognitive development (Piaget, 1965). This means that, apart from deductive reasoning abilities, adolescents can also think inductively, going from specific observations to more general conclusions. In other words, they are more capable of thinking scientifically. This potentially paves the way for principled and systematic thinking about what is possible in one's life, understanding better other people's perspectives and the causes of their behaviours (Shaffer and Kipp, 2007). In general, older adolescents are more likely than younger counterparts to reason and make decisions by anticipating a wider range of consequences of their actions, and to learn from the success or failure of their decision-making (Byrnes, 2003). At this stage, adolescents may also begin to question everything they encounter, from their parents' authority, to everyday realities such as wearing uniforms at school.

Adolescents' advances in autonomy mark the progression from childhood to adulthood where the young person is more capable of self-motivation and self-regulation. Beckert (2007) suggests that, for adolescents, autonomy encompasses the ability to act, think and feel autonomously. In a similar vein, Steinberg (2008) offers three characterisations of adolescent autonomy: emotional (emotional independence in relationships with others, especially parents), behavioural independence (independent decision-making abilities) and value autonomy (independent beliefs and principles). Autonomy includes self-governance, managing one's own behaviour and acting on personal decisions; independent reasoning and decision-making without excessive reliance on validation from others including social norms, a feeling of self-reliance and choice-making; and independence from parents (Steinberg, 1999, 2008).

In this way, during adolescence, individuals can have an increased ability to reflect upon the source of their knowledge and are more able to engage with multiple perspectives and challenge the quality of evidence on which a particular idea or perspective is based. Educational experiences that stress logic and reasoning through studying philosophy, science and mathematics at this stage can help provide the kind of exposure necessary for adolescents to achieve formal thought and intellectual autonomy (Kroger, 2007; Sigelman and Rider, 2009).

In principle, adolescents are more able to think about the future, and consider the logical outcomes of possible events; and are more likely to take on others' perspectives, thus having the potential to foster empathy and develop concern for other people, and thereby be encouraged to have an interest in social justice and ideological issues (Lerner and Steinberg, 2009).

In reality, however, adolescent actions are largely subject to their feelings, as well as affective and social influences, in a way that is usually different from adults. This results in their having less advanced cognitive capacities for resolving real-life dilemmas and problems than when they are dealing with hypothetical situations. In other words, an adolescent might appear to be competent in reasoning, but fail to demonstrate this ability in real-world situations or real-life problem solving due to motivational or emotional factors (Byrnes, 2003).

Moral reasoning in adolescents

The development of formal operational thought and the advancement of an adolescent's ability in perspective-taking as described above has led Kohlberg (1984) to propose more advanced moral judgement and moral reasoning in adolescence. Wainryb *et al.* (2008: 263) summarise that:

> Adolescents are not consistently principled moral thinkers . . . nor are they morally confused and selfish individualists . . . Adolescents make autonomous moral judgements in some situations and focus on personal goals in others.

Kohlberg's research pointed out that, at this age, an adolescent's moral reasoning has gone beyond the stage when, as a child, he/she tended to view rules as absolute and fixed. During his/her early years, a child responds to what is good or bad, right or wrong, based on his/her own self-interest and by obeying authority. From early adolescence, he/she can more readily take into account his/her own views and others' perspectives at the same time. As a result, adolescents are more capable of considering rules critically, and can selectively apply rules in different situations in their own life. Because of this, adolescents are more able to base their consideration of rules on the goals of mutual respect and cooperation. Piaget (1932, 1965) regarded this shift as a progression from moral realism to moral relativism. Perspective-taking thus allows for fair reciprocity. Consequently, schools, social institutions, communities and families can achieve a great deal by engaging young people in discussions of moral issues. This kind of social interaction is key to the young person's understanding of virtues and vices and in developing them accordingly (see also Lerner and Steinberg, 2009).

During adolescence, however, the moral behaviour of individuals does not always match their enhanced ability for moral reasoning due to certain contextual factors influencing how they act in real-life situations. Similarly, despite becoming more sophisticated in thinking about pro-social phenomena, adolescents are not always consistent in empathising with others (Steinberg, 2008).

A closely connected aspect of moral development is the young person's changes in their abilities to think politically and about religious and spiritual matters, which can become more abstract, more principled and more independent (*ibid.*). With increased self-awareness, adolescents may also experience conflicts in terms of freedom, choice, responsibility, how to live their life and how to be in the world.

It is also a time when adolescents begin to realise that there may be a discrepancy between their own values and those of others. A person might need to make a decision based on what he/she values most and what is important in his/her life, rather than basing it on what others value or expect him/her to do. For an adolescent, this may involve ideological views of the world as the result of his/her increased cognitive abilities and social awareness contributed to by the immediate environment and those significant adults around him/her.

These aspects were not specifically investigated in our interviews with young people. However, what has been identified by the literature points to the importance of education in cultivating a young person's thinking, moral reasoning, compassion, empathy, autonomy and other human qualities.

Changes in emotions

Adolescents' cognitive abilities have a significant impact on their emotional life because changes in the way the individual reasons about the world during adolescence can bring new possibilities for his/her reasoning about emotions (Rosenblum and Lewis, 2006). In this way, adolescents become more capable of understanding and analysing their own and other people's 'personalities'. They are also more able to recognise complex multi-faceted emotions of self and others, and to introspect and examine their own emotional life as well as being more ready to experience emotional responses to relationships (*ibid.*).

Generally, adolescents experience wide fluctuations in their daily emotional states (Larson and Richards, 1994). They undergo dramatic changes in their motivation, sexual interest, emotional intensity and social relationships. Some claim that these could have been brought on by hormonal changes or the accumulation of multiple life-changes, each of which individually and collectively could contribute to the emotional upheaval during this time (Coleman and Hendry, 1999). Stereotypically, adolescence is perceived as a period of rebellion (against parents) and of emotional turmoil. Some research suggests that adolescents' 'mood swings' and negative emotions are greater than those of either children or adults (see, for example, those cited by Rosenblum and Lewis, 2006). We have also seen a few anecdotal accounts of these from the adolescents themselves in Chapter 4. However, there is other research which indicates that most adolescents typically have a much smoother and less tumultuous transition. Turmoil is not necessary a characteristic of adolescence for most individuals (Coleman, 1974). This is because they tend to deal with the changes one at a time.

After mid-adolescence, the individual becomes more capable of showing empathy, as well as understanding how others feel. Adolescents have a heightened sensitivity to others' evaluations of themselves, and this is part of their increased self-awareness. At the same time, the search for greater emotional autonomy brings increased conflict with authorities, such as parents and teachers at the school; greater mood volatility; and increased risk-taking behaviours, such as recklessness and the tendency for sensation-seeking (Greene *et al.*, 2000).

Adolescence is a crucial time when the young person learns to experience, understand and express feelings and emotions appropriately and to act accordingly. This requires a greater cognitive–emotional integration. For example, it involves the capacity to evaluate one's emotions and behaviours to see if they accord with abstract principles, social norms and personal goals, and to consider the long-term consequences of one's actions. Young people learn to make decisions and behavioural choices by becoming more aware of the emotions and feelings involved and sometimes by analysing them. One developmental task facing adolescents, as they learn to regulate their emotions and behaviours more purposefully, is to understand how the emotive and cognitive aspects of decision-making mutually influence each other (Steinberg, 2005).

Thompson (1994) maintains that emotional regulation consists of the ability to recognise, monitor, evaluate and modify emotional reactions. It comprises being able to respond to emotions in socially sensitive and culturally appropriate ways, which nevertheless permit spontaneous and authentic reactions. Adolescents' ability to function adaptively and appropriately can be hindered by the misidentification and misdirection of emotions (Kostiuk and Fouts, 2002). Emotional regulation can result in more positive emotional experiences, and fewer negative ones, and in an improved ability to make decisions. It can also enhance motivation, empathy, self-esteem, understanding social relations, and so forth.

Peer group belonging

Adolescents often experience the need for more personal independence; for instance, by becoming emotionally distant from their parents (Steinberg, 1987, 1988). This is part of their desire to become more autonomous and break away from childhood. Steinberg (2008) gives three examples to show how adolescents are far less emotionally dependent on their parents than when they were children: (1) older adolescents don't rush to their parents when they are upset, worried or in need of assistance; (2) they de-idealise their parents; (3) their emotional energy can find an anchor in relationships outside the family. Blos (1967) regarded the detachment from parents at this stage as part of the human's individuation process. With increased emotional independence, adolescents may accept responsibility for their choices and actions.

As adolescents pull away from their parents in a search for autonomy, the peer group takes on a special and significant role. To some, it may even become a safe haven in which the adolescent can test new ideas and compare physical and psychological growth. He/she not only seeks feedback and a sense of belonging from their peers, but his/her psychological well-being is also claimed to be connected with peer relations and other social relations. La Greca and Harrison's (2005) survey identified positive peer relations, best friendships, the presence of a dating relationship, and affiliation with a high-status peer group as some of the elements that are helpful in protecting the adolescent from developing social anxiety and depression; whereas negative interactions in best friendships are likely to cause high social anxiety and depression. Similarly, there is a strong connection between the young person's behaviour and peer relationships, friendships, family bonds and schooling experience. For instance, young people are less likely to engage in risky and delinquent behaviour such as substance abuse and aggression if there is a strong positive bond in any of these relationships – peer, family and school (Elliott *et al.*, 1989).

Indeed, peer groups for the young person are so important that some adolescents may change their behaviour in order to gain peer acceptance, as we have seen in one of the interviews in Chapter 4. Research with adolescents supports the claim that closeness in peer relationships is positively correlated with popularity and good social reputation (Cauce, 1986), self-esteem (McGuire and Weisz, 1982), and (positive) psychosocial adjustment (Buhrmester, 1990).

In general, young people at this stage tend to have a need for belonging, social acceptance and recognition, and respect from others for who they are (Driekurs *et al.*, 1982). They also seek a loving and intimate personal relationship which is connected with their freedom, enjoyment and happiness (Glasser, 1985). In addition, they are likely to be experiencing a desire for passion, imitation and identification, but at the same time, a desire for rebelliousness and exploration of negative identity (Erikson, 1968; Mitchell, 1972: 447).

However, not all adolescents are equally concerned with being a member of a group. The feelings of social distress tend to be greater for those adolescents who strongly desire group membership but do not experience a sense of group belonging. Some research has shown that adolescent girls value group membership more than boys (Brown *et al.*, 1986; Brown and Lohr, 1987) and are found to be more identified with their peer groups than boys (Kiesner *et al.*, 2002). Steinberg (2008) suggests that being popular for mid to late adolescents is less important than genuinely having friends, and having friends is less important than having good friends.

Not belonging to peer groups can have a negative effect on the adolescent, such as feelings of being excluded. Social exclusion refers to the perception of being excluded from desired relationships or devalued by valued relationship partners or groups (MacDonald and Leary, 2005: 202). Exclusion from social groups can cause pain, anxiety and depression in adolescents. Baumeister *et al.* (2005) demonstrated that social rejection also caused a decline in self-regulation. In their research, those adolescents who received information that no one in their group wanted to work with them were more likely to eat more snack foods, give up sooner on frustrating tasks and have a harder time paying attention in dichotic listening tasks. The studies support the view that social rejection undermines a person's sense of purpose.

Emotional intimacy

During adolescence, young people begin to have a more sophisticated understanding of all kinds of relationships, including friendships, romantic relationships and closeness with other people. Emotional intimacy involves a reciprocal relationship in which a person's innermost thoughts, feelings, dreams, desires and concerns are shaved with another – a sharing of minds as well as a sharing of bodies. From mid to late adolescence, individuals begin to learn more about their own emotions and those of others and become more comfortable with their own body and sexual feelings (Steinberg, 2008).

At this time, friendship becomes increasingly more important than family bonds. Adolescents tend to place emphasis on trust and loyalty as defining features of their friendships and are more self-disclosing as well as being more responsive and sensitive to friends' needs (Steinberg, 2008). Friendships with the opposite sex in early adolescence help 'set the stage' for romantic relationships in later adolescence (*ibid.*). Romantic relationships during adolescence apply to individuals of the opposite sex as well as those of the same sex.

Emotional intimacy and romantic relationships occupy a central place in an adolescent's world and romantic partners can be a major source of emotional support. At the same time, romantic experiences can also help the adolescent to successfully establish autonomy (Bouchery and Furman, 2006). Romantic relationships can influence the adolescent's intimacy and identity formation and the nature of his/her subsequent close relationships in adulthood such as marriage (Erikson, 1968). In addition, romantic experiences increase the adolescent's sense of relatedness to others, which helps him/her to establish autonomy and become less reliant on parents (Furman *et al.*, 1999).

From an educational point of view, due to adolescents' increased needs for romantic friendships, dating and sexual experiences, it is necessary that adolescents learn to express love and passion and receive intimate or sexual advances in a manner that is consistent with their internalised values, such as respect for another person and wanting to be respected.

Motivational problems and apathy in adolescence

Adolescent motivation has been variously defined by psychologists, educationalists and other theorists. In Chapter 3, we argued that motivation consists of the integration of the cognitive and the non-cognitive. Following this kind of idea, Hidi and Ainley (2002) have explored adolescents' interest as a motivational concept, as they believe that the notion of interest 'incorporates affective and cognitive factors' and explains why individuals choose to engage in certain activities (p. 247). These authors argue that cultivating interest is essential to enabling the self-initiating activities that result in joy, a sense of achievement and learning.

However, many adolescents, and especially those in mainstream secondary schools, are found to be uncommitted to academic work, have negative attitudes towards learning and are disengaged from the school's social and other activities (Buckingham, 1999). Adolescents often feel powerless. The futility of agency or political action leads to cynicism in other aspects of adolescents' life.

Adolescent apathy is a multidimensional trait characterised by a lack of goal-setting, energy and interest; indifference to changes; and having difficulty in making decisions assessed by him/herself, teachers, parents and friends (Handelman, 1999). Apathy in schools includes putting in minimum effort to achieve grades rather than having a genuine interest in learning, disengagement from school activities, a lack of curiosity, emotion and motivation, a lack of effort to do work, an absence of (political) activism, and a lack of exercises of agency. Apathy is becoming increasingly common in most large comprehensive secondary schools in the UK. Brophy (2004: 307) suggests that students' apathy 'is the ultimate motivational problem facing teachers'.

Eccles *et al.* (1998) noted that children's beliefs and expectations about their own competences tend to become more negative during adolescence. This is because young people at this age are better at understanding, interpreting and integrating evaluative feedback; they engage in more social comparison with their peers; and their increased self-awareness makes them more realistic in their own self-assessment. They now can judge themselves in relation to impersonal standards. At the same time, often, the overall culture of the school and its academic structure is geared more towards competition and judgement-based assessment. This may explain the phenomenon of adolescent apathy in schools in general.

When an individual is motivated intrinsically, he/she performs the activities for their own sake and out of an interest in the activities themselves or the subject matter itself. Hidi (2000) holds that this psychological state of interest involves focused attention, persistence, increased cognitive functioning and affective involvement. Hidi points out that such interest can be nurtured and developed. As we argued in Chapter 3, this kind of interest is an evaluative perception that depends on factors such as how a topic is explained to the students, or contextualised in a class.

During adolescence, overall student interest in subjects tends to decline (Eccles and Wigfield, 2000). Although it is contested which direct factors contribute most to adolescent apathy, a few have been generally recognised as important and are discussed below.

As we mentioned earlier, school culture is sometimes characterised by a disciplinarian and authoritarian approach to adolescents' behaviours and this clashes with the young person's desire for autonomy in mind, feelings and decision-making.

Hidi and Ainley (2002) point out that, to embark on a higher level of learning in secondary schools, which is quite different from the discovery-based methods of primary education, it is a prerequisite for the young person to have a certain set of competences such as a high-level of personal discipline, focused attention, organisation skills, persistent effort, self-responsibility and self-regulation. All these require long-term processes of training and nurturing. Adolescents often arrive at secondary education and find themselves being confronted with challenges that they are not prepared to deal with. As we shall see later, schools are not always helpful in making the adolescent connect with what they are doing in schools or understand why they should want to do it.

Adolescents are increasingly interested in social interaction and relationships. At this age, a young person might have more interest in social activities than academic ones, especially as the latter are structured within the authoritarian culture mentioned earlier (Hidi and Ainley, 2002).

In some areas, adolescents' substance abuse can lead to increased apathy both in academic work and more generally. Drug-use inhibits short-term memory, and decreases creativity, energy and motivation; it also alienates the young person and drives him/her further away from the school community (Kimberly, 2010).

Some adolescents engage in part-time work which diminishes their involvement in school life (Greenberger and Steinberg, 1981). Youth employment can sometimes contribute to a cynical attitude towards work later in life, partly due to the fact that adolescents are not treated with respect in workplaces. It also reduces the amount of time the young person spends with family and weakens his/her ties with peers (see Steinberg and Dornbusch, 1991; Steinberg *et al.*, 1991; Steinberg *et al.*, 1993, for the negative impact of part-time work on adolescents). Furthermore, as these authors point out, work promotes 'practical knowledge', and the adolescent becomes less interested in the 'abstract knowledge' of school and can develop a more cynical attitude towards education.

Becoming oneself

With the overwhelming combination of the onset of puberty, physical change, increased sex drive and cognitive maturity, is also the gradual movement towards a more sophisticated sense of oneself. Many psychologists have argued that adolescence is a crucial time when a person begins to form his/her identity (Erikson, 1968; Kroger, 2004; Steinberg, 2008). Identity is an ongoing dynamic process throughout human life. It is an emerging way of perceiving or defining oneself which involves a sense of unity and continuity over time. In this way, identity includes a persistent and continuous state of being oneself despite different social contexts and various other conditions. In addition, identity is an overarching concept involving both a person's conception of him/herself and his/her awareness and understanding of others' recognition of him/her as a person.

Adolescence is a unique time during which the young person undergoes pronounced changes through which he/she learns to find his/her place in society, form loving bonds and personal relationships, and make decisions about his/

her life ahead. The adolescent's increased capacity for meta-thinking allows one not only to reflect on one's own identity but also to consider many other possible roles (Adamson and Lyxell, 1996).

Adams and Marshall (1996) maintain that personal identity constitutes the structure for understanding who one is and that it can offer directions (in a consistent, coherent and harmonious way) to the person's life by clarifying one's commitment, values and goals. It can give the individual a sense of self-control and can enable the person to have a sense of their potential and future possibilities and choices.

As Steinberg (2008: 269) writes:

> The changes in identity that take place during adolescence involve the first substantial reorganization and restructuring of the individual's sense of self at a time when he/she has the intellectual capability to appreciate fully just how significant the changes are. Although important changes in identity certainly occur during childhood, the adolescent is far more self-conscious about these changes and feels them much more acutely.

Thus with increased self-awareness and self-consciousness, as well as changes in thinking and his/her ability to hypothesise, the adolescent is more likely to ask him/herself questions such as: 'What am I really like?', 'Who will I become?', 'What things are important to me?'

Identity formation is multi-faceted and each aspect contributes to the changes in ways that an adolescent views him/herself in relation to others and within the broader context of society. Steinberg (2008) examines an adolescent's changes in identity formation from three angles: (1) changes in self-conceptions which are connected to the ideas an adolescent has about his/her personal traits and attributes; (2) changes in self-image (or self-esteem) which are linked to how an adolescent feels about him/herself as a person; and (3) changes in the sense of oneself, i.e. the sense of who one is, where one has come from and where one is going. We will make use of these as a framework to review the key points from literature about the topic. We will examine this from the angle of an 'identity crisis' (Erikson, 1968).

Changes in self-conceptions

Self-conception changes in structure and content during adolescence, and it becomes more differentiated, better organised and more integrated (Harter, 1999, cited in Steinberg, 2008). In contrast to children whose self-description of traits and attributes is disorganised and fragmented, the adolescent is more capable of organising and integrating different traits and attributes in a logical and coherent manner. An adolescent's self-conceptions tend to be more abstract and more psychological. Late adolescents are more able to cope with opposite and conflicting traits in their self-description than mid-adolescents and children, as we have seen in the interviews presented in Chapter 4. With increased self-awareness, an adolescent's self-conceptions are more multi-faceted and he/she can have a much more complicated view of him/herself. Some researchers suggest that adolescents with more complex self-conceptions are less likely to be depressed (see Chapter 8 in Steinberg, 2008).

Steinberg points out that despite the stereotypical view of adolescence as tumul-tuous, there is some stability in the adolescent's basic personality traits and temperament over time.

Changes in self-esteem

Self-esteem concerns how one feels about oneself, which can be high (when one feels positively about oneself) or low (when the feeling about oneself is negative). Research suggests that during early adolescence, with increased self-consciousness, the individual's self-esteem becomes lower and he/she has a more unstable self-image. One suggestion is that this is because heightened self-consciousness can result in a feeling of shame about oneself (Reimer, 1996, cited in Steinberg, 2008). One's self-esteem tends to become more stable from mid-adolescence. Hence, the transition from primary school to secondary school can be some-what more disruptive to the adolescent than the transition from secondary school to college.

Harter (1999) suggests that some aspects of adolescence appear to contribute more to one's self-esteem than others. For instance, how one feels about one's physical appearance is considered to be one of the most important determin-ants for an adolescent's overall self-esteem (*ibid.*). This is followed by one's social relationship with peers. Less important factors are one's academic ability, athletic ability or moral conduct. Thus, academic achievement becomes a lower priority for most adolescents. For girls, who generally are more concerned with physical appearances than boys, popularity amongst peers and intimate rela-tionships with others can have greater self-esteem impact.

Other factors contributing to the adolescent's self-esteem include social classes and ethnic groups. Research in North America suggests that male, middle-class adolescents, and African American adolescents have higher self-esteem than females, working-class adolescents or adolescents from other ethnic groups (Steinberg, 2008).

'Identity crisis'

Erikson (1968) identified a number of stages in human identity development and noted that the ascendancy of each stage is determined by the successful completion of those that come before. Development at each stage constitutes a 'crisis' to be resolved before further development is possible. Crisis here implies not only a threat of catastrophe but also an opportunity characterised by 'increased vulnerability and heightened potential' (p. 96). Erikson coined the phrase 'identity crisis', which refers to self-exploration and involves elements such as conflict and stress, an emerging ability to generate future ideas of oneself, and readiness for change (Kroger, 2004).

In general, very few individuals go through adolescence without some kind of turmoil. According to Erikson, many adolescents may find themselves in a state of 'identity crisis' when they are confronted with a temporary experience of uncertainty and confusion as they struggle with options and possibilities. Young people's attempts to resolve these dilemmas include experimenting with different social roles, looks, sexuality, values, friendships, ethnicity and occupations. They may be tempted to identify, and sometimes over-identify, with selected role models and personal heroes. For example, some young people might want to model themselves according to celebrities – well-known footballers, business tycoons or popular singers. Minority youths might explore several patterns of identity formation: a strong ethnic identity; bi-cultural identity and assimilation; or alienation from the majority culture (Kroger, 2004).

Some troubled youths, when finding this process of exploration and integration too difficult, may seek 'negative identity resolution' (Erikson, 1968). Negative identity resolution is when the adolescent derives:

> a sense of identity out of a total identification with that which he is least supposed to be [*rather*] than to struggle for a feeling of reality in acceptable roles which are unattainable with his inner means.
>
> (Erikson, 1968: 176)

Negative identity resolution suggests that identity in adolescence is a shifting process constantly being explored, lost, regained and re-explored. Erikson envisaged that in an ideal world where the social, the ego and other elements come together in a favourable way, the optimum identity formation means that, at the end of adolescence and the beginning of adulthood, the young person would have 'a feeling of being at home' in their own body, a sense of well-being, the knowledge of where he/she is going, and 'an inner assuredness of anticipated recognition from those who count' (Erikson, 1968: 165). In our research interviews with young people, even the older adolescents didn't seem to be that clear in terms of where they were going with life and studies. If we follow Erikson's claim, it may suggest that identity formation is a long process and that it will take more time to finally 'form one's identity'.

Social and cultural influences play an important role in a young person's identity formation. These include those from religion, education, the adolescent's close community (such as family, peers and others), work/employment, legal and political systems, and other socio-cultural practices. However, Kroger (2004: 47) cautions that:

> All such orders regulate attitudes and behaviour of their young members, and all are capable of becoming too cooperative in the provision of labels that may not ultimately serve the best interests of youths seeking self-definition.

This means that it could be counterproductive to offer ready-made role models or predetermined roles to the young person who is in the process of actively searching, exploring and experimenting with different alternative roles and identity models. The adolescent may be helped in his/her own self-defining when there are opportunities to explore different possibilities and options for him/herself. This search and exploration requires society and community's tolerance towards role experimentation, but '*not* to treat their experimentations as the final identity' (*ibid.*). Many social institutions and communities could facilitate and assist this process, in particular, by helping young people recognise their individual talents and true nature, as well as identifying and supporting their unique needs in order to achieve their identity.

Coleman and Hendry (1999) reviewed some of the empirical investigations into adolescent identity development and suggest that it is not until late adolescence that the young person can experience 'achieved identity', i.e. when he/she has experienced, confronted and resolved his/her identity crisis (Marcia, 1979). This means that, by early adulthood, many young people are able to 'find themselves' and commit to work, values, loving bonds and personal direction.

Adolescents and their ideas of a future

Adolescence is an important time in a person's life when the individual begins to accept his/her physical characteristics and sexual orientation, and establish more independent social relationships with other people. The young person becomes emotionally autonomous from their family/parents and has enhanced social, emotional and academic capacities. He/she also begins to think about their preference for an occupation, examine their intellectual and other potential for social and civic engagement, and make important decisions about intimate relationships, such as a commitment to a more stable romantic partnership or marriage, about choices for work, as well as decisions about academic studies and/or vocational training. Above all, the adolescent begins to contemplate his/her own values and beliefs, and how they relate to the wider world. All of these will have significant implications for a young person's future life.

Most research into adolescents' future orientation tends to focus on four domains: (1) further and higher education; (2) career and work; (3) social relations; and (4) family and marriage (Seginer and Lilach, 2004; Seginer, 2008). On the one hand, Seginer (2008) maintains that future orientation consists of the images that the individuals hold concerning their future life and most of these images are reflected in hopes and fears. Zhang and Zhang (2007), on the other hand, suggest that future orientation concerns how the adolescent anticipates and constructs his/her personal future. It is a multi-dimensional and multi-stage phenomenon that can be described in terms of a person's motivation and evaluation of his/her own needs and wants. These authors point out that for an adolescent, future-oriented planning involves both exploration and commitment and is greatly influenced by the particular family, relational, educational, socio-cultural and economic contexts within which the young person finds him/herself.

Apart from contextual influence, Keating (1980) maintains that cognitive and affective development can have significant impact on the adolescent's future orientation in a number of ways. First, and as we pointed out earlier, formal and reflective thinking allows the adolescent to hypothesise and critically engage in examining different future possibilities and making decisions on the necessary strategies and related courses of action in order to pursue them. This point was echoed by Elkind (1980).

Second, the adolescent's increased ability in meta-cognition can help them to reflect on and conceptualise their own thoughts. In this way, he/she has the capacity to evaluate their goals and alter their strategies and actions accordingly. Adolescents set goals based on their intentions and what they perceive as valuable (see our discussion on evaluative perception in Chapter 3). Evaluative perception motivates the adolescent to set up future goals towards certain life styles, work choices and family relations that he/she finds valuable as a person. Then he/she will work out how to achieve these goals through some form of planning and problem solving, often with the support of teachers, families and peers, educational institutions, other organisations and social agencies. Furthermore, the adolescent can evaluate the possibilities of achieving their goals and carrying out their plans based on their self-awareness and their evaluative perception mentioned earlier. Keating and other authors such as Nurmi (1987) point out that the evaluative stage is always accompanied by emotions.

Third, formal thinking and emotional maturity can enable the adolescent to better conceptualise the thoughts of other people. This also suggests that adolescents are more open to the influence of significant others around them with regard to their ideas for future directions.

As we have seen in Chapter 4, our interviews with young people in early adolescence showed that they appeared to be unclear about their future goals, whereas those who were in mid and late adolescence seemed to be more capable of expressing their short- and long-term personal goals and were more articulate about their ideas for a future. This echoes research findings that as adolescents become more mature, their level of purposefulness concerning their future increases. They become more able to make plans and commit to that future, including orienting their academic studies and work-related training towards achieving these goals (Nurmi, 1987).

Seginer (1998) proposes that when adolescents explore their future opportunities, set goals, and commit to achieving them, they simultaneously form their self-identity. He further points out that an adolescent's future orientation also consists of existential domains of the self as well as consideration for others and questions concerning communities, nations and mankind. As we pointed out in Chapter 3, education plays an important part in enabling the adolescent to understand him/herself, forming an identity and finding meaning in his/her present and future life. Activities both inside and outside school can encourage the adolescent to further explore who they are and who they want to become.

In Chapter 4, we noted from the interview conversations that many young people in their early and mid-adolescence appeared to have done little exploration with regard to questions about their future life, in terms of what they can do now in order to live a good life in the future. This, we suspect, is because they have hardly any idea of what constitutes a good life. We believe that an exposure to a wide range of educational activities can broaden the adolescent's horizons and perceptions. Similarly, parents, teachers, peers and others in the adolescent's life, as well as other institutions, can play a big part in helping the young person to begin considering the idea of a good life and to plan for their future accordingly.

However, it is clear from the interviews presented in Chapter 4, that if the above group and institutions use language dominated by instrumental reasoning such as the kind being used by some of the young people in our interviews, i.e. 'having a lot of money', 'a nice girlfriend' or an extravagant life style, then it is likely that young people will perceive their future in instrumental terms.

How education, schools and other individuals can offer such help is the focus of the second part of this book.

Conclusion

Adolescence is a period of transition from childhood to adulthood. This does not mean that this is all it is, as we shall see later, but this idea enables us to gain an overview of many of the studies mentioned in this chapter.

The studies that we have cited contain a puzzling paradox. On the one hand, some of the studies indicate that adolescence is a time of greater preoccupation with oneself. Some adolescents believe that no one is capable of understanding them or how they are feeling. As we saw, the young person is in the process of developing a more fixed and clear set of identities and is more aware of him/herself and has a much greater sense of his/her own future as something that he/she will live.

On the other hand, other studies indicate that adolescence is a time of development when one becomes more aware of and connected to other people. At the same time, adolescents are more able to apply impersonal standards (such as consistency) and principles to their own thinking processes. This suggests that adolescence is a period of opening up to the world. Consciousness is less egocentric at this stage.

The puzzle is solved in two ways. First, the two halves of this sharpened duality really constitute two sides of the same coin. As one becomes more aware of oneself as someone and something discrete in the world, one also becomes more conscious of the world as something distinct from oneself. Amplified self-consciousness requires augmented other-consciousness. For instance, when a person becomes more self-reflective, this means that he/she is also more capable of being aware of his/her thinking processes in impersonal terms. Hence, one becomes more able to criticise one's own ideas as well as those of others. To be more conscious of oneself as a person is to be more aware of oneself as part of the wider world. The realisation that one is one self among many others is the Copernican Revolution of one's life. This revolution, however, can take several years. Therefore, we can find marked differences between the younger 14-year-olds and the older 16-year-olds, in terms of their self-understanding, articulation of who they are and what they are to become and to do with their life, etc., as we noted in Chapter 4. This indicates a fundamental feature of the developmental process that young people undergo during adolescence.

Another point that is implied in our discussions in this chapter is that adolescence is not just a preparation for adulthood despite it being an important transition phase in a person's life. If it is mere preparation, then what happens during this time will have no bearing and be meaningless for the young person who is experiencing it. What we have seen suggests that, on the contrary, adolescence is significant in many ways. This is the time when one identifies one's talents and gifts, cultivates one's interests, and establishes friendships and other interpersonal relationships. Often the people the young person meets, and the activities they engage in, and the experiences they undergo will determine, to a greater extent, who they are and what kind of person they are going to be.

Considerable emphasis has been laid over recent decades on the centrality of the cultural context of schooling to the adolescent's growth and development. Curricular activities, pedagogy and teacher/student relations, peer friendships, classroom environments, institutional culture, and wider practices and contexts beyond the school can be crucial in enhancing a positive experience of adolescence. However, too often, as we have seen, schools tend to regard the different interventions to enhance the adolescent's social and emotional development as instrumental to their academic performance and attainment, which sadly misses the true meaning of education.

In light of our understanding of the adolescent's developmental process, we will explore the educational implications of it in the second part of the book.

6
Human-centred education

Introduction

Human-centred education involves three basic principles. The first is that the individual should not be treated merely instrumentally, but rather respected fully as a person. The second is that the main aim of education ought to be the development of the individual as a human being. The third is that education should be directed to the individual as a whole.

For secondary education, the process of development involves becoming more human within a given social context. Part of what we mean by 'human-centred education' is as follows: by facilitating the development of the person as a human, education ought to help prepare the young person towards a more human life. Of course, this idea of 'becoming more human', appealing though it may sound, has not yet been clearly explained.

In this chapter, we will clarify this idea, and thereby give more substance to the framework so far established. The purpose of this chapter is to consolidate the theoretical skeleton and empirical results of the previous chapters in order to have a more complete conception of human-centred education. In particular, we will explain what we mean by 'becoming more human' and derive from it some educational principles, which we will employ in the second half of the book. Therefore, this chapter concludes the more theoretical part of the book and serves as a bridge to the discussion of educational practices in the second.

Being human

The human-centred approach is different from some versions of person-centred education, which tend to stress the essential qualities of being a person, i.e. self-awareness and rational autonomy (Rogers, 1979). The notion of the person is obviously important, but it tends to focus exclusively on the ideas of autonomous action, rationality and self-conscious cognitive states, and thereby ignores important aspects of the human condition, such as friendship, work, humour and being humane. The concept of being human is richer in content and wider in scope than that of a person. Being human is an embodied way of being a person. In short, we emphasise the concept of the human, in contrast to that of the person, because that of a person usually focuses exclusively on the idea of reasoned autonomous choice, following Kant. In fact, Kant's own vision of personhood was probably much richer in moral content than the contemporary neo-liberal conception, which tends to involve a disembodied minimalist notion of freely reasoned choice. Kant's own notion of reason involved that of respect, dignity and community.[1] Kant's richer notion is perhaps harder to defend, but this minimal contemporary notion of autonomy is too weak to support a full justification of educational practices. It might be a part of the picture but not the whole of it.

The issue is not what is unique to humans. We are *not* looking for, say, meta-cognitive processes that whales could not possibly undergo or emotional dispositions that gorillas necessarily lack. In the sense that we are after, 'human' is not a strictly biological term that refers to the genetic patterns underlying membership of the species *Homo sapiens*. It is rather a term that refers to the valuable qualities that form part of our way of being. As pointed out by Thomas Hill, Kant uses the term 'humanity' to indicate relevant moral properties that humans typically have and which, according to Kant, underlie our moral experiences of each other and ourselves (Hill, 1991). This is why Kant's notion of personhood includes some aspects of the idea of being human.

Clearly, the concepts of being human and becoming more so, are both evaluative. This does not prevent them from also having an empirical content. To use these ideas educationally, we need to clarify the empirical content of these concepts. The approach we will take is to identify what counts as a flourishing life for a human, and to specify the kinds of qualities or virtues that are part of such a life. Later we will see how educational processes might strengthen, facilitate and nurture such qualities. These qualities do not have to be moral ones. As we argued in Chapter 2, the process of learning sometimes needs to involve the

[1] Kant, Immanuel, *Groundwork for the Metaphysics of Morals*, Cambridge University Press, 1998.

development of qualities. These qualities may be specific to subject areas, such as literature and biology, or to social roles, such as being a teacher or a lawyer. However, now that we are trying to define the broader concept of being human, we shall examine the non-moral virtues pertaining to the quality of one's life as a human being.

Human flourishing

At the beginning of Chapter 1, we argued that the main priority of education should be to facilitate the development of the individual rather than to promote socio-economic and academic ends. To explain what this priority means in practice, we must start with a brief renewed explanation of what it signifies in principle. Such a development needs to be guided by some vision of what human life ought to be like. This is a very important point because words like 'development' and 'improvement' have implicit value assumptions that need to be made explicit. To understand what it means to be human in the relevant sense requires making these value assumptions more explicit.

How should we conceive the value of living for the person who is living that life? We cannot answer that question adequately simply by showing how useful a person's life is. Although this is an important dimension of most people's lives, what we contribute to our family, friends and society is *instrumentally* valuable. We need to understand better first how to conceive of the non-instrumentally valuable aspects of our lives – life for living's sake.

We shall employ the term 'flourish' to indicate this group of values. Often writers employ the term 'happiness' in this context. This, however, wrongly suggests that what is valuable in life is purely or only hedonic, like subjective pleasures or feelings of gladness. Although feeling happiness is an important part of human life, it is not the only relevant value, because, as we shall see, what causes our happiness can also matter. Another word that is used for this kind of evaluation of our lives is 'well-being'. The term 'flourish' has one advantage over 'well-being': it is more dynamic. It carries the idea that when a person's life is going well, the various parts work together in a mutually supportive way, or symbiotically, like a plant that is flowering.

What is it for a human being to flourish? To answer this question, we do not need to assume that human flourishing will be the same for all individuals at all times in all contexts. Of course, there are huge relevant differences between individuals, and any theoretical account of flourishing must be able to take into account those differences. However, this does not preclude the idea that we can describe the general contours or features of the concept of flourishing. It means rather that such a description must be sensitive to individual and cultural differences when they are relevant.

What does it mean for a human person to flourish or to live a flourishing life? To recap, an answer will provide the general normative framework for understanding the concept of human development needed for a vision of human-centred education. Among other things, it will help us to articulate the aims of learning outlined in Chapters 2 and 3.

The concept of flourishing has five necessary ingredients:

1. Valuable kinds of activities.
2. Appreciation.
3. Self-perception.
4. Synergy.
5. Fullness.

These are described in more detail below.

Valuable kinds of activities

Of these, the first is primordial in that it indicates the kinds of processes, activities and experiences that are non-instrumentally valuable for a human person; they constitute parts of a person's life. An account of 'flourishing' must include a specification of the kinds of activities that are non-instrumentally valuable in a human life.

Their valuable nature has to be understood in terms of the structure of the individual's web of desires (Thomson, 1987). Because of this structure, these activities can be described using certain desirable characterisations or evaluative descriptions. For instance, skiing is desirable in that it is exhilarating; sitting on the beach is relaxing; and so on.

The kinds of activities that are non-instrumentally valuable for a person are defined by the structure of that person's desires or wants. This idea is not as complicated as it may sound. Often people want very specific things. However, beyond the specifics of what is desired, we can give a general description of what is desirable about what we want, and so define the structure of our wants (Thomson, 2005).

Of course, there will be many similarities between the kinds of activities that different individuals find valuable, but for a person's life to flourish, the activities and experiences that comprise that life have to be tailor-made to fit the nature of the individual as well as being appropriate for the social context in which he/she lives. For instance, there might be some important individual variation in what counts as a good friendship. Some people are more expressive; some are more intimate; others require extraordinary frankness of their friends. So, the experience of friendship has to be well suited to the nature of the individual. Furthermore, intimacy, expressiveness and frankness have different social expressions in different cultures. In this sense, the activities and experiences have to be appropriate to the social context in which the person lives in order to be valuable in a way that he/she can appreciate. Despite these social and individual differences, most general descriptions of different people's webs of desires will be similar. Of course, from the point of view of defining what counts as flourishing for an individual, the fact that there is an overlap between most humans is not directly relevant.

Most of the kinds of activities that are valuable for humans involve other people. Even many apparently solitary pursuits such as painting, computer programming and composing are creative activities whose products serve or are used by others. This suggests an important point, namely that the non-instrumental value of such activities consists in part of how connect to other people. This brings us to the need for appropriate appreciation.

Appreciation

In order for a person's life to be valuable in the living of it, he/she has to have experiences and perform activities with the appropriate kind of appreciation of their value in each case. For example, one enjoys lying on the beach by finding it relaxing; one appreciates a serious debate by becoming engaged with the issue. Appreciation requires perceiving the value of an activity under the relevant description. (This was a theme developed in Chapter 3 in relation to motivation.) It is not enough to perform a valuable activity. One has to engage with it or appreciate it.

Proper appreciation can be difficult to attain; one can be distracted by desires, clouded by anxieties and dulled by sadness. Negative emotions are negative not only because they feel bad, but also because they prevent the person from appreciating the valuable aspects and components of his or her life, including other people. For example, worry can destroy the joy of being with a friend, and anger can embitter even the most pleasant work. Positive emotions such as joy are so not only because of how they feel but also because they enable an appreciation of the valuable aspects of activities, including their relation to other people. Awareness has to be clear, clean and focused to appreciate fully the value of what one is doing.

For many activities, especially those that involve others, the relevant appreciation may involve connecting to the valuable aspects of the other people involved. For example, one can bring the value of another person's happiness or enjoyment into one's own activity by properly appreciating that enjoyment. In this way, one can enhance the non-instrumental value of the activity for oneself. The important idea here is that one is connecting directly to things of value beyond oneself.

Self-perception

A flourishing life requires the appropriate kinds of evaluative self-perception (see Chapter 3). This pertains to time. With regard to the present, as we saw earlier, the life of a person has a primary value. For a person's life to flourish, he/she has to perceive or appreciate that value in an appropriate way. I have to perceive and feel myself as valuable. This is a fundamental form of self-respect, which does not depend on what one does or has done. In a similar vein regarding the past, for a person's life to flourish, she needs an appropriate sense of her identity, broadly conceived. As we have already seen, flourishing requires perceiving the valuable activities that constitute the person's life *as valuable under the relevant descriptions*. Now we can add a related point: he/she also needs to perceive some of those activities in general in the past *as processes that form a valuable part of her life*. In other words, the person needs to have a sense of her past activities and experience constituting his/her life up to now as something valuable and worthwhile. Likewise, with regard to the future, in order to flourish, one needs to have the sense of one's future life as something with worthwhile possibilities.

Synergy

'Flourishing' contains the idea of flowering through harmonious functioning. All the bits work together. Thus, in a flourishing life, means and ends come together synergetically. More precisely, the kinds of activity that are non-instrumentally valuable for the person are also instrumentally valuable, and vice versa. Furthermore, this symbiosis allows for the strengthening and continuing development of the person in accordance with his or her nature.

Fullness

A flourishing life would have to be full in the sense that it does not omit important kinds of valuable activity or experience. For instance, suppose a person does not have (or hardly has) any aesthetic experiences or activities in his or her life.

All other things being equal, such a life would not be full or complete, and the person cannot be flourishing, even if he/she does not feel any lack. In a similar vein, we might say that thinking is a natural human function and a human life without thinking is missing something. Likewise, a life without close relationships with others would be incomplete.

This brief conceptual outline of human flourishing and development is in some ways broadly Aristotelian (Thomson, 2003). Like Aristotle's and other accounts, such as Nussbaum's, it relies on some notion of human nature. However, there are some very important differences, as we will now relate.

First, whether or not humans share a common nature is not directly relevant to this specific issue at hand. As a matter of fact, at a broad level of generality, people do have a lot in common. However, our account appeals to the idea of an individual's nature and allows for variation between individuals.

Second, the idea of the individual's motivational nature is and has to be empirically specifiable. We cannot remain content with a list of typical human functions, which we take to be objectively valuable without any further explanation. The motivational nature that an individual has must be discoverable through empirical observation, at least in principle. The contours of human nature are to be mapped broadly through evolutionary theory and psychology. Such a project has many potential pitfalls, such as relying on a false opposition between nature and nurture and depending on a reductive account of socio-cultural influences.

At the same time, the empirical specification for a person's motivational nature will have evaluative implications. The general and structural features of our web of desires as individuals will be inescapable, given one's upbringing and social background. However, we should not assume that because some aspect of our desires is, in some sense, natural that it is therefore morally good. For example, suppose that aggression is part of human nature. This would mean that humans have aggressively motivated desires, which do not depend on specific cultural influences. We would have such desires in almost any culture. This fact (if it is a fact) does not condone aggression.

Third, in this context, the term 'nature' here does not mean innate or natural as opposed to socially acquired. It indicates the relevant features of a person's life or motivational nature that are valuable in a practically inescapable way. This obviously includes the social upbringing of the person. Furthermore, even the genetic cannot be opposed to the social. Even the high-level content of genes is environmentally dependent. When it is described in terms of its effects on an individual's personality or nature, what a gene does depends on the environment the individual was raised in. One cannot specify the former without the latter. Because of this, we cannot oppose the genetic with the social (see Chapters 2 and 3 in Thomson, 1987). However, we are employing a wider concept than the genetic, namely the idea of the nature of a person as determined by what features of his or her motivational character are practically inescapable. These points raise many theoretical concerns that are best pursued more deeply outside this book.

Human functions and valuable activities

The primary kind of value that defines flourishing for humans must take into account the general nature or characteristics of human life. More specifically, what is valuable has to have an empirical basis. This basis is not constituted by the satisfaction of our desires *per se* or by what causes us pleasure but rather by the structure of our wants. Our desires or wants are structured by the most general descriptions of their motivational source or nature (for the arguments for this, see Thomson, 1987 and 2005). Activities and experiences that answer or fit this structure are non-instrumentally valuable, and a flourishing life must involve the appreciation of such activities. Such 'needs' will include those related to:

- *Physical*: one's physical condition and the ownership of material things
- *Cognitive*: the cognitive including the perceptual and aesthetic
- *Emotional and social*: emotional and social/friendship (of various kinds including the sexual)
- *Action related*: action/accomplishment/work and autonomy of action
- *Self-awareness*: self-awareness and auto-evaluation, autonomy of self, including the spiritual

Strictly speaking, these are not needs at all but rather broad headings for labelling the motivational nature of our desires.[2] The physical will include desires related to physical comfort and hygiene, as well as health and pain. People have desires that pertain to ownership quite apart from the instrumental benefits of possession. The second grouping, the cognitive, includes our desires to explore, know, understand, synthesise and explain. It also includes the perceptual, which contains desires related to sensory stimulation, and the aesthetic, which contains desires pertaining to artistic and musical appreciation, as well as those that pertain to order and tidiness. The third group, emotional desires, include the

---

[2] Needs are special kinds of necessary conditions for well-being or for the avoidance of serious harm (see Thomson, 1987, 2005). For a list of such needs, see Max-Neef *et al.* (1991), Chapter 2, p. 18.

desires that we have when we feel specific emotions, plus the desire to feel certain emotions. The social category includes the desires that we have with regard to our friends, families, colleagues and strangers, as well as our community and society; it encompasses our desires for friendship, belonging, group life, social standing and social recognition. Since this is such a broad category, we might divide it into five sub-groups: family, friends, colleagues, community and society. In the fourth grouping we also have desires related to achievement, and directed towards planning, doing and initiating; our desires pertaining to work and to making a difference fit into this category. Finally, in the fifth grouping those pertaining to auto-evaluation and autonomy include our desires to perceive and feel about ourselves in certain ways, such as have dignity, self-respect and a sense of one's life as valuable. The spiritual includes desires for transcendence.

Before we move forward, however, some words of caution. Although they are heuristically useful, these kinds of lists are misleading, however carefully they are constructed. The point is that such a catalogue is not like a shopping list of items that can be counted. They are not objects; they are headings for intensional descriptions.[3] Furthermore, the categories themselves are contestable. For example, the emotional and social are very intimately linked and we might wonder whether they should be separated. Can the sexual be included in the social on the grounds that sex is usually an act of intimacy? Should the aesthetic be included as a sub-set of the cognitive since aesthetic desires usually pertain to sensory perception, which is cognitive? Or if the aesthetic involves transcendence then perhaps it ought to be a sub-category of the spiritual? Should our moral desires be a separate category or are they adequately covered by social and auto-evaluative desires? Is the spiritual a separate category, or can such desires be subsumed under other categories such as the aesthetic?

More words of caution: quite apart from these difficulties, the groupings overlap, not only because of their intentional nature but also because a specific desire is usually motivated by more than one of the above considerations. For example, sexual and socially motivated desires are intermingled. Indeed, in our everyday lives, in our activities and wants, each category impinges on the other. For example, auto-evaluation or evaluative self-consciousness modulates each of the other categories because it permeates and transforms the whole of our way of being. For this reason, for example, desires to own things are hardly ever purely such.

---

[3] An intensional description is referentially opaque or non-extensional. Roughly speaking this means that it is from a point of view. Intensional descriptions characterise the intentional nature of psychological states.

Maslow has a hierarchy of human needs, which are actually drives (Maslow, 1954). Needs are inescapably necessary conditions for avoiding serious harm; they are not linked to motivational drives or forces, which may be a problematic concept. What we are presenting here is quite different. It is not a hierarchy – we are not claiming that one kind of desire comes into operation only after the lower ones have been satisfied. In addition, it is not a list of drives or even needs. It is rather a compilation of different kinds of high-level descriptions one can give of desires that indicate their motivational nature and will define their structure. It only consists of headings as an abbreviation of these characterisations. It would require much empirical study to fill these headings out. However, one also might think of such functions, which are general patterns in our desires, as needs because they form part or aspects of a valuable or flourishing life fitting for human beings (Thomson, 1987, 2005). They are necessary for such a life, not as means, but rather as aspects of it.

Qualities

In Chapter 2, we argued that some learning involves the cultivation or strengthening of qualities. Training in mathematics is not just a question of knowledge of equations, or skill in applying them to solve problems, but also consists of the development of the kinds of (non-moral) virtues that a good mathematician needs, such as diligence, persistence, curiosity and sticking to the point. Such virtues do not replace knowledge and skills; indeed they require them. Nevertheless, these virtues are more than traditionally conceived knowledge or skills because they involve caring in the appropriate ways. Following what we argued in Chapter 3, this caring requires, and can be fostered by, the relevant kinds of appreciation or evaluative perception. So, for example, a good scientist cares about the evidence or the details of how an experiment was set up. In practice, this means, for instance, that he/she might perceive a piece of evidence as dubious or an observation as unsystematic, or see one procedure as better than another.

Let us look at these qualities in more detail. In his *Nicomachean Ethics*, Aristotle advanced his famous doctrine of the mean, according to which the virtues are a mean between two extremes, which constitute vices. This is not the same as advocating moderation. For example, although courage is a mean between cowardice and foolhardiness, there are moments in life that call for immoderate physical courage. Following this, one might say that the virtues have a corrective aspect. For example, one person might lack generosity whereas another might be over-generous to the point of neglecting him- or herself. The virtue of generosity is a mean because it is a corrective to these two extremes.

This point about the virtues being a corrective implies that their cultivation may differ from person to person and between cultures. The required path of development for the person who is foolhardy will be different from the one for the person who is fearful. In a society in which people are very obedient, independence of mind might be an important virtue, even if it is not always recognised as such. Loyalty or solidarity would be an important virtue in a society of people who have independence of mind, even though it might not always be recognised as such. Because of such variations, we cannot list all the virtues that people need in a way that is independent of context. The same point applies to individuals. The virtues are also personalised in the additional sense that, because people have varied temperaments, each virtue will express itself differently in each person. For example, eloquence in a person with a strong comic talent will be different from articulacy in a person with a serious character.

However, none of this implies that what counts as a virtue is purely subjective or a matter of opinion. Nor does it mean that we cannot make generalisations about the nature of any virtue, but it does imply that, insofar as it involves the nurturing of virtues, learning requires a personalised, guided process. It means that a factory model of education can only provide something superficial. The corrective aspect of the virtues also explains why it is difficult to make a clear-cut list of all the virtues or to assign priorities to them.

The qualities that a person needs as a part of learning depend on the nature of the area studied. We can think of such qualities as similar to the virtues required for a social role. For instance, the learning of mathematics involves the strengthening of certain qualities of mind whereas literature involves a different set of sensibilities. With respect to qualities, learning for gymnastics is different from that for boxing. However, we need to avoid thinking that these learning processes should be subject-driven in the way that writers such as Hirst and Peters (1970) advocate. We argued against falling into this trap in Chapter 1, when we discussed the relative priority of human developmental needs as against academic goals.

It is not part of this book to examine the vexed question of what counts (in the context of secondary education) as a discipline, although in this book we have made the minimal assumption that there are important methodological differences at least between natural sciences, mathematics, social sciences, and humanities and the arts, despite the overlaps between them. However, such a division cannot pretend to be complete because it ignores many areas of learning such as gymnastics, metalwork and nursing. Furthermore, it is not part of this book to investigate the qualities or virtues associated with the learning of each area of activity or discipline. Nevertheless, a human-centred curriculum would require such an exercise because such a curriculum has to involve a series of activities that help build and strengthen the appropriate qualities.

There are qualities or virtues that a person should foster independently of his or her roles as a human person. These are defined by the general contours of flourishing and by its specific individual human content. These qualities are not those required by the 'shoulds' of social morality but rather by the 'it would be better if' of personal ethics.

Following Aristotle, we argue that, for each area of life, there is a corresponding set of virtues or character qualities (see Nussbaum, 1988). We can choose as the relevant areas of life, the provisional simplified classification of the types of desire given on page 129 of this chapter.

It would be a mistake to assume that there is only one quality or virtue per category, especially given what we have said about the corrective nature of the virtues. Moreover, there might not even be a single word in English for the corresponding general grouping of virtues. We will give a brief overview of each area.

The emotional and social qualities primarily involve being able to appreciate and care for other people (see Chapter 3). It is a question of being appropriately open in one's feelings to the reality of other people. This requires having inner strength, emotional stability and openness. It also requires happiness in the sense that when people are unhappy, they are usually preoccupied with themselves. Caring for others also requires that one cares for oneself.

The cognitive virtues constitute one's epistemological relationship to reality, and to truths and to new ideas about reality. The basic quality is one of understanding. This would include being honest in the broadest sense, which requires being critical and logical, seeking counter-evidence, and avoiding irrelevance, cognitive dissonance and error. It would also involve being creative in the sense of looking for new ideas and connections, being open to the views of others and being able to reformulate or reframe problems. As we saw in Chapter 2, understanding involves having appropriate appreciation of relevant facts and facets of the world. Understanding also requires having good judgement, which involves knowing when and how to be critical, and when and how to be open or creative.

As we saw in Chapter 3, the virtues concerning action relate primarily to being proactive, and to having direction or something worth caring about. Such a person is self-motivated and able to take initiatives, including in the way they work with others. This requires determination, as well as carefulness.

The qualities concerning self-awareness involve an appreciative but critical understanding of oneself that permits one to have a direction in life that accords with one's own nature and talents, and enables one to know what one is less good at. It allows one to respect and care for oneself.

Each category interplays with the others. For example, one can exercise dignity in the way one owns things by being generous and fair. Practical wisdom is the group of virtues that allows one to be excellent in the other areas. For this reason, Aristotle held that practical wisdom was one of the cardinal virtues, a virtue that other virtues depend on. One can see why practical wisdom is central by bringing together different ideas. First, virtues are more than skills because they require caring for the appropriate things in the right way. In more contemporary language, they involve internalising standards, which is one of the reasons why they are educationally so important. In order for young people to do well, they have to understand the relevant practical and contextual meaning of 'well', and this means caring about that. Second, as we have seen, virtues are corrective and circumstantial, without thereby being subjective. Together these two points mean that to nurture the virtues requires a person to be able to reflect critically regarding what he/she cares about. For example, she has to be able to see how solving a mathematical problem involves systematic and logically consequential thought and she has to be able to reflect critically upon what she cares about in mathematics. It requires critical distance to one's own desires and tendencies. Therefore, the educational process has to encourage such reflection. How it might achieve that, we shall examine in Chapter 7. However, critical reflection on what one cares about is not sufficient for practical wisdom, even if it is necessary. It is also necessary to care.

There is another aspect of flourishing that tends to be ignored in contemporary society, especially in an achievement-oriented culture that often glosses over the subjective or inner aspects of life. As we noted earlier, it is not enough to participate or engage in the valuable kinds of activities listed above. It is also necessary to appreciate them appropriately. Although this idea might be included in some of the qualities already mentioned, nevertheless it needs highlighting. A person who is over-anxious or insecure cannot easily appreciate well the activities that he/she might be enjoying. Some people do not really even enjoy their holidays because they are absent from the present moment. The capacity to appreciate fully what one is doing is a quality vital to the well-being and flourishing of a person. In a way, it is one aspect of what one might hope would be covered under the broad umbrella of the humanities and arts, although traditional literature classes often stress literary analysis rather than appreciation. Likewise, one can study art without appreciating the act of seeing. Nevertheless, appreciation need not always be aesthetic because it covers all forms of evaluative cognition. Appreciation needs to be signalled as a quality apart. Furthermore, as we noted in Chapter 3, such appreciation has intimate relations with our feelings. Not only is it blocked or enhanced, but it is sometimes also constituted by what one feels.

To flourish, one has to find life circumstances that enable a synergetic relation between important intrinsic and instrumental values. For example, one has to find financially viable work that fits one's talents and interests, that one can identify with and that involves good relationships with colleagues. In a similar vein, one's friendships have to have an analogous and ongoing symbiosis between means and ends. This feature of the flourishing life shows the necessity for practical wisdom along the lines defined by Aristotle.

Back to education

In the first chapter of this book, we explored the idea that the development of the individual needs to be the primary aim of secondary education. We saw that this involves treating the person non-instrumentally, and how instrumentalising the process of learning and education deprives it of its real meaning, as well as embodying a fundamental misunderstanding of values. To provide an initial indication of what treating education non-instrumentally means in practice, we compared it to the requisites of meaningful work.

The educational process is about learning in the broad sense described in Chapter 2. It follows from what we have said about the nature of practical wisdom that a primary quality that education should develop is one of caring about and being engaged in one's learning processes. Education should aim to help young people care about their learning. This involves a struggle against apathy in its myriad forms. If we tried to envisage how young people should be when they leave school, then as a first attempt one might respond: to have the skills and qualities necessary and sufficient to know how to learn. One might affirm this by saying that education requires a process of learning how to learn. However, this statement does not quite hit the target because the art of cooking means little to the person who has no appetite. Thus, likewise for education, it is not merely a question of transmitting knowledge and imparting skills, even those that pertain to learning itself. The issue is also how to awaken, develop and channel the relevant forms of caring, a process that we discussed in Chapter 3.

In this part of the chapter, we will discuss some of the principles that comprise human-centred education. We will divide this discussion into two parts. First, it is necessary to discuss education as a part of the adolescent's current life. Time at school is a significant part of adolescence and, during this time, the student ought to be treated and respected as a human person. Second, it is necessary to discuss the principles of human-centred education as applied to education as a preparation for the adolescent's future life as an adult. These discussions will serve as a bridge between the more theoretical arguments in the first part of the book and our later attempts to envisage the structure of a new, more human-centred curriculum design, learning appraisal and feedback, pedagogy and learning environment.

Respect the individual person

It is a travesty of adolescence to regard it primarily as a preparation for adulthood, just as it is disdainful to think of an adult's life as a preparation for retirement (or death). Likewise, it is contemptuous to regard a person merely as a means towards increased national competitiveness, whether this person is child or adult. All of these ways of thinking treat part of human life merely as an instrument for something else, which is what we have been critiquing all along. Thus, the educational process, to be caring, has to respect and attend to the present needs of young people, which signifies above all, providing the space necessary for young people themselves to address those needs.[4] Indeed, we are talking about human persons, their development and their lives. This matters much more profoundly than anything else. Other things only matter in relation to that.

For an education to be caring, it must take into account the current needs of students. To identify those needs is a judgement that is both empirical and evaluative, which is required to construct a curriculum, to determine the appropriate pedagogy, to provide learning feedback and to design the learning environment.

Cognition

As already pointed out in the previous chapter, during adolescence, the mind of the young person is becoming more active, with a greater capacity for abstract self-reflective thought. It is the time when he/she asks questions and rejects bad reasoning. This means that adolescents will be developing new relationships to

---

[4] 'Needs' is of course an evaluative term but we have answered the theoretical point by arguing that evaluative terms can have empirical content; think of 'pain'.

authority, much more challenging than the acceptance they tended to have as younger children. When a person's autonomy is developing, resistance to teaching does not equal resistance to learning. The learning institution has to respond to this kind of need. If a young person has a mind that is demanding, then teachers and educators need to know what will feed it and be able to help young people to eventually feed their own intellectual development. For the young people, pursuing their own inquiries and meeting their own learning needs requires a lot of confidence and self-responsibility. How can the school encourage this?

Some schools fall at the very first fence by not taking the time to explain to students why they are learning what they are learning. Young people need an overview of the curriculum. Such meta-knowledge helps a young person to learn better and to be able to make his or her own curricular choices. However, the point now is that failure to explain and discuss the curriculum constitutes a failure to meet their needs as human beings. It amounts to treating the young people as vessels. Additionally, it contradicts the views of learning and motiva-tion sketched in Chapters 2 and 3, which stressed the intentional or aspectual nature of both. In practice, this means that context matters. Motivationally, it is very important how things are perceived.

Without necessarily doing so explicitly, schools do set a general context in which young people study courses and attend school. For example, in very expensive private schools, the context might be something like the following: to become the leaders of this country, you will need to understand the art of rhetoric and self-presentation. In many mainstream schools, the context might be: if you want to avoid being unemployed, then you need some qualifications to set you apart from the crowd. In others, the message might be just: get this done because that is what everyone has to do in their youth. In each of these hypothetical cases, the underlying message is negative because it appeals to arrogance, fear or obligation. An institution needs to ask 'What is the intention behind this institution?' It needs to make its intention clear to the students and to employees. We will return to this kind of institutional (re)framing in Chapter 11.

Each specific area of study also needs a set of contexts. It is remarkable how little time and attention is paid to explaining to young people why they are studying X and Y and the subject as a whole. The student needs to know the organising principles of a subject, as we stressed in Chapter 2. The student needs to be able to see the forest as a whole from the viewpoint of a helicopter rather than getting lost in a maze of details like an ant. It is possible to grasp the organising principles of a subject in a short time.

Schools can respect young people by challenging their cognitive powers. As we have seen, young people are developing more abstract reasoning capacities and the capacity to reason hypothetically and multi-dimensionally, but these capacities can be developed only by actually employing them. In Chapter 4 we noted that some of the younger students found it difficult to articulate their ideas. This returns us to the recommendations regarding linguistic capacities from Chapter 2. We noted that linguistic capacities greatly affect one's ability to learn the concepts and organising principles of different areas of knowledge. This suggests that students need time specifically directed to their cognitive learning needs, and that young people who cannot express themselves well verbally probably need more opportunities to talk in order to build their confidence.

Another way in which schools might respect the young person is by giving him or her more choice about what he/she studies. The claim that the student should be offered more choice sounds good, but this requires that the student be given the background and guidance to be able to make choices well. Choosing requires that one understands what the criteria for good choices are and how choices are to be made. It is not easy to choose well in conditions of ignorance. Choosing what to study when one does not know what the subjects consist of is very difficult. This means that the student needs guidance to make good choices. However, this type of guidance requires a personal element and trust. It involves a mentoring relationship. Building the capacity to make reflective choices is a vital part of a person's education, which can be built into the curriculum.

Motivation

Adolescence is a period of the development of autonomy. This is part of the process of the flowering of a sense of oneself. With this flowering, there ought to come the growing realisation that one has to live one's own life and that it is up to oneself what that life will be. This sense of freedom ('My life is mine; I can do what I want with it; the future is open') ought to bring with it an increasing sense of self-responsibility ('It is up to me'). Education can nurture these qualities but the institutional setting often encourages passivity.

This is one of the reasons why educational thinking ought to stress learning rather than instructing. No one likes being told everything. Even small children rebel against being told or taught and often prefer to run off and explore for themselves. A resistance to being taught does not always indicate an unwillingness to learn. It indicates a wish to do so on one's own terms. It is for this reason that teachers need the art of being invisible guides and implicit facilitators, as well as overt teachers.

For this reason, young people need to have the opportunity to learn from experience and by doing, both inside and outside the school setting. It is great if they have the chance to do social work, work in a business, visit different institutions and experience a taste of the gamut of activities the city or town or area they live in has to offer. It is good if they also have the opportunity to reflect upon those experiences as a group of peers. Many schools do provide these kinds of experiences but usually not often or enough. Students need opportunities to learn without feeling that they are being taught in order to heighten their sense of self-guidance.

This process of increasing self-guidance ought to lead the student to connect to things of value beyond him/herself. This is not a question of simply finding out what is interesting in an area of knowledge such as history or biology, but more of finding a passion that engages the student. Perhaps it is too easy to assume that young people are interested in little except friends, sex, music and sport. It requires much individual attention to the young person to find out what she or he is interested in and why, and what the next step is. In some cases, it is a question of building on those interests. Why do many young people find football more interesting than history? We want our students to read more; let us give the young person encouragement to read lots about football and to write about it. Then let us encourage him/her on to the next stage, the economics of football perhaps. Or perhaps, it is better to challenge the student to care for something else. Some students characterise themselves as lazy, but this evades the real issue. Laziness requires that one has something to be lazy about. The person who is disengaged does not fit this precondition. If a student appears to be passive, and does not connect well to what he/she is learning then perhaps the young person needs to be heard and understood. What is the problem? As we discussed in Chapter 3, chronic passivity can be a symptom of other emotional problems. The school has to be able to show that it cares in this way for the student as a person by helping him or her cultivate wider interests and finally passions that fit his or her nature. This is the precondition for the student being able to evaluate him/herself and think critically about what he/she can improve, and how and why.

Young people often experience school as a place of coercion. The alternative to the feeling of coercion is not simply having more free choice. In any case, free choice without criteria or the capacity for choosing may amount to little more than playing roulette and may be a source of anxiety. Within a large impersonal institution, such choice may reinforce the feeling that no one cares. The alternative to the feeling of coercion is the perception of non-coercion. If I value what I am doing then I will not ask: 'Do I have to do it?' If the school sends messages that amount to 'You are coerced into doing this' then students will feel coerced.

People of all ages need variety, as well as routine. There should be discussions amongst educators and with young people to explore what counts as variety. Physically, it is hard to sit in desks in the same buildings day after day, year after year. It is easy to get hypnotised into the ways of the institution. Change requires a radical rethinking of a learning institution and the way that it frames the activities for students. For instance, school leaders may consider questions such as: 'Do all learning activities have to be in one school?', 'Can students swap schools for some days?', 'Can training and courses take place from time to time in a new building, with new people in order to create some freshness and change for young people?', 'Can some of the more able students attend some courses at local universities?'

Emotions and relationships

As we saw in Chapter 5, young people can be volatile and emotionally dependent on their relationships with peer groups. Some are tempted to try to escape their own feelings, often as a result of the harshness or dreariness of their everyday lives, through drugs and drink. As Steinberg pointed out, young people tend to underestimate the dangers of such behaviour patterns (Steinberg, 2005). There are alternatives, which involve facing up to one's feelings, accepting them and moving forward more positively. In the interviews cited later in Chapter 10, a few students mentioned that they had been looking for emotional support from the school, which had not been forthcoming.

As some of the interviews in Chapter 4 revealed, young people can be idealistic, and this is a quality that needs to be nurtured so that it does not turn to cynicism. Educational institutions can provide more opportunities for adolescents to begin to discuss questions such as: 'How can you contribute best to society and to the world?', 'How can society be better organised?' As well as discussion groups, young people may be offered the chance to put their idealism into practice through social work and to reflect on their experience.

During adolescence, young people are trying to discover new adult-like and intimate relationships with individuals of their own age. This process is often painful and exhilarating, and young people often need but lack the space to talk about these processes in a mature and self-reflective way. They need to have space to understand blame, anger and fear as well as integrity, loyalty and honesty within themselves. They also need to see how to deal with the anger and violence of others. In Chapter 3, we noted that the development of one's emotions involves feeling them in appropriate ways in appropriate contexts, but that this aspect of emotional development can be very challenging for young people who may be susceptible to mood swings. The opportunity to discuss such matters in a group will help the developmental process.

A learning institution needs to foster significant relationships between teachers and students as people, as human beings, beyond the instrumentalisation of their roles. As we noted in some of the interviews in Chapter 10, often students do not see their teachers except as teachers. It is difficult for them to see beyond the role. This implies that they expect to be perceived and thought of primarily as only students rather than as persons. This means that the relationships are perceived primarily as instrumental or functional. Insofar as this is true, the young people do not have a sense of the institution caring for them as persons. So, while variety is important, this should not be at the cost of having only impersonal and purely functional relationships. If students have seven different teachers every day, and only a few minutes at the beginning of each day with their form teacher who provides the only continuity, then there will be fewer opportunities to develop significant relationships with adults.

Identity

As we saw in Chapter 5, kids are trying to form a sense of themselves as persons. This is a major part of the process of increased self-awareness and independence from parents. Often, this involves identifying oneself with one's peer group and with role models. As we saw in Chapter 4, as they get older, some young people also begin to find more critical distance from these identifications as their sense of themselves becomes stronger. This process is integral to that of discovering and creating one's future direction in life.

How can a secondary educational institution better respect and care for the student as a human person as a whole? Given their age and given the social context, we have listed the kinds of things that might fit this requirement and which constitute the principles of human-centred education. This list may not be complete. Nevertheless, we can see that much of the respect and care consists of providing young people with the opportunity to work through these aspects of their lives with the guidance of a mentor.

In order to help make the list more comprehensive, we might compare the elements we have just cited with the list of typical human functions given earlier in the chapter. We have not yet examined what counts as respect in terms of the physical ownership and perceptual interests of young people. This would require discussing, for instance, the plan and design of school buildings, or school meals and timetables, all topics that we cannot cover here.

Preparing for the future

We do not live for the future. Thus, because school life is a huge part of a young person's current life, it requires the kinds of respect that we discussed in the previous section. Nevertheless, education does involve enabling the young person to prepare for his or her future life. The main preparation that some schools currently provide is the opportunity to acquire a set of qualifications (exam results). Of course, these are supposed to represent, or measure, the qualities, skills and knowledge that prepare a person for his or her adult life. Nevertheless, the certificates in themselves are not a preparation at all; they are vouchers. Although as a ticket they have an important value, the main preparation consists of the qualities, skills and knowledge that the young person develops and acquires through the educational process. We will postpone our discussion of measurement, assessment and exams for later in Chapter 9.

Work

At this age, a person is trying to get a sense of him/herself and work out what kind of life he/she wants. It is very important that students are encouraged to do this for themselves with guidance so that they will value their own education and personal development, and indeed themselves. As we noted from some of the interviews in Chapter 4, it is very easy for young people to have a narrow conception of what their lives might be. To overcome this, they need several educational processes.

The first is to identify, develop and follow their interests. For a person's life to flower, he/she needs to identify the kind of work that fits his or her nature and talents. People who dislike their work usually dislike life. One might say that the happy person has made his hobby into his work, a change that requires the disciplines of good self-knowledge. Having identified one's work-hobby then there is the process of nurturing the talents one has and the character traits that enable one to work in that area.

Second, young people need help to broaden their horizons in a practical sense. To see beyond one's own horizons requires encounters with new possibilities. As we noted in Chapter 4, young people may have an idea of their tastes and even of their talents but usually have a very limited conception of the kinds of work that can be done.

The third process is to improve one's understanding of the criteria according to which one should evaluate one's life. People tend to have a very material conception of what a happy life consists in. What counts as an ideal, full and happy life? What qualities do you need to develop to become such a person? Young people employ their own concepts to evaluate their present life, but can they evaluate these concepts critically? What are the assumptions within those concepts?

Young people have to make important choices about their livelihood quite early on in life. Few understand well the options before them, and the likely implications of their choices, or what would count as a good or bad choice, and few apply critical and sympathetic self-reflection to their own decision-making process. How would a young person choose if he/she really understood what his or her talent was and had a strong feeling of self-worth as well as developed passions and interests? This is an entirely different kind of process to trying to fit people into predetermined careers.

Finally, students need more opportunities to practise the art of making decisions. School usually provides a very well-defined institutional framework. What has to be done is usually determined by the teacher and the authorities, and the young person has very limited input into this. Few have an understanding of the rationale for the processes they undergo. This sends them a lesson in passivity, which the school needs to overcome in order to help young people develop the art of living autonomously. This would indicate the need for a curriculum that allowed the students more study choices and that provided opportunities for in-depth personal guidance about such choices.

Relationships

Most young people and adults will fall in love, get married and become parents. As well as having the opportunity to discuss current relationships, adolescents also need the space to understand better what all these future relationships involve and what counts as being a good spouse, a good parent, etc. Giving and receiving love can be a very difficult and sometimes painful process for people, especially if they are not used to sharing their expectations and if they do not know how to express their feelings. One's capacity for a flourishing life depends crucially on the qualities that one has in relationships with family, friends and strangers, such as the willingness to care for others by listening, understanding their needs and accepting. Equally, young people who grow up and are educated in an environment in which they are listened to and cared for, and where their needs are respected, and where they are accepted for who they are, are most likely to have the willingness and capacity to offer the same to their partners and children.

Part of the preparation for a flourishing human life is to be able to relate pro-fessionally to others. Education will need to address questions such as what it means to follow orders and take initiatives, how one reacts to criticism, and what kinds of standard apply in the context of different jobs and why they apply. These questions cannot be addressed by simply following a highly subject-oriented curriculum. Instead, they rely on a confluence of approaches, which will include encouraging young people to connect with the values of work, and to connect their work with own their interests. This in turn requires some experience of the world of work beyond the school campus.

Some young adults need some simple guidance in household management. For example, if a person cannot live within his or her means or fails to understand how quickly compound interest accumulates, or in general lacks the skill and vision to care properly for him/herself, then the educational system should provide the opportunity to address these needs. Some of this knowledge and skill is pretty much commonsense, and not all students will need it.

Values and direction

A requirement for a flourishing life is a positive and proactive attitude. This includes, in the broadest sense of the term, an entrepreneurial approach. Such a person will not only seek to solve problems but also to create new and fruitful opportunities. A person should leave school with the ability and wish to learn for him or herself. As we saw in Chapter 2, knowledge can be regarded as answers to questions.

However, this positive attitude includes much more than being enterprising. Although it is not easy to cultivate, this preparation includes finding a good relationship within oneself, to one's emotions and desires. Adolescence is the time of life when a person can first become conscious of his or her responsibility for the quality of his/her own life. Few people are encouraged to do this except in materialistic and monetary terms, and few understand or appreciate their responsibility for their own feelings and state. For example, people who complain a lot tend to feel depressed more easily. People can go through the whole of their life without realising this, and thus do not have the opportunity to improve in this respect.

Another ingredient for a good or flourishing life is to have direction. This is not something as fixed or specific as a life-plan and not as instrumental as a set of goals or a life project. Every young person should be encouraged to begin to consider where he/she is going in life and what counts as improvements in life. At this age, young people have an extraordinary opportunity to expand their horizons and see themselves in a new light that might transcend the expectations that they have been unconsciously living down to. Therefore, part of the preparation for adult life should be to have the possibility to taste new opportunities.

A person's quality of life is determined in part by what they perceive as possible for themselves.

Conclusions

We have outlined the basic principles of human-centred education, bringing together the argumentation of the first three chapters of this book and the empirical conclusions of Chapters 4 and 5. In the second part of the book we will apply these, albeit in a general way, to curriculum, pedagogy and assessment. After examining the views of some young people of their educational experience, we will consolidate all of this into a view of a human-centred educational institution.

Further reading

Nussbaum, M. (1988) *The Virtues.* Midwest Studies in Philosophy.

Helm, B. (2010) *Love, Friendship and the Self.* Oxford: Oxford University Press.

Thomson, G. (2003) *On the Meaning of Life.* Belmont, CA: Wadsworth Press.

Wolf, S. (2010) *Meaning in Life and Why it Matters.* Princeton, NJ: Princeton University Press.

2
Rethinking secondary education

As we indicated in the first part of the book, the human-centred approach has much in common with holistic and other alternative methods. At the same time, it advocates some of the elements from the traditional state educational system. We are attempting to combine the best of both worlds in a new vision.

When stated in bold terms, the distilled essence of both the traditional view of schooling and the alternative holistic conception are unsatisfactory. On the one hand, the mainstream idea that teachers should mainly impart knowledge to students and cultivate skills in the hope that what they retain will be good for their development requires an overhaul. This view has many deep problems, and this is perhaps why political discourse about educational goals often eschews the language of the traditional view even when the actual practices in the classrooms embody it. On the other hand, the alternative conception of education that insists on students' directing and managing their own learning without 'interference' from adults seems like an unrealistic vision for the majority of the young people. In many cases, it actually results in lower academic standards. More to the point, it has no conceptual space for external academic standards, because these are supposed to be impositions that distract from the natural growth of the child.

Put the other way around, the state system puts emphasis on producing academically skilled and knowledgeable people, and on treating all students equally. In other words, the 'most honorable' intention of state education is to produce equally knowledgeable and skilled people regardless of their social backgrounds and personal attributes. Given the numbers of children and young people involved, its particular strength lies in its central academic task that, in many ways, makes schools look like an academic machine. It has a set of well-defined expected academic outcomes, uniform standards and a whole system of monitoring. It is reminiscent of a franchise.

In sharp contrast, alternative schools or schools with holistic educational ideals are much more interested in the personal development of each individual young person, and are more willing to treat the student holistically and on his/her own terms. This is reminiscent of home cookery willing to depart from the set menu.

Whereas the one stems from an Enlightenment rationalist tradition that is willing to employ economic procedures such as cost–benefit analysis in the educational sphere, the other has its roots in Rousseau's romanticism that is willing to forgo such rationality for the sake of being natural. In the first part of the book, we have tried to show that this rationalism and romanticism constitute a false dichotomy in the field of education, and we have argued that to resolve this we need to transcend the idea of a dichotomy of reason vs. emotion.

As we have seen, the vision of human-centred education, by clarifying the aims of education (see Chapter 1), and by highlighting the focus of education as the cultivation of human/humane qualities or virtues (see Chapter 2), can integrate the overly knowledge-based and skill-intense system of schooling with an education that has the unfolding of the child's natural attributes at its core. In this way, human-centred education that aims at the flourishing of the whole person in a harmonious way can also assume a broader array of responsibilities, including nurturing qualities and virtues, encouraging personal attributes and unfolding of personalities, building social relations, practising citizenship, developing ethical characters, and more. The central task of the second part of the book is to explain how such a vision plays out in practice in secondary schools.

Bernstein (1977) argued that curriculum, pedagogy and assessment constitute the core triad of educational practice and that changes in one would intimately affect the others. In this second half of the book, we will apply the theory developed so far and our understanding of adolescence to Bernstein's triad in order to see what a human-centred education is like in practice within an educational institution such as a secondary school.

According to Bernstein, curriculum, assessment and pedagogy are the key interlocking pillars that support the educational system or schooling, and that they mutually inform each other in the process of education. Applied to an English secondary educational system for 14–16-year-olds, we can see that there is indeed a close connection between the conception of the national curriculum as a set of outcomes, the tendency to regard pedagogy as national curriculum delivery methods, and the idea of national testing as a way to assess the quality of delivery and to measure the student's attainment of those set learning outcomes. It is almost unimaginable to change one of these conceptions without altering the other two.

Of the three, however, we think curriculum is primary in the sense that it defines the educational aims of the practice. Pedagogy would be second in line because it is the range of activities that facilitate the learning processes that are defined by the curriculum. Assessment of learning would be third as it allows both teacher and student to understand better how well the designated activities have helped in facilitating learning. This is how we will structure part of the second half of the book. This will lead to an examination of the culture of a human-centred learning institution, after we have reviewed the views of young people about their current experiences in secondary schools.

7
Curriculum

Introduction

There are several disputes about what a curriculum is. In the first section of this chapter, we will try to offer a simple definition of the concept of curriculum, and argue that the disputes are not really about the definition at all, but rather concern mainly how curricula should be developed and used, and by whom. We will also separate out the different issues. In the second section, we will review the principles already argued for in this book that are needed to construct the skeleton of a human-centred curriculum at secondary school level. Third, we will suggest a provisional outline for a curriculum based on those principles. In the last section, we will answer some of the questions that arise from the outline.

Definition and disputes

What is a curriculum? The standard definition makes it roughly a programme of study involving a body of knowledge to be transmitted (Blenkin *et al.*, 1992), and this kind of definition is contested for good reasons. It emphasises knowledge and implies that study is the only activity that is educational. It seems like a bookish definition. We want to avoid building a particular conception of learning and of education more generally into the definition of the term 'curriculum'. Consequently, we need to steer clear of unwarranted assumptions in coming to grips with the concept itself (as opposed to arguing for a particular conception). For example, suppose we defined 'curriculum' as an instrument for governments to control schools: we would be assuming that only governments can draw up curricula and only for that purpose. It is better not to build such assumptions into the definition. Likewise, one might be tempted to define a curriculum as a set of courses and their content and programme for a specific end. For example, Peter Grundy (1987: 11) has suggested that a curriculum is a 'programme of activities (by teachers and pupils) designed so that pupils will attain so far as possible certain educational and other schooling ends or objectives'. However, this presupposes that education should consist of only courses with a predetermined content, which exists independently of the students. This definition is clearly vulnerable to serious questions. The definition needs to be more open than this. It needs to have fewer limiting assumptions. Of course, it is impossible to formulate a definition that makes no presumptions, but this is a rather abstract point that we will not dwell on.

The arguments as to how a curriculum should be shaped and used and what it should contain are more substantial and require an appeal to principles that lie beyond the definition of the term. For example, it is very difficult to determine who should construct a curriculum, and a good answer to this question needs the backing of a theory of political power as applied to education in a particular country. In a similar vein, we could ask how prescriptive a curriculum should be. The answer might depend on who constructs it, why and how. In short, these kinds of questions can't be settled within or through the definition itself.

After these cautionary comments on the making of the definition, let's begin by distinguishing language and reality, the map and the territory, or in this case, the curriculum and what actually happens in the classroom. A recipe might say 'cut two onions into fine slices'. This sentence is distinct from the actual action or slicing operation. As we shall use the term, curricula are on the language side of this divide. They are like maps rather than land, and recipes rather than the actual cooking. This does not mean that good cooking must always follow a recipe or that good education must adhere to a curriculum; that would be a different point.

Some writers, such as Catherine Cornbleth (1990), have suggested that a curriculum is what actually happens in the classroom. The idea is to allow educational processes to be open-ended without predetermined learning outcomes. Such open processes can be guided by the constant evaluation and reformulation by teachers and students as part of the learning process itself. To capture this idea, it might be clearer to say: '*A curriculum should indicate the kind of classroom processes that teachers should facilitate and it should not try to specify end-products. A curriculum shouldn't be pre-cooked and rigid, but open-ended and open to changes in direction and content from the interaction during the process itself.*' In other words, the curriculum is still a recipe, albeit one that allows for improvisation, defined by a process and not by a result.

Cornbleth's comments are – in part – an articulation of an alternative view of what practical reasoning and planning actually are. According to an Aristotelian view on this topic, practical reasoning cannot be reduced to a set of rules to achieve pre-specified end-states but rather, must be conceived of as the contextualised exercise of general virtues and sensibilities such as wisdom and caring. Practical reasoning cannot be like having the right computer manual in your head. In part, reasoning happens spontaneously during practice. There are reasons for being sympathetic to this Aristotelian reform of the concept of practical reasoning and planning. It is logically impossible to define the right or best choice in terms of a set of rules. Rules always undermine choice (Thomson, 2002).

However, advocating such a praxis conception of reasoning does not imply that a curriculum is the learning and growth that actually occur during an educational process. Such a definition would deny the possibility, within the discourse of 'curriculum', of separating the intentions from what actually happens. For instance, absurdly, it would mean that if no one turned up to school, the curriculum would be empty, or that if the children fought, then the curriculum would be fighting. Thus, we need to make a distinction between what actually occurs from what ought to happen, or what would be good to happen (according to an unspecified someone), even when the plan is open-ended and subject to revision (or even an overhaul). We can separate the curriculum from how we should use it as practitioners. Likewise, a musical score can be very specific about how the music is to be played or it could be very vague, leaving room for improvisation on a loosely defined theme.

Furthermore, if the curriculum is like a set of guidelines or a recipe, a map or plan, then it is broadly a kind of prescription or recommendation, so long as we include hypothetical recommendations in this category. Of course, in ordinary parlance, the word 'prescription' usually carries strong paternalistic overtones of authority, which writers such as Goodson (2005) object to. However, a curriculum does not have to have the characteristics of a command. In the context of national curricula, one might be tempted to identify 'curriculum' with prescriptions that are insensitive to contexts, highly detailed and specific, rigid, authoritarian and non-participatory, but one needn't. A curriculum could be a suggestion. Even when it is a suggestion, a curriculum is supposed to express or indicate a reason for action and, because of this, it is unavoidably recommendatory rather than just purely descriptive. It is not a prediction about what will happen in the class; it is a recommendation about what ought to happen. This does not mean that it is necessarily authoritarian.

In this way, a curriculum is a special kind of plan for learning. What makes it special is what distinguishes it from a lesson plan. This is to say that a curriculum provides a second-order general framework for first-order lesson-plans, which form part of pedagogy. It is a recipe for making maps, or a map for making recipes. Stenhouse (1975) was the originator of the recipe metaphor. With this metaphor, Stenhouse allowed for scrutiny of or experimenting with: (1) the ingredients to be used; (2) the practices or pedagogy of the teachers; (3) description of what is happening in the classroom; and (4) variation according to different students.

In this conception, the curriculum offers a set of suggestions or guiding principles for recommended activities, as well as further guidelines for facilitating these activities (pedagogy), and approaches to reviewing students' engagement with the activities (assessment). It therefore seems that Stenhouse had Bernstein's triads embedded in his conception of educational planning.

Perhaps the word 'plan' has potentially unwanted implications insofar as it is tied closely to instrumental or means–ends reasoning. To signal this, we might sometimes use the word 'intention' instead. Rather than referring to 'planning', we can talk about 'forming an intention'. For curricula, the intention is a second-order one because it is an intention regarding other intentions that are pedagogical. The plan could be defined around close-ended results or open-ended processes. The former would involve instrumental reasoning but the latter would not.

Through this definition, we recognise that, even with a detailed prescription/ suggestion, such as a national curriculum, how each teacher approaches each of his/her classes will be very different. A national curriculum is effectively a framework for teachers to plan their own classes. However, as a matter of historical fact, it was probably established as a set of second-order *instructions* rather than as a suggestion, proposal or request, but that is a different point.

Other disputes

So a curriculum is like a second-order educational plan. Given this, let us briefly separate some of the disputes of educational theorists regarding the definition of 'curriculum'. Our aim is to show that these are distinct issues not necessarily directly related to the content of a curriculum. Some of the issues concern the curriculum as such; some pertain to how it is used; and others are about the intentions from which it was constructed.

Politically authoritarian   One major contention is authority. So the first question at issue is: who devises a curriculum and for what purpose? A curriculum can be a top-down tool for government policymakers to regulate the 'standards' of schools and the 'performance' of teachers, with little or no participation from the student end-users; but a curriculum doesn't need to be such a tool. It could be a set of mild suggestions from a government department, or home-brewed by teachers and students, or indeed a mixture of these.

The extent of planning   There is another issue, distinct from one concerning political authority, which concerns the second question: how much should one plan? Often the deepest learning experiences and the most powerful classroom interactions are spontaneous, and could never have been planned. Of course, such spontaneous learning should not deny the need for a curriculum or some educational planning. However, if one has a detailed and specific national curricula plan, which leaves little space or time for the unplanned, then such spontaneous interactions will be limited. A plan could be very lightweight: it might indicate a general direction that the class or group should go with a great deal of interaction. In such a case, as we have already shown, the slightly strict word 'plan' is inappropriate and the term 'intention' is better. However, without some kind of plan, one cannot have any idea of whether the process has worked well or not.

The terms of a plan   This leads to the third question: in what terms should the plan or intention be framed? For example, a curriculum could be framed in terms of specific learning outcomes or in terms of the qualities and nature of the processes of learning and interaction. It could be divided into subjects or classified on non-academic grounds.

One or many?   Connected to this is a fourth question: should there be just one universal plan for everyone at a certain stage in his/her education? While a national curriculum provides some choice, nevertheless, it is still one single second-order framework for all teachers to use in their first-order pedagogical planning. The answer to this question depends on how we should reply to the second and third ones: an open-ended, process-oriented plan to have multiple options would be more generally applicable than a very specific outcome-specific plan.

The nature of planning   There is still one last issue: what is the nature of such planning? According to one standard conception of practical reasoning, planning involves trying to figure out which means are most effective and efficient in attaining a set of specified goals. This is the prevailing paradigm of means–ends or instrumental reasoning. Such an instrumental conception of planning tends to treat people and activities as merely instruments for the attainment of a set of goals. A symptom of such a curriculum is an obsession with standardisation and high-stakes testing (Noddings, 2003). Another quite different view of planning is one that creates spaces for individual or collaborative learning processes, which have a direction or a goal that does not instrumentalise the value of the learning activities.

There has been a lot of debate in England over the last decade about whether the national curriculum is too heavy-handed and detailed or whether, in its specificity and detail, it offers a rich resource to schools (see the contrasting views in Ron Dearing's 1995 report and Tim Oates' 2010 review). Should the curriculum be regarded as a rigid command from educational authorities, or rather as suggested guidelines for practitioners? On the one hand, it is argued that educators ought not to have to continuously reinvent the wheel, and hence, this requires a detailed national curriculum. On the other hand, it is contended that such a national curriculum prevents teachers from thinking critically and creatively about what they are doing. Either approach to curriculum construction further affects the ways that teachers should be trained and educated. However, that is a different matter.

Is the problem with the curriculum itself or with those who use it slavishly rather than creatively? The national curriculum is often conceived of in the following terms: it defines what needs to be done and why, and therefore, teachers' pedagogy amounts to delivering the national curriculum. Consequently, the type of critical self-reflection that teachers need to engage in consists in asking and answering how they should best *deliver* this curriculum. If this really is the implication, then it is problematic because it requires the view of learning as acquisition and teaching as transmission that we rejected in very fundamental terms in Chapter 2. It regards the student as a vessel into which mental items should be placed.

Authors such as Goodson (1991) believe that the national curriculum and its centralised model of schooling takes autonomy away from teachers as professionals, and such a discourse of schooling essentially disenfranchises those involved in the educational process, i.e. teachers, students and parents. However, our aim is not to evaluate this discussion about the social and political implications of a centralised national curriculum. How the curriculum should be used and with what intentions it was created is a different issue from the evaluation of its educational content. At the same time, we acknowledge that the concerns behind the national curriculum are fundamentally social and political, and that a national curriculum is intended to provide equal access to academic content for all pupils and students (curriculum entitlement) regardless of socio-economic background.

Let's now summarise the main points of this section. We have tried to give a definition of 'curriculum', which, insofar as it is possible, is not tied to any specific conception about how curricula should be. To do this, we separated some of the main issues regarding curricula from each other, as well as from the definition. Often writers do not distinguish these different dimensions of discussion, especially in relation to the national curriculum, which is sometimes deplored because of the heavy centralised authority that was apparently behind its formation. We have separated these different issues in order to prepare the ground for the idea of a more human-centred conception of a curriculum.

The human-centred principles

What does human-centred education say about how curricula should be constructed for young people in secondary schools? We will answer this question first by examining some of the criteria that a curriculum should adhere to. We have already covered many relevant points, albeit in a different guise, especially in Chapter 1 about the aims of education, in Chapter 2 on learning and in the last two sections of Chapter 6. Stepping back from the details, we can summarise a few principles. The curriculum should:

1. Treat students as human beings and, therefore, be designed primarily with their actual needs and development as human beings in mind.
2. Treat each student as a person and not merely instrumentally, i.e. as a means to an end. Therefore, the curriculum should not be designed with the needs of national economic growth or with requirements for academic standardisation as primary concerns.
3. Allow space for the development of the human being rather than just the academic and vocational, and even in these areas, it should be holistic and include relationships with others and recognise the importance of the non-cognitive part of the whole person rather than simply seeing it in opposition to the cognitive.
4. Be constructed in terms of developing the needed and relevant virtues or qualities, and not only skills and knowledge. This approach focuses on the unique nature and talents of each person more directly as central to the learning process. At a general level, such qualities would include thinking independently, the abilities to express oneself, to be persistent, to listen, to be creative and, above all, to be caring and to connect to things of value beyond oneself.
5. Allow the individual to recognise and act in accordance with the claim that he/she is responsible primarily for his/her own development, and provide

opportunities for the young person to find fields or activities that he/she is passionate about and that contribute significantly to his/her flourishing as a human being. It should encourage the proactive aspects of a person's nature.

6. Be constructed in ways that enable the young person to identify his/her own goals in life, as well as involve him/her in determining the learning paths and plans that will allow them to further explore their life's trajectories.

7. Not make standardised testing or assessment an obsession.

There are several clarifications we would like to make in relation to these principles:

Curriculum does not exclude academic learning

It should be clear that these principles do not at all preclude academic learning. On the contrary, we have argued that considered attention to the full human being ought to increase the intellectual capacity of each student because blocks to the exercise of intelligence are often emotional and motivational. Consequently, academic learning should fit into, and be reinforced by, the other aspects of the curriculum because learning can never be purely academic. Indeed, what we call 'academic learning' is, at heart, the cultivation of certain qualities, such as a sensitivity to the strategic questions in a field of enquiry, a systematic approach to investigation, and a care for detail without neglect of the overall picture. Of course, these qualities take varying forms in different fields but, nevertheless, they both form the very core of much academic learning and, at the same time, constitute a transformation of the person. In this sense, in accordance with the argumentation in Chapter 1, what we call 'academic learning' should be regarded as serving the needs of the person. One cannot justify a curriculum element on *purely* academic grounds. Therefore, it would be going backwards to justify a human-centred curriculum on the grounds that it heightens academic ability and improves exam results! The academic qualities that students develop through education constitute a strengthened relationship to the world, knowledge and inquiry.

Earlier we said that academic learning should serve the needs of the student. This point needs to be deepened. Some core academic values centre on the discovery, creation and articulation of knowledge and insights. For instance, there are key epistemological values, such as: to know something requires having some justification or reason or evidence for it; in the absence of any evidence, one should suspend judgement. Another example is that insights need to be expressed in unambiguous language. Key academic qualities involve sensitivity to such values (cf. Chapter 2). Once developed, these qualities become part of a person's way of being, intrinsic to his/her character and outlook on life.

As we saw in Chapter 3, other core academic values, though stressed less often, pertain to the opening up of curiosity, creativity, and imaginative and appreciative perception. For example, a person who can connect to the reality of the past would be more disposed to imagine the life of a medieval peasant and thereby ask about medieval housing, food, work and life conditions. This is a form of appreciative perceiving and connecting that we discussed in Chapter 3.

These are central ways in which the very core of academia can serve the needs of the individuals. The problem is that academic schooling tends to focus on knowledge and low-level skills at the expense of the core where the academic and the personal converge.

Curriculum must be based on the primacy of life not knowledge

There is an enormous pressure on curriculum developers to pack it with everything. This pressure not only arises from the false assessment needs that we will discuss later in the book, but is also motivated by a false dichotomy: if a curriculum is not full then it is academically weak. This is a false dichotomy because it links academic strengths and standards primarily to knowledge. It is worth noting that in 2006, the Association of Teachers and Lecturers in England called for a change to the national curriculum, suggesting that it be replaced with a 'framework of entitlements' to ensure the following: (1) physical skills of co-ordination, control, manipulation and movement; (2) creativity; (3) communication; (4) information management; (5) learning and thinking skills; (6) interpersonal skills; and (7) citizenship. This so-called 'framework of entitlement' seems to swing the curriculum to the other end, i.e. towards the rejection of knowledge per se.

Some writers claim that academic skills and qualities have only secondary importance in relation to knowledge. For example, Hirst and Peters (1970) argued that the skills students should acquire are derived from the varying needs of the different disciplines. Because of this, knowledge comes first, and skills and qualities second, as derivatives. If one were to construct a curriculum based on this assumption then one would ask oneself 'What should someone know at the age of 16 who has studied biology?', with the idea that this knowledge should form the foundation for continuing studies at A level (cf. Chapter 3). Try to answer that question for each subject. In broad terms, the answer that one would find is close to the actual content of the national curriculum. However, this reasoning is fundamentally flawed. It is exactly the point at which we need to remind ourselves of the primacy of life and that knowledge does not really have needs. This is the point at which one would need to revisit the arguments about the aims of education, outlined in Chapter 1, in support of the human-centred conception of education.

As we have seen, ignorance is not a lack of knowledge. It is a much more complex negative quality. Lack of knowledge concerns us because of what it expresses. It is a symptom, not the disease. Let us imagine that José is an articulate, intelligent, proactive and sensible 16-year-old who is quite balanced and mature. Let us also suppose that José has carved out for himself a relatively clear understanding of what he wants to do after he leaves school at 18. For example, suppose that he is a lover of animal biology. Let us leave aside the knowledge that José might need directly and indirectly for these specialised studies. Apart from this, what should José know? What knowledge should José have and why should he have it?

This question is quite difficult. Let us start with physics. Does he need to know Ohm's law or what a Wheatstone bridge is? In physics, one might decide that: one needs to know a few very basic things really well, such as the law of conservation of energy and Newton's laws of motion; one also needs to know that everything is composed of matter and what this means, and to have an idea of electromagnetic force and gravity. A person aged 16 ought to have a few basic concepts such as mass, force, momentum, conservation, etc. He/she needs to know how to use these concepts and see how mathematics works in physics, as well as understanding the scientific method of hypothesis testing with controlled experimentation. In fact, these understandings are difficult to attain in any permanent sense. Even university students in the humanities have a mild phobia against science, and probably do not know any of the above basics well, despite the fact that they been taught much more than this.

What is it that constitutes ignorance in physics for a person who will *not* undertake specialised study in that area, such as José? In answer to this question, we should start with the qualities. For example, a person needs to be scientific in his/her approach to problems. In addition to being methodical and logical, this requires the understanding that physical changes have some underlying mechanism and are not magical. Energy is not created out of nothing. One of the qualities that we might want a person to show is some love for the study of the physical universe as such, the opposite of the phobia that many have. This quality would stimulate a person to be curious about the physical world and would help him/her not to be overwhelmed by the technical language of physics. Confidence is a virtue. Given the relevant qualities or virtues, we can work out the kinds of skills that a student needs and, from there, the knowledge required.

In general, the point is that the knowledge that people need in order to avoid ignorance is much less than what is usually thought (i.e. they need the basic concepts and the principles and a wide overview), given that person has the relevant qualities. The qualities matter more than the knowledge itself, even though developing the virtues often requires learning knowledge.

The integration of the academic and the vocational

There is an allied pedagogical point from our discussion in Chapter 3 that we need to remind ourselves of. What is imposed upon me will probably not stay with me for long and have little meaning. It will be something external. In contrast, what I learn for myself will tend to stay with me and be much more meaningful in the sense of making more connections to other knowledge I have. In a similar vein, just as they do not contradict academic learning, the curricular principles listed on pages 157–8 do not exclude vocational training; they advocate that the curriculum must not turn the individual into a mere means for economic development.

A person's productive work life should be based primarily on his/her character traits and talents (Dewey, 1902) rather than on projections regarding future global economic competition in different international markets. Plato seems to have had a similar idea in *The Republic* when he constructed a model of educating the people who would contribute to the ideal just state. He advocated that children and young people should be educated according to their different natures, attributes and interests. One cannot justify a curriculum element on purely economic grounds, even when it is motivated by the democratic intention to provide the same education for all (Noddings, 2003). This point does not negate the importance of effort and work; indeed, the quality of an adult life is largely determined by whether the person loves his/her work or not. Yet for many people, it is not easy to discover one's talent and to understand the work conditions one needs to flourish, and as a result, many people drift into work that they do not really enjoy. As we saw in Chapters 4 and 5, adolescence is a time of intensive self-discovery, and so the curriculum should include space for experiments, exploration and exercises in self-knowledge related to the work aspects of life.

Indeed, the academic/vocational distinction should be, and has been, contested because it helps perpetuate the class system in the UK (Booth, 2011). The point we are making is *not* that education should be an agent of social change, which is a different discussion, but rather that the educational system is rife with self-fulfilling social expectations: some young people do less well because they are expected to. The national curriculum and its companion, standard testing, ensure that a certain number of young people will fail, and these young people are put on a vocational track because they are expected to do less well 'academically', and as a result they do fare less well. These expectations, insidiously implicit as they are, constitute a lack of care because they cause many young people to live in a less fulfilling way.

In summary, given the above curricular principles (pages 157–8), a human-centred curriculum ought to provide space and time for the young person's own needs. This includes, above all, time for relationships and discussions about relationships as well as collective reflection on what counts as development for each individual. The curriculum needs to provide the student with deeper relationships and longer-term trajectory at its core. A purely buffet-style model, where each student is a solitary consumer, cannot do that.

A human-centred curriculum will ensure that the individual will have some decision-making power in relation to his/her education. For this to happen, he/she needs to be able to make sense of his/her activities over a period of time and see how they fit together. Therefore, the curriculum must provide opportunities for the young person to think about his/her own development and paths through education.

At the same time, the curriculum must offer guidance that the student cannot provide for him/herself, and activities that are challenging in the right way. Furthermore, young people should have the opportunity to taste everything that education has to offer. But it is no good offering a book to a hungry body and food to a person who has just eaten. This indicates the need for self-designed, but guided, study plans.

The curriculum needs to propose a wide variety of activities and experiences. Each individual's time is divided up daily and weekly into a variety of activities including those that do not involve sitting in a classroom, and which take the student outside the school.

In addition, the curriculum needs flexibility. A person should be able to take an advanced mathematics course at the age of 14 if he/she has the interest and is capable to pursue such high-level studies, and have the opportunity to study elementary music at the age of 17. A student who is in love with computer programming needs to have lashings of the subject.

Lastly, it is important to have a clear idea of how well the student is learning so that the young person can continue to improve and so that teachers and others can understand how best to support his/her learning. The curriculum needs to provide space for such feedback, reflection and adjustment. However, the curriculum should not fall in the trap of becoming a means for good assessment results, a point we shall return to in Chapter 9.

All of this indicates that the curriculum needs to avoid being too crammed and cramped or too fixed for the sake of testing and assessment. It really needs to focus on the essentials for the development of the individual as such. The curriculum we propose focuses on cultivating young people's qualities or virtues. This is a focus that is increasingly appropriate given the challenges brought by information and communication technology (ICT). Given an explosion of information, often consisting of different versions of facts and multiple perspectives on the same topic, a young person needs the capacity to select and synthesise information, to interpret and interrogate the accuracy of claims and the plausibility of arguments. He/she needs to be both open and at the same time critical towards different perspectives. Above all, he/she needs the capacity and motivation to reflect for him/herself.

A suggested skeletal curriculum

We invite readers to think about how to construct a curriculum based on the principles and guidelines outlined above. Our own thoughts have led us to make the following very schematic suggestion for students aged 14–16. We would divide a curriculum based on such principles into seven sectors as follows. However, it is worth noting that these different curriculum times are often mutually supportive.

1. Direction time
2. Group time
3. Individual project time
4. Cognitive development time
5. General knowledge time
6. Exploration time
7. Speciality time

Direction time

The meaning of this sector is to direct learning and enable the person to be responsible for his/her development and own his/her learning processes. In effect, during this time, the student constructs aspects of the rest of his/her curriculum, together with the mentor, given an overall framework and other external limitations. However, this process of construction is itself deeply educational, and we will now examine its four main elements.

The first element relates to the processes involved in learning within the institution itself. The main aim is for the young person to identify, with the guidance of a personal mentor, what activities he/she needs to undertake at specific time periods, say a week, a month, a term and a year. This identification can take the form of recognising the qualities that he/she needs to develop, skills that he/she needs to improve, including key ones such as reading, writing, arithmetic, critical thinking, etc., as well as, of course, the areas of knowledge that he/she needs and wants to learn. Through this process, the student identifies his/her programme of activities for a period of time, such as a term.

Some students will need to set specific goals for some areas, and will have more freedom in others. The mentor will work with the student to consolidate personal goals and trajectories. The guidelines for reporting back to the mentor would have to be elaborated. To be able to plan well, the mentor and student need to have feedback from teachers and facilitators about different aspects of the student's learning activities and work. In line with our previous commentary, this feedback should be framed primarily in terms of virtues or qualities that the student needs to strengthen, as well as specific skills.

Young people may have problems connecting to the meaning of learning. To address this, the student needs to understand the point of what he/she is doing/ learning, and to be able to make sense of his/her time in education, including his/her life at school and at home. So, although the curriculum would provide space for each course/subjecct teacher to explain the purposes of a specific element within the overall programme, the personal mentor has, as part of his/her role, to help the student frame and make sense of the whole. One of the great limitations of education as currently practised in most schools is that there is seldom an institutional space (or time slot) specifically for young people to conceptualise what they are doing as a whole and why. This activity is very important because it embodies the critical self-reflection about practice that people need throughout their lives: 'What am I doing and why?'; 'Given this, how can I improve?' An education should inculcate this critical self-reflective quality about practice. Often, schools do try to foster this quality but with regard to particular projects, rather than the young person's education and life as a whole.

To further enable the student to connect to the overall meaning of learning, the mentor needs to help the young person develop his/her curiosity in order that he/she may connect better to the activities. In order for this to happen, it is important for the student to ask questions, and so part of the art of teaching is to nourish and nurture the ability of questioning. Even if a young person has a genuine interest in certain areas of knowledge, there may still be obstacles that he/she needs to overcome, such as lack of confidence, inability to manage distractions or failure to understand academic standards. The mentor will review these challenges with the student, encourage him/her to overcome the blocks and ask questions that can help connect to the content.

The second overall element is that the young person needs time to help identify his/her talents, interests and preferred field of work in later life. Indeed each person has a character that defines his/her outlook on life, strengths, weaknesses and approaches to things. Often these character traits also define what sort of work a person would best do even more than his/her skills. As we mentioned earlier, many people drift into their work blindly, without taking self-conscious and informed decisions. Therefore, we propose that part of the educational process is to help young people understand enough about themselves to avoid the boredom of work that they don't like, or falling into a passive approach to life.

The mentor plays a significant part in guiding the student through this process of increased self-discovery so that students can identify what they most deeply like doing and why. This will include creating new spaces and activities beyond the classroom, as we shall see. With the help of the mentor, the young person can understand better what counts as good preparation for his/her future life as an adult on individual terms that make sense to him/her. Mentors might encourage students to use writing as a way to work things out, or to read books that can stimulate thinking about these issues.

The third element is that some young people have emotional problems that may plague them throughout lives if they do not have the opportunity during adolescence to face themselves and try to work through these difficulties, and overcome them. We will designate the group part of the curriculum for this purpose. However, if the problems of an individual are too difficult for the group, then the issue will be returned to the mentor, who may refer the individual to a counsellor or psychologist.

In general, what are called 'behavioural problems', including chronic apathy or laziness, are to be dealt with at this individual level. Often, the so-called behavioural or discipline problems are associated with lack of engagement with the activities imposed on the young person. So direction time would be invaluable to engage students in their own learning processes. However, if the young person has behavioural problems then the mentor will discuss these with him/her, and the two will decide on an agreed set of goals for the student to attain. The mentor may assign written work of self-reflection and other activities to help the young person understand that it is in his/her own self-interest to overcome these difficulties. If these remedial actions do not work, then this indicates that the partnership is too limited and needs to be expanded. The next step would be for the mentor to visit the young person at home with his/her parents or guardians in order to explore and understand the young person's realities and the challenges he/she faces, and seek support from the student's families for their process of self-improvement. If necessary, there may be several home visits.

Fourth, as we have seen, this individual part of the curriculum is itself a learning process in which the student has the opportunity to develop qualities that relate to self-respect, compassionate self-awareness, self-guidance and practical wisdom. However, it also provides the main opportunity for the student to strengthen and maintain his/her motivation, and this requires focusing on two aspects that we have not so far stressed in this section: improvement and challenge. The student needs to improve in all of his/her endeavours and this requires understanding or internalising the standards that constitute 'better' and 'worse'. Mentors and teachers see both good and bad pieces of work and thus can understand well the differences between them. Typically, students do not. The mentor needs to have material at her disposal that enables her to coach the student in a way that helps the young person to understand the relevant standards that constitute improvement.

While a school will need to set aside a specific time allocation for students to participate in general activities, the time allocation of the different elements of the curriculum should nevertheless depend on the individual needs of the student. It should not be automatic. Since a student will have a mentor over a long period of time, the mentor can judge the educational needs of the student over a longer period. Each term does not need to be balanced, just as an appetiser does not include dessert. A student might want to concentrate heavily on one or two areas of study in one semester and broaden his/her fare in the next one.

Furthermore, in helping a student construct his/her individual programme of activities and setting goals and priorities, a mentor should not permit a student to evade challenges. Good education is challenging. However, an activity can challenge a person only if it meets the student in his/her present condition. To meet a challenge, one has to be ready. To put it another way, challenges require preparation. For this reason, a demanding education cannot be conceived as a set of discrete activities.

Group time

The meaning of this second aspect of the curriculum is for young people to share experiences and emotions with other people of roughly their own age, but not necessarily limited to it. The direction or general aim of these sessions is to provide the opportunity to build care, especially for other people, and responsibility for one's own feelings.

This time would have two main components. Some of the group time would be directly experiential: for example, using drama, group dynamics, role-play exercises, group team-building sessions and other activities to explore emotions, feelings and emotive perceptions. These sessions do not always have to be in a formal setting, such as the classroom. In this way, the young people can feel, sympathise, empathise, laugh and cry together, and in this manner, they can learn to build caring attitudes. Often people are blocked from their capacity to care for others and themselves by their own anger, fear (anxieties) and sadness. The activities during group time would help young people unblock these feelings and experience them directly.

Second, some of the sessions would be organised as discussions, which might be preceded by brief presentations by the students. Other sessions can be organised using creative outlets, such as art, music, poetry and drama. These activities can encourage young people who are not particularly verbal about their feelings, personal experiences and relationships to find an alternative and non-threatening way to express themselves. The focus would be on the current personal needs and concerns of the young people. In terms of the themes for discussion, this element of the curriculum ought to be quite open-ended and process-oriented so that the group can identify its own topics. The curriculum might specify some options that the group can choose which relate to the students satisfying their own needs now and for their future life as well as some fixed givens. The choices would include time to discuss questions pertaining to relationships with one's peers, friendship and intimacy, the limits of responsibility, how to deal with one's own feelings and problem-solving activities – e.g. should you tell your parents that your older brother is taking class 1 drugs? The programme could involve written discursive pieces of work as well as the creative activities mentioned above. However, this part of the curriculum concerns primarily the experience of feelings and emotions, and reflection on them, and not writing as such at all.

The underlying reason for this aspect of the programme is that some of the key qualities that young people need to develop relate to caring about others, living and working in a group, and understanding one's own emotions and those of others. These qualities are also needed to develop and maintain one's sense of self-worth through one's own feelings. This is a key to the flourishing and well-being of any person.

Maturity with regard to one's own emotions is not the same as managing or controlling those feelings. As we saw in Chapter 3, the idea of managing one's feelings can imply their degradation, namely the idea that emotions are energies to be harnessed and resources to be exploited. This makes feelings instrumental to some purpose and tends to emphasise the idea that they are obstacles. While such ideas can be appropriate, as we saw earlier, emotions and feelings are primarily part of one's being and an essential part of one's life. In this sense, they are not tools any more than one is oneself. For this reason, we emphasise the experience of feelings rather than their control or management (Macmurray, 1961, 1962).

The student should have opportunities to experience feelings directly, and afterwards, to reflect on how he/she relates to the other people in his/her group and the qualities that one needs in order to get on well with others, such as seeing things from the point of view of others. This part of the curriculum also provides an excellent opportunity to develop other qualities, such as being an attentive listener. These sessions will sometimes be potentially explosive, with young people feeling and expressing anger, depression and despair, as well as desire, joy and hope. Nevertheless, we need to stick to the principle that secondary education is a process of development that ought to involve the person as a whole, which means interaction between young people on their own terms.

Of course, in this time slot, the mentor needs to be a skilled facilitator, with some training in counselling, working within established guidelines for such encounters. Indeed, we can see that the role of the mentor (for personal growth time) is quite far removed from the normal work of a teacher who is specialised in an area of knowledge. In this sense, our proposed curriculum requires re-conceiving the teaching profession. This will be an important theme in Chapter 8.

One could add a last but relatively minor component in the group time: a practical preparation for adult life. With regard to future needs, there might be topics related to the practical side of adult life, such as money management, work and household management, parenting and being part of a family, and other homemaking topics. Some of these would be conducted as group discussions, but others would be brief presentations perhaps from outside speakers, including the parents of current students.

Individual project time

We propose that each individual has time to develop and work on his/her own project. This project might include vocational training or work experience, or social work, or simply be focused on academic work in the form of an inquiry or a long paper, or a combination of the above. The aim is for the student to have learning experiences that relate directly to their planned life-projection and future work or course of study. This could include a definite project or question, a portfolio of art, a business plan, various design projects, or a paper on the student's work experience.

Ideally, the project would include some combination of experience and study related to the kinds of activities the young person is really interested in and might want to pursue later in life. This is an important ingredient in the curriculum because it allows for more ownership of the learning process; such an experience may help inculcate in the student more care for the quality of his/her work. If the student does become engaged then the project might be the basis of transformation and of greater involvement in other areas of learning. With the help of the tutor, such links can be made. As we saw in Chapter 6, proactive engagement with regard to one's own learning processes is one of the main qualities that education ought to develop. This means creating and using opportunities for the transformation of care, and an individualised project is ideal for this.

The project should be designed so that the young person can connect to the valuable content of material and activities beyond him/herself. Therefore, it should be a self-initiated process of delving into something deeply. As part of a regular review, the student and tutor would examine the processes to develop an understanding of how the student is working. Also, the project should be designed so that it might relate to the adult life of the student. In this way, it ought to contribute to developing a sense of self and the understanding that one's future life is in one's own hands. Furthermore, the linking of a written research project to activities that are beyond the school reinforces the experience and feeling of self-guided learning, and thus helps the young person cultivate a sense of self-responsibility.

The student would co-design this project with the guidance of the personal mentor, but of course, the mentor would need to receive input from other tutors/teachers in the designing of it. Once the student and his/her mentor have completed a general design of the project, then a more specialised tutor/teacher would be assigned to work with the student on the details and supervise and guide his/her work.

It is important to note that the use of information and communication technology (ICT) has become a basic fabric of contemporary life for the majority of the young people who have access to the technology. As a result, there is a greater responsibility for curriculum activities to direct the young person in terms of how to source the materials they need, how to distinguish good and helpful sources from non-helpful ones and how to use the abundance of information to support their own learning.

Cognitive development time

The current education system is dedicated almost exclusively to the systematic study of subjects or disciplines, in part because of the assumption that this is the main way in which students can develop their cognitive abilities. However, as an aim, this fails to meet the conditions of full human development. As a strategy, it does not address the motivational problems that students face. Furthermore, it ignores an important point that we have been concerned to stress throughout the book: the difference between pointing outwards and inwards. In studying a subject or an area of knowledge, what is really fundamental in terms of the student's experience is directly connecting to the content. The study of history should be an exercise in understanding the past, which requires making it alive or real (see Chapter 3). In physics, one needs to see how fundamental laws apply to concrete interactions. It is similar for the study of all areas of knowledge. In other words, the student's attention points outwards. However, the development of skills also requires movement in the opposite direction. It requires pointing one's attention inwards as well. One needs to reflect self-consciously and perceive in new ways what one is doing. In this case, the emphasis is no longer on the past, the characters in the novel, the flower, the forces in a roller coaster; the focus is oneself, on *what I am doing*. It is partly for this reason that we recommend a distinct time period for the development of cognitive skills. This is a quiet space where the student looks at his/her own development explicitly and directly without the pressures of trying to understand something else.

As we stressed in Chapter 2, what is sometimes called 'literacy' (or in our case, 'language capability') is a crucial foundation for a person's work in any field, academic or otherwise. The basis is primarily the capacity to listen and talk, and read and write. Much of this concerns how the student directs his/her attention. From this basis, more abstract thinking capabilities can develop, including comprehension, systematic analysis, argumentation, deduction, criticism, questioning, and making the relevant connections and formulating strategies.

The meaning of the cognitive development part of the curriculum is to devote attention directly and exclusively to these capabilities in small groups and sometimes on an individual basis, starting from the fundamentals. These are coaching sessions.

The needs of the individual are not easily determined. For example, if a person does not know how to read well, this may be because he/she is distracted by his/her own thoughts and feelings, or because he/she is overwhelmed by the words. Many young people do not have the idea of proactive reading, of looking for the main point and seeking the structure. Many do not have the idea that one can understand the big picture without comprehending the specifics of some of the details and vice versa; nor that we need them for different purposes. Some young people read too fast and cannot find the voice of a writer. For some, it is a question of self-confidence; for others, simply a lack of practice. Some see books and the written word as profoundly alien and as belonging to a different world from theirs. There needs to be a space in the curriculum for a coach who is an expert in these kinds of issues to address the weaknesses of each individual. One cannot expect students who have fundamental obstacles to overcome in their cognitive development to be able to do that in the context of learning a subject matter without some special attention. It is a bit like expecting someone to play a sport well without having any training sessions.

As we said in Chapter 2, the idea of 'literacy' may not be entirely clear because it is sometimes associated with the language, say English, as a discipline or subject, and this fosters the idea that literacy is a specific study-track that some students will specialise in and others not. While this might be true of the study of novels, drama and poetry and of the cultivation of literary sensitivities, it does not apply to basic language and thinking skills. Everyone needs such skills because language is part of being human and therefore is integral to living. Language is not merely a tool for communication. On the contrary, it is closer to us than any tool: it defines our thoughts and experiences. For this reason, this time would include opportunities for the young person to learn new vocabulary and to increase his/her word sensitivity.

The time for cognitive development is *not* remedial. It addresses each person from where they are, and defines the next step forward. So, this part of the curriculum would include training and practice in critical thinking and problem-solving at all levels. When they are ready for it, students would have the opportunity to understand epistemological values and principles more reflexively than they do in normal subject-time. They should be given the opportunity to challenge the views of authors, question accepted knowledge and embrace uncertainty.

This cognitive time is also the opportunity for developing capacities related to what is called 'numeracy'. This is not the same as teaching mathematics as a subject. The point is that three of the main qualities that constitute numeracy are being systematic in solving a problem, being logical in one's deductions, and looking for relevant facts and discarding the irrelevant. A person who lacks these qualities would not be able to do mathematics well, although the qualities are far from being sufficient for appreciating mathematics. However, these are much more general thinking capacities that apply outside mathematics and which, of course, affect one's general outlook on life.

The tutors/teachers who lead these small groups during cognitive development time would also need access to the written work of the student from other classes and would need feedback from the other teachers who see the student on a regular basis, including the student's mentor, who helps the young person construct his/her individualised programme.

General knowledge time

The school will offer courses in areas of knowledge for the sake of general education. We suggest that some of these could be in brief and concentrated units that build into modules. Let's take history as an example. If a young person has absolutely no grasp of the history of Britain (e.g. thinks that the Roman Empire dissolved a hundred years ago and that the Second World War happened during the Victorian period), then there is little point in his/her trying to learn details about the War of the Roses, or how the plague spread around Europe in the Middle Ages, or about the events leading up to the Industrial Revolution. Consequently, it would be useful to have a brief overview course of British history that lasts, say, a few days in quick short bursts. A similar course could be offered on world history. Short courses then might be offered on more specific aspects of history. The idea of these classes is not to make a historian out of a student, but to give them a general idea of how the past leads to the present.

We could adopt a similar argument for a few other areas of knowledge or topics. Since most people, including adolescents, cannot concentrate well for more than 20–30 minutes, these would consist of short classes concentrated over a short period of time for intensive learning. On the one hand, students must be ready for such knowledge learning; there is no point someone attending a class of this type who will not learn. On the other hand, since some students would already have the general knowledge that is being offered in the early classes, these courses would be organised in modules from the basic to the more advanced. The mentor is responsible for helping the student choose the appropriate modules, and for overseeing this process. This should be a simple and minimal part of the curriculum but its content depends on what the student has already learned.

The key is for the young person to see the relevance of studying such knowledge. The tutors/teachers and mentors are there to help the student become aware that absorbing pieces of knowledge is not the main aim of learning here. As we discussed earlier, the need for knowledge must be linked to the qualities to be nurtured in order to enable the development of the person. Usually, such links are established through 'direction time' and 'group time', and become clearer through the young people's work in 'individual project time'. Without 'direction time' and other activities, young people can feel that they are being coerced into learning knowledge.

Exploration time

Everyone needs some space for exploring new activities and areas of knowledge that one might find interesting. As we discussed in Chapter 5, young people need diverse experiences and encounters in their everyday lives, which is part of the exploration and understanding of themselves, their unique traits and talents, and direction for future life. This part of the curriculum provides opportunities for students to broaden their horizons and try out new things for fun.

First, any student should be able to attend a class session or activity group that is new to them under the guidance of his/her mentor. This may mean that the student is an observer in some, and an active participant in others.

Second, in addition, the school or learning centre would offer special activities that students could participate in for a short while as a taster. For example, a school might offer samplers, which would be an intensive and brief course in a subject or topic that would not be part of the normal curriculum and which would broaden the students' horizons. These could be related to potential areas of work, for example, a participatory seminar on what lawyers do and 'why is the law important to us?'; or a presentation given by a nurse about healthcare. A taster will help both the mentor and the students to decide if such activities would be of interest to them.

Third, exploration time may also involve the student taking courses and participating in activities outside of his/her own learning environment. The school could organise outings and other special events. Such activities can be both academic and experiential. For instance, through special arrangements, adolescents can attend master classes or lectures in local universities or colleges. For experiential activities, they may go to concerts, visit job centres, attend woodcraft workshops, train to become a fireman, visit and help out in care homes for the elderly, or read to young children in primary schools.

Fourth, during the exploration time, the young person is given little direction, but more caring. This means that the mentor will invite the student to share his/her experiences during the exploratory time, and encourage him/her to draw insights from these encounters.

Speciality time

Each student will have broad areas that he/she will specialise in. These need not be very specific; it depends on the individual. However, as the young person begins to have a better sense of the directions that his/her life might take, he/she will appreciate better the value of studying in those areas and take on more of the ownership that is required to make efforts to improve. He/she will take courses that offer knowledge that is important for this specialisation and improve the relevant skills that help the process of forming the qualities needed in those general areas.

Exploration time and speciality time, together with direction time, allow the young person to consolidate his/her interests, and help the person develop a sense of direction in life. (Refer to Chapters 4 and 5 for more information on the adolescent's need for exploration.) This, in turn, motivates and guides his/her project work, and enables a positive attitude towards cognitive and general knowledge development.

For the reader to understand the skeletal curriculum we are proposing here, it is necessary that we briefly discuss the roles of the teacher in such a curriculum, even though this will be the topic of the next chapter. As pointed out by Stenhouse (1975), a curriculum defines the roles of the teacher and the accompanied pedagogy, as well as the assessment of the student's strengths and weaknesses. In this skeletal curriculum proposal, teachers have diverse roles, including:

- the role of mentor who facilitates, accompanies and guides the student's learning activities and curriculum construction, and who provides personal feedback to the student in terms of his/her development;
- the role of a specialist tutor teacher who has good knowledge of a particular subject area and who can help the student to develop those qualities needed within the specific field;
- the role of counsellor who can provide support to the young person's personal, social and emotional needs in a friendly and caring way.

The teacher will also play other roles such as that of a good listener, friend, co-learner, parent, and so forth.

A single person cannot perform these diverse roles, as they demand a wide variety of different qualities and abilities. Thus, educational institutions should offer access to different adults, who together can provide for the young person's multiple developmental and learning needs.

Response to objections

Perhaps, the main objection to the curriculum guide outlined above would be that it could leave many young people more ignorant than they are now. By taking away time from traditional knowledge-based or subject learning and by removing the pressure of exams, the result of the proposed curriculum would be that young people would end up knowing even less than they do now. Some young people will not learn knowledge for themselves; they need some external incentives and imposed structure to their day, without which they would be even less educated than they are now under the current system. The objection is that the proposed curriculum disadvantages young people who cannot benefit from the freedom it offers.

The reply to this objection comes in two parts. First, as we have already seen, there are different kinds of ignorance. It is inadequate to define 'ignorance' simply as not knowing something, and leave it at that. There are deeper kinds of ignorance, which consist of first not being aware that one does not know, and second, not even caring. There are young people who wilfully refuse to care. The proposed curriculum attempts to give space to treat these forms of ignorance as close to the root as one can within an institutional setting.

Second, admittedly it does this by allowing the young people to spend less time learning in a traditional classroom setting. However, there are two allied points that nullify this as an objection: (1) the logic of the argument has taken us to this conclusion. In other words, this proposal for the curriculum is a consequence of what we have argued earlier in the book: namely, that the development of the person has priority over purely academic attainment and that qualities are more important than knowledge. (2) There is a huge danger in not allowing for these other forms of learning. In other words, sticking to the idea that we have to doggedly impart knowledge will prevent the students who will not learn, who are motivationally inert, or anxious and angry, from finding a new way for themselves. In short, it would be ignorant of us to stick to an ignorant definition of ignorance! Needless to say, the transmission model of the curriculum has already proven to disenfranchise many young people in English state schools (Hope, 2006).

Another kind of objection, which comes from the opposite direction, is that the above curriculum outline puts too much store on the traditional subjects and disciplines. Many schools that provide alternatives to the mainstream fare of subject-divided lessons do so with multi-disciplinary projects. Students research and write projects on topics or themes such as the importance of water, which cross the artificial boundaries of different disciplines. This makes sense, it is argued, because knowledge does not come naturally divided up into subjects such as geography, chemistry, history and mathematics. What counts as one subject as opposed to another is arbitrary; it has changed and continues to do so.

However, this ignores some of the strengths of learning by discipline. As we saw in Chapter 2, understanding does not consist of acquiring discrete bits of information. It requires knowing how to apply basic principles and key concepts in different contexts. It involves understanding epistemological criteria and internalising standards in the context of different kinds of knowledge. Understanding is more than knowledge. Adolescents ought to have the abstract level of thought necessary to understand and apply the principles of different areas of knowledge such as the physical sciences, the social sciences, the arts and humanities. One can admit that there are some fundamental epistemological differences between these major disciplines, without committing oneself to a diet of traditional subjects.

Despite the above, the idea of student projects has immense advantages over other pedagogical approaches. First, it allows for greater ownership of work because it permits the young person to work on questions of his/her choosing, even if the mentor guides the process of selection. Second, projects can be question-based rather than topic-based and thereby reinforce the process of questioning and answering that we stressed earlier. Indeed, if done well, a series of projects can introduce the idea of asking better questions about a particular area. Third, project work can involve a wider range of skills and qualities than writing set papers. It involves conceiving, planning, researching, reading, writing, summarising and reporting. For these reasons, we have opted for a possible combination of both approaches.

A further objection to the outlined skeletal curriculum is that it requires too much of the mentor. The success of the whole programme depends very much on the sensitivities and abilities of the mentor and what is required of him/her are seemingly impossible tasks. For example, the mentor has to be able to know what is happening in all the courses of the learning centre or school. He/she has to know what is good for the student and when. Once again, this demands a radical rethinking of teaching and pedagogy.

The last objection may arise from the concern for curriculum evaluation, or in other words, monitoring how well the curriculum is working in helping the young people learn and develop. The challenge would be that the proposed curriculum framework does not allow rigorous evaluation, for example by using standardised tests. Indeed, we argue that this is precisely the strength of our curriculum proposal. There is no prescriptive content in this outline, and therefore the curriculum is not geared towards externally imposed content and outcome. Rather, the proposed curriculum outline requires the student to own his/her learning and become more aware of the virtues and qualities the curriculum intends to develop in him/her. The kind of feedback and other ways of demonstrating learning to various stakeholders will challenge much of our contemporary thinking on measuring and assessment.

Conclusion

After establishing a definition of 'curriculum', we have proposed a set of principles that underpin a human-centred curriculum. In particular, we have argued that the curriculum must be centred on the young person's needs as a whole human being, and not just academic subject knowledge or vocational skills. This means that the curriculum will focus on nurturing the nature and talents of the individual, helping the young person identify his/her goals, and cultivating the relevant qualities that would enable the young person to live fully both during adolescence and in adulthood.

A curriculum that focuses on the qualities or virtues can offer a compelling learning experience in which the young person is actively engaged with what he/she has chosen to do and is more likely to take responsibility for his/her own learning.

We have acknowledged that there are inevitable challenges associated with such a curriculum proposal. In particular, because this approach respects the person as a whole, treats the student as a subject rather than an object, and stresses the meaningfulness of curricular activities, it can result in very varied educational practices within different institutions.

First, our curriculum proposal points to the need for different roles of teaching staff. So far, we have highlighted the differing parts that mentors, tutors and teachers play in the proposed curriculum. Because the new curriculum stresses the educational significance of teacher/student relationships, it is not easy to predict what these teachers may actually do, especially in the case of the mentor. This challenges the current way in which teachers are trained and evaluated.

Our curriculum proposal further highlights the tension between a mainstream approach to teaching as curriculum delivery and an alternative conception of teaching as facilitation. We believe that a human-centred curriculum can resolve this tension, and will explain this in the next chapter.

Additionally, although our curriculum outline does not require standard attainment tests (SATs), nevertheless, it does demand a framework for feedback and for monitoring the student's progress over time. This challenges us to reconsider the current conception of assessment. In order to create a regulated space for measuring learning, current national curricula tend to have knowledge, skills and competencies broken down into small units. Standardised assessment is more like ticking items on a shopping list than providing personalised feedback to advance a higher quality of learning. We will attend to this issue in Chapter 9.

The final challenge is directed towards the school as an institution. What kind of institution does a human-centred curriculum require? Is it an institution which is centrally controlled and managed by the educational authority and which has relatively little autonomy; or is it an organisation which has relative independence; or is it a community such as a learning centre, facilitated by professional mentors, tutors and other staff? In addition, there is the concern for the learning environments, the shared spaces, and resources, such as IT facilities, arts rooms, musical equipment, science labs, theatre, sports fields, and so forth.

Indeed, following Stenhouse, a curriculum not only defines educational planning, pedagogy and assessment, it also impacts on the context within which the curriculum activities take place. It requires a certain institutional culture. We will address this issue in Chapter 11.

Further reading

Booth, T. (2011) Curricula for the common school: what shall we tell our children? *Forum*, 53, 31–47.

Kliebard, H. (1989) Problems of definition in curriculum. *Journal of Curriculum and Supervision*, 5, 1–5.

Schiro, M. (2007) *Curriculum Theory: Conflicting Visions and Enduring Concerns*. Thousand Oaks, CA: Sage.

Thornton, S. and Flinders, D. (eds) (1997) *The Curriculum Studies Reader*. London: Routledge.

8

The teacher and the art of teaching

Introduction

What should the work of a teacher be? What are the implications of the skeletal curriculum outlined in the previous chapter for the role of teachers and for pedagogy in general? These questions need to be answered in the light of human-centred education and its principles established in the first half of the book.

As we have pointed out, human-centred education aims to integrate the strengths of both traditional approaches to education and their alternative counterparts. Whilst there are no clear-cut differences between these two 'systems' of thinking, nevertheless, we can still outline the elements of a traditional view of the teacher's work, and tease out the strengths and weaknesses of this view. Likewise, we can do the same for alternative conceptions of the teacher's role.

After this, we will present a human-centred vision of the role of the teacher and of the art of teaching that combines elements from both of the other views, and which also transcends both. This vision follows from the curriculum outline argued for in the previous chapter. As theorists, we need to take an integral view of the main pillars of education: curriculum, pedagogy and assessment. Within the overarching culture of the school, these pillars are mutually constitutive and defined by the same principles and support the aims of education.

Critical background

In order to redefine the role of the teacher and to reconceptualise pedagogy, let us briefly review our earlier discussions concerning the forces and dynamics that tend to shape teaching in state education.

There has been a global trend that the drive for excellence has been justified largely by a goal external to education, namely to compete effectively in the international marketplace. There has been increased pressure from policy makers that education must serve as an instrument for the nation's economic growth and global competitiveness. Thus educational institutions are subordinated to economic goals, which has a direct impact on the way teaching and teachers are conceptualised (Smyth and Shacklock, 1998; Fielding and McGregor, 2005). We critiqued these tendencies in Chapter 1.

This economic driving force has led to an increased centralisation in education in many parts of the world. For instance, the British government's requirement that all government spending should be accountable became a motivating source for attainment targets in order to measure the effectiveness of schools. These targets are measured through complex uniform standard attainment tests (SATs). The move towards centralised control of the curriculum, teaching and exams can undermine teachers' autonomy and professionalism (Furlong *et al.*, 2000; Sachs, 2003). The teacher can become the person who 'delivers' the national curriculum – wording that recalls the transmission theory of learning critiqued in Chapter 2, and which seems to relegate the teacher's role to that of a postman of information. Furthermore, what is being delivered is detached both from the teacher who does the delivering and from the student who is supposed to receive the 'content' of the delivery regardless of whether he/she wants it or not.

The resulting influence on pedagogy is more significant than it may seem. In countries such as England, teachers have their worth judged by students' output, and other externally imposed measures that resemble industrial or commercial quality assurance. We shall argue that the introduction of management techniques into teaching, with learning outcomes and targets defining teacher performance, misunderstands the nature of the art of teaching, and the nature of learning.

Teaching is often a process of facilitating and guiding. This means that the teacher cannot be held responsible for all aspects of the student's progress. The other side of the same coin is as follows: the claim that students ought to take responsibility for their own learning implies that there are limits to a teacher's responsibilities, although this is not an excuse for bad teaching. Given this, defining the quality of teachers' work only in terms of student outcomes ignores the fact that students are autonomous persons, in much that same way that measuring the performance of a salesman in terms of sales figures disregards the autonomy of consumers.

The introduction of management language, such as performance appraisals (which are linked to teachers' pay scales), target-setting and auditing of curriculum deliveries, is gradually orienting education towards commercialisation. Teachers are forced to work within a defined pedagogical framework, which is packaged and pipelined towards predetermined measurable outcomes. This management language and its accompanying practices are thoroughly instrumental in the pejorative sense discussed and criticised in Chapter 1.

The increase of purely instrumental management thinking in teaching has two detrimental effects on the sincerity of educational discourse. First, as Smyth and Shacklock (1998) point out, the current language in the educational field suggests that there has been some development in terms of teacher empowerment, which is in fact often illusory. According to these authors, there are discrepancies between the language of policy discourse and that of educational theory. For instance, in policy language the phrase 'benchmarking and standards' has as a counterpart in educational discourse: 'monitoring consistent and compassionate teaching'. In policy language the phrase 'systems' policies and priorities' has counterparts in education such as 'emancipatory possibilities', 'teacher and school effectiveness' and 'teacher and school identity formation' (p. 35). Because key phrases in educational discourse actually have counterparts in policy and management language, certain key words in education actually have different meanings than would normally be assumed. They are like euphemisms. For instance, words such as 'choice', 'autonomy', 'collaboration', 'self-management', 'team-work', 'partnerships', 'networking', 'collegiality', 'flexibility' and 'responsiveness' have a more functional and a less human meaning than one might suppose (p. 23).

Second, a similar effect has occurred in the government's rhetoric. For instance, the UK government's 2006 'Every Child Matters' initiative laudably says that teachers should focus on:

- the connection between children and young people's achievement and well-being
- maximising the opportunities for them to reach their full potential

These goals express an intention to nurture the holistic development of young people as human beings. However, at the same time, the role of the teacher is closely bound up with a prescriptive national curriculum and knowledge-oriented national standard attainment tests, despite more recent attempts to loosen this kind of rigidity. Fielding and McGregor (2005) point out how political and educational rhetoric is skilfully creating an illusion to disguise the real picture:

> Despite the fact that 'transformation' is replacing 'school improvement' and 'networking', 'collaboration' and 'personalisation' look set to become the new orthodoxy, there is little acknowledgement that we are only tinkering with a moribund system.
>
> (p. 1)

In other words, unfortunately, despite an improvement in the rhetoric and despite the changing aims of the new secondary national curriculum in England, teaching is often a question of *delivering* the national curriculum for exams, and thus it remains wedded to an instrumental view of education and a narrow conception of learning.

Now let's take a closer look at the how the role of the teacher and the art of teaching is conceived in mainstream education, which, for lack of other terms, we simply call the 'traditional' view. Later, we will examine alternative education, which is an umbrella term referring to non-mainstream education.

The traditional ideal

The traditional view of the functions that a teacher should perform is that he/she would enable students to learn by transmitting knowledge and motivation. The teacher is primarily a knowledgeable enthusiast. As a consequence, the standard ideal of a teacher in a mainstream secondary school is that of a person who has three prime qualities:

- being knowledgeable in his/her field or subject area
- being a lover of the given area of knowledge
- having the willingness and ability to impart both knowledge and the love for the subject to young people

Other required qualities follow from these. To illustrate this definition, we shall describe the work of John, a newly qualified teacher (NQT) of science in England, to show how an energetic state secondary school teacher perceives his role and teaching.

John made a deliberate choice to enter the teaching profession because of his two passions: science and working with young people. He believes that a pedagogue should kindle enthusiasm in willing young minds to help them inquire into the magical world of science. He reports that, during his training, more experienced colleagues told him that 30 per cent of his students are expected to learn what is taught, 30 per cent will learn much less, 30 per cent will fail, and the remaining 10 per cent will leave the system without having tried to understand what is taught at all.

John said that within a short time into his teaching practice, he realised that only a relatively small proportion of his teaching was about expert knowledge (that has been set by the curriculum), and that the majority was mostly devoted to enthusing. Working with large groups of students (aged 15–16), he soon developed strategies to get the young people involved in the study of science. He summarised these to include

- setting an interesting classroom environment decorated with scientific material and posters;
- using stories of great scientists to encourage students to become interested in the subject;
- making the subject knowledge relevant to students' reality and interests as much as possible;
- occasional mild persuasion (by painting a bleak picture of a future without knowledge);
- questioning in order to induce critical thinking;
- being playful in teaching – having a laugh, telling jokes, using games in the classroom;
- putting students in groups for debate and discussions;
- encouraging students to work cooperatively on problem solving;
- assessing and monitoring students' attainment, and providing them with contents appropriate to their academic level, and so forth.

In some ways John's approach ticks all the traditional boxes about what an enthusiastic teacher can do to help students learn. His enthusiasm about teaching also makes his exhausting day both exciting and rewarding on a personal level. As the key actor on his classroom stage, he has developed a great rapport with his students, and feels that he has made it possible for these young people to respond, and even to learn.

An implicit assumption of John's role is that the teacher should be at the centre of the process of learning. His job is to make his audience, the students, respond to him by putting himself at the centre of the stage. Like many teachers who conceive their profession to be teaching within the standard model, John perceives his role as a teacher to include the following:

The teacher as a knowledge provider – The teacher is responsible for passing on information and knowledge in a subject (through topic work in John's case) to students in ways that are appropriate for their age and their intellectual capacity. Teachers like John do not rigidly deliver the content of the curriculum, because they often feel it important to also include their personal overview of the field of knowledge and its applications for the student, provided that there is sufficient space within the school's tight timetable.

The teacher as a passionate lover of the subject – Most teachers are like John in that they see this aspect of the role as most important, i.e. being passionate about the subject and working with young people, and being able to get their students' attention and retain it. If the student is not interested and does not particularly like a topic, the teacher can manage to attract their interest through his/her own passion for the subject, which can motivate students to learn more about the subject.

The teacher as the assessor – Many teachers see one of their key roles as assessing students' curriculum learning. Their evaluation helps identify students' needs and place students within the correct group for input appropriate to their competence. John says that assessing students' learning also provides feedback about his own teaching, giving him a valuable opportunity to monitor his own practices.

The teacher as a role model – Within his particular subject of study, John feels that he also acts as a role model for the students: as a scientist. As a good teacher, he exemplifies the approaches and practices of good scientists in science labs or in the classroom. In particular, he questions rather than merely passively absorbs already existing information. He affirms: 'We learn science in order to discover new things that the world needs; for instance, we ask ourselves: "How we can develop vaccines for AIDS and malaria?"'

It is reasonable to assert that most teachers would support John's summary of the role of the teacher, although some may add other roles, such as crowd control, pastoral care, target achieving, parent liaison and lesson planning. However, the three qualities mentioned earlier (being knowledgeable, being passionate about the subject, and being able to impart both) seem to be primary. There are other qualities that a good teacher ought to have, such as being able to explain something complex in a set of simple steps, but these are all skills and dispositions that basically follow from the three qualities. For example, this ideal would also include a teacher being a generally nice and kind person.

It would also include the teacher being strong and firm enough to maintain discipline. At many points, this picture of the ideal teacher, and the consequent vision of a school, especially at secondary level, is strong and healthy. Therefore, before we challenge the ideal, let us review what is good about it.

Strengths

First, it does indeed take a lot of expert knowledge to be able to teach the fundamental concepts and principles within a discipline (such as a science or humanities subject), which may be quite complex, and explain them in simple, logical steps. Moreover, it requires expertise to show how such concepts are used in practice in a variety of contexts. For example, it needs solid proficiency to be able to show students how to write up the results of their experiments in a scientifically acceptable way or how to assess a literary text or to construct the parameters of a student art project. Often, such knowledge and experience is required to see what is causing problems for students. In brief, we need teachers to be very knowledgeable in a specific field because otherwise students will not be learning correctly or at a sufficient depth or level that challenges them.

Second, in a similar way, the idea of having academic subjects seems also both intuitive and reasonable, despite being old-fashioned, because although there are many overlaps within the social and natural sciences, and although knowledge does not come packaged as subjects, nevertheless the basic concepts, principles and methodology of each broad subject area tend to be distinct. As we argued in Chapter 7, a curriculum without subjects and only using multidisciplinary projects would lack important ingredients, which are the distinctive approaches to discovery and creation. Of course, this is not an argument for only traditionally taught subjects, nor does it argue for a particular way of drawing the lines between subjects in any particular context.

There is a third point: the importance of academic values in education. As we saw earlier, some (though not all) of the values embodied in academic education are related to truth. For example, they pertain to the need for evidence and the need for systematic and careful thought. These specific epistemological values pertain to the avoidance of error; some relate to exploration and discovery, such as the need for creativity, insightfulness, originality, playfulness and open-mindedness; others relate to dialogue, such as the value of listening, generosity of interpretation, being open while respecting the views of others and being clear. An institution will be more purely academic insofar as it treats these values as important and non-instrumental. For example, in such an institution, the quality of being hard-working would be regarded as valuable because it serves academic ends.

There is much to be said in favour of such values and the institutions that embody them.[1] In particular, outside of their schooling, most people have few opportunities in their lives to appreciate such values. Much of adulthood tends to be dominated by economic considerations, and other values become instrumental to that. The academic aspects of an education require students to connect to values that form an important part of their being.

Weaknesses

These assumed qualities follow from the focus in state or mainstream education on knowledge and skills. However, as knowledge experts, the teachers' primary role is imparting knowledge, cultivating skills, helping students accumulate and retain facts and information, and of course, enthusing them to pursue knowledge within subject domains. The pedagogy appropriate for the transmission model of learning includes a dependence on pre-determined educational goals and prescribed outcomes.

There are however a few problems. First, this traditional conceptualisation of teaching contains an emphasis of great importance: it places the students' 'learning' at the centre of educational concern. The main weakness, however, is the conception of learning that it is wedded to, which we outlined and criticised in Chapter 2: learning as acquisition. As the knowledge provider, the teacher is supposed to pass on what he/she knows to the young person. This makes education mostly a question of teaching, teaching mainly an issue of *transmission* or delivery of previously defined knowledge, and learning a question of acquiring mental items. Goodson (2005) cautions that:

> At the level of rhetoric 'transmission' has come to characterise a particular view of practice and an associated view of knowledge as a commodity (p. 31).

We explained in Chapter 2 what is mistaken about treating knowledge as a commodity, when we discussed how this ignores the intentional or aspectual nature of cognition, and cannot account for the quality of understanding.

The importance of expert knowledge and intellectual ability assumes that the focus of learning is to acquire 'knowing-that' and academic skills. However, as we discussed in earlier chapters, knowledge and skills are only valuable when connected and integrated as part of the students' character and life. Many young people would claim that they usually do not understand why they have

---

[1] Schools are not automatically academic institutions. They can become more of an economic institution when academic learning becomes purely a means to training people for a competitive economy, at which point grades become a form of currency and all study is a method of earning.

to learn what they are being asked to learn. We can see that, according to the traditional view, learning is often about mastering information and grasping knowledge, a cognitive model that we critiqued extensively in the first part of the book.

In short, the traditional picture of the ideal teacher makes sense only when given a curriculum that is based primarily on the acquisition of knowledge and skills, either for academic or vocational purposes. As we have seen, however, this view of the curriculum is thrown deeply into doubt by the arguments of earlier chapters, especially the following claims:

- education should be human-centred rather than knowledge-centred;
- knowledge is not an entity or commodity that is to be imparted;
- the core of academic education does not consist of acquiring knowledge.

Given this, let us recap briefly the main points so far: the primary goal of the education process should be the development of the person, and this is best defined initially in terms of the qualities that strengthen a person, rather than just the skills and knowledge that he/she acquires through the processes of learning. The value of those qualities is determined by how they contribute to or form part of the well-being and quality of life of the person.

Furthermore, we also argued that, in the final analysis above, even an academic education is, in fact, more concerned with qualities than skills and knowledge, despite appearances to the contrary. We argued that the core of academic training is the nurturing of virtues such as being curious, being careful in making inferences and using words, being sceptical (i.e. challenging unsupported claims and looking for evidence) and being creative in making connections. This is more than a set of complex skills; it is something of a different order, namely, being deeply interested in particular aspects of the world and taking responsibility for what and how one knows. A real academic takes responsibility for his/her field of knowledge. Of course, for many individuals, the qualities that a purely academic education seeks to foster would be different from those pertaining to an education centred on the person as a whole. There might be some overlap, but not an exact match. In short, these points indicate why the ideal of a teacher as a specialist enthusiast might not be sufficient: it does not dig deeply enough into the nature of the kinds of learning that there ought to be in schools.

There is a second problem with the traditional model, and this stems from the discussion of motivation in Chapter 3. The enthusiasm of a teacher may not suit all students. One cannot always expect a young person to be able to immediately step into someone else's shoes and replicate the passion that fired a teacher in his/her youth and duplicate the experiences that led the teacher to his/her passion. Yesterday's parties do not make tonight's celebrations. The enthusiasm that a teacher has now may be difficult for a younger person to understand. These statements require two important qualifications. First, of course, we do not want boring teachers who are not interested in their subject area. Second, a student who already has a predisposition to like biology will definitely benefit from an enthusiastic biology teacher. Clearly, in a group, there may be several students who are in this position. A teacher's enthusiasm may fire only those who are already predisposed to like the subject. However, a student who is taught by an unenthusiastic teacher may follow his/her interest in a subject for a short while, but it may peter out later because of the uninspiring teacher.

Despite the caveats, the central point remains: in effect, the student has to find for him/herself activities that generate enthusiasm. This follows from the intentional nature of motivation described in Chapter 3. In fact, the idea of conveying passion and enthusiasm misunderstands the nature of the relevant kind of motivation. Motivation is not an emotional cream dolloped on top of a dry cognitive cake. On the contrary, the motivation and the cognition are all mixed up. It is rather a way of connecting directly to the content of the subject matter. As we argued, motivation involves an evaluative perception of the subject matter.

During our research interviews we heard about Daniel, who wanted to become a scientist at the age of 14 because his science teacher had made the subject feel like magic. Daniel fell passionately in love with science. Unfortunately, unbeknown to him, Daniel was not strong in logic and abstract thinking. After a few years, he found that mathematics and other science subjects were too much of an enigma for him to comprehend, and once he moved to sixth form and met different teachers, his passion for science quickly dried up. Daniel left college early, and is now a self-made poet and songwriter, which seems to be more in tune with his natural talent, even though he had spent very little time on the study of literature and English at school.

Daniel's story depicts the other side of teachers' enthusiasm. It can influence children and young people positively, but it can also mislead. It may be good only when the passion stimulated by the teacher is connected appropriately to the child's own perception of his/her talents and dispositions. As we have seen, the development of a young person's motivation is a delicate process that takes time and this is why we advocate a curriculum with space for such processes.

Finally, the idea of the teacher as a role model has limited applicability within the traditional view. Within this view, often teachers can only be exemplars, as purveyors of information. They have limited opportunities to be role models in a broader and more realistic way. In fact, students also often have a very limited sense of their teachers as human beings. In most cases, adults cannot be themselves when they work as teachers within an institution, and without opportunities for teachers to engage with young people in a more meaningful manner, they cannot serve as role models.

Sam, a young participant in our research, told us the following story about his maths teacher 'Dr J'. One day Sam went to see Dr J in his office. Because the office door was open and Dr J was sitting with his back to the door, Sam could see a photo on Dr J's laptop screen. When Sam knocked Dr J immediately closed his computer. He invited Sam to sit down and was about to talk about his maths homework. However, Sam was much more interested in the photo that he had just seen, and asked: 'Sir, did I just see a photo of a band? Which one is that?' To Sam's surprise, Dr J decided to run the slideshow of his photos for Sam, which was of a band playing on a stage. Sam noticed that the lead singer who played the guitar was Dr J himself, although the hairstyle and the clothes made him almost unrecognisable. When Sam asked, Dr J admitted that he was the guitarist, and told Sam about his band, the songs he wrote and that one of his songs was going to be played on the radio. Sam found this 'just so amazing'.

This story illustrates that students rarely have the opportunity to know their teachers as persons, especially in secondary schools. It captures what Walker (1973, in Goodson, 2006) portrayed as the contradictions between teachers as teachers, and teachers as persons.

Diagnosis

To explore how we got stuck with the idea of teaching as the transmission of knowledge, we need to return to some of the earlier discussions. Why is the idea of knowledge-based teaching so resilient?

The root problem is that the standard model of the ideal teacher tends to value academic learning for its own sake, over and above the development of the student as a person. This means that the needs of the subject tend to dominate and dictate the curriculum. Curriculum designers tend to ask 'What does a young potential scientist need to know and need to be able to do at the ages of 16 and 18?' and map out a plan of study from there. Therefore, if a student chooses to study science then he/she does so as a candidate scientist, with the possibility of a university degree in the subject in mind. Given this assumption, there are very many complex concepts and pieces of knowledge that a young student needs to know and understand how to apply. From this point of view, it is very hard to cut the curriculum, as most cuts would look like a travesty to the integrity and complexity of the subject. In effect, an academic subject generates its own requirements, such as: 'A person who is knowledgeable in the field needs to know X' or 'Anyone who is a scientist must understand Y'. Thus, a student who treads the path of GCSE and A level in a science subject becomes viewed as a mini-scientist subject to these requirements. Compliance is rewarded with the trappings of success, such as praise, and with the possibility of further progression towards mastery of the domain. Eventually, the roles become reversed: the student who was subject to the discipline becomes master of the subject.

The problem arises because we rightly want expert scientists to design the science curriculums in schools. However, expert scientists are precisely the people who will tend to put the demands of the discipline above the needs of the students (or indeed, will conceptualise the latter in terms of the former). Suppose one were asked the question 'What does a 16-year old taking GCSE in science need to know and be able to do?' then any self-respecting scientist would produce a relatively substantial list of areas to be covered. In contrast, if a knowledgeable outsider were asked 'What does a 16-year-old need to know about science?' the answer would be quite different, as we saw in the previous chapter.

Furthermore, teachers in their work need to identify with some of their students, and thus, in terms of teaching the subject, it helps a teacher to think of his/her students as mini-scientists or scientists-in-the-making rather than as accidental tourists or as passers-by. The teacher might have as a self-directed guideline: 'I'll try to make scientists out of as many of the students as possible.'

The problem is that we *do* want our science curriculum to be constructed from a deeply expert knowledge about science, but at the same time, we must acknowledge that if we want science education to be directed towards young people's holistic development, then the study of science may feature relatively low on the priority list for many young people.

That may sound harsh. However, although we elected to discuss science, we could have chosen almost any subject area. One could say: this area of knowledge has taken hundreds of years of human devotion and sweat to develop, and it deserves respect. The problem is: respect from whom? Clearly, experts in the field care for the width and depth of the knowledge contained in their subject area, and respect the labours of love that have gone into constructing and discovering that knowledge. The question is: where should the typical 15-year-old be in relation to this or that area of knowledge? How much of their time and energy should be devoted to the study of science (or any subject)? Fifteen-year-olds also deserve respect, and this includes having the space to be able find their own self-respect. In other words, a discipline may have demands but so do adolescents. It is a question of priority, and we have already argued that the priority has to be the human person as a whole. We have also argued that respect for this person as whole within education requires providing the young person with a curriculum that is less task-directed and more holistic, more embracing of the variety of interests and points of growth that he/she has.

In this subsection, we have tried to answer the question: why is the idea that education is fundamentally about imparting knowledge so resilient? This resilience is apparent in teacher training courses, such as the Post Graduate Certificate of Education (PGCE) in England. Teacher training is locked into a tight triangle with standard attainment tests and the national curriculum; none can be changed easily without changing the others.

To conclude, the traditional view of the teacher and teaching has certain strengths and weaknesses. This view limits the teacher's role to enthusiastic knowledge-provider. However, following on from Part 1 of the book, academic learning is important only in relation to the holistic development of the person. Knowledge itself cannot be an end. The mainstream conception of teacher and teaching is situated within a narrow understanding of learning (Chapter 2). It is located within a system that views education and the person instrumentally and thereby ignores the primacy of a person's life. Furthermore, this view neglects the part that a young person ought to play in determining his or her own learning.

An alternative view

We have sketched the traditional idea of a teacher in mainstream education. In contrast, there are many alternative educational models and grass-root secondary schools which include but are not limited to: Rudolf Steiner schools, the small school movement, home schooling, free and democratic schools, small self-managed learning groups, learning centres, and most recently, the schools-within-the-school model for larger state schools. Although these approaches are very different from each other, nevertheless, some share a common conception of teaching. In this part of the chapter, we shall distil and examine a typical conception of teaching and the role of the teacher in alternative institutions such as these. As we did with the standard view, we will look at both the strengths and weaknesses of these alternative approaches.

Let's start with a specific case of an alternative model of education, and use it as an example to illustrate some of the typical views expressed in the non-mainstream approaches to teaching. Beth has developed a community-based learning centre, which offers an alternative approach to education in which young people can make their own choices and manage their own learning pace. Some of the young people have joined the centre because their parents reject the state model of schooling. There are some who have joined because, in a state institution, the youngsters would be withdrawn and passive, and there are others who have special learning and behavioural needs.

The work of the centre is based on the idea that individuals study in accordance with their own interests and learning approach or learning style. According to Beth, young people need to set their own goals for life and learning and to work with others in order to achieve them. In the centre the young people work in groups of six students and plan and carry out their learning with support from adult facilitators. According to Beth, the adult facilitator's role consists of the following:

- To provide an environment within which the group can learn and work together
- To facilitate and support the group's needs
- To challenge the students to attain deeper levels of thinking in terms of their goals and how they might be achieved

Anything beyond this would be seen as an imposition on the young person. The teachers facilitate meetings where the students come together and reflect on questions such as 'What am I good at?', 'What do I like?', 'What makes me happy?' and 'What is important to me?' By addressing such questions in a group, each individual identifies his/her own needs for development and thereby sets both short-term and long-term learning goals.

Beth explains that these goals are diverse: some are social, emotional or behavioural, according to the particular background of the young person. For instance, for 14-year-old Ellis, who has a history of challenging behaviour in the classroom, his short-term goal is to be able to sit quietly and listen when it is not his turn to speak during group discussions. Some goals are cognitive, while others are vocational, and most are academically oriented. Beth says that it is important to help young people develop academic capabilities and attain recognisable qualifications, which can give them confidence to learn and prevent feelings of alienation. For this purpose, the young people can study academic subjects with private tutors who are not from the centre. Vocational training and apprenticeships are alternative options for those young people who are not interested in academic subjects.

The learning group operates in a similar way to home-schooling groups. The young people follow a very flexible timetable with most studying in the mornings, either individually or together. The afternoons are usually for sports, social events and visits. There are frequent visits to parks, public libraries, museums, workplaces, nature reserves and other field trips.

Strengths

This pedagogical approach has some obvious strengths, especially in contrast to the traditional view of teaching, in that it fosters self-motivation. This is important in several ways. First, it allows students to live in their activities rather than performing them for the sake of external rewards or punishment. In other words, it nurtures the disposition to engage in activities for their own sake, as opposed to the purely instrumental view previously outlined and criticised, which has a Medusa touch, turning all activities into mere instruments. In this way, the alternative approach respects the dignity of the person. It does not treat the young person merely or mostly as a means to some set of social or economic ends. It also avoids defining the young person essentially as a student, i.e. merely in terms of his/her role, but instead views him/her as a person.

Second, under this approach, young people will feel ownership of their learning. They will not feel that these activities are imposed on them as the kind of passive drudgery that we discussed in Chapter 3. In other words, they will not feel alienated. On the contrary, the approach may even blur the distinction between work and pleasure or hobby. As young people develop their autonomy and sense of independence, they naturally want to learn without being lectured to or told what to do and need to be in a space that is non-authoritarian. For young people to care about their learning, they may need to feel that what they are learning is their own and this alternative approach is strong in that way.

Furthermore, as Rousseau said, there is a tendency for people to gravitate naturally towards what they are good at and what suits their nature and talents. As we noted in Chapter 7, likes and dislikes can constitute a guide, although not an infallible one, to which work activities we are best suited for. Therefore, the facilitation approach leaves youngsters to follow their own interests and promises to allow them a good chance to find the kind of work that they would be suited to later in life.

Finally, the approach may encourage entrepreneurial qualities. Such qualities do not have to be restricted to starting new commercial businesses. They consist of having a proactive, initiative-taking disposition to any aspect of life – the opposite of passively waiting for others to initiate action.

Weaknesses

There are some weaknesses in the conception of pedagogy as facilitation, though these should not be taken as a vindication of the traditional view.

It is often impossible for a child or a young person to know what he/she needs to know, especially if he/she does not know it already.[2] Of course, a young person can consult outside sources, but the question of which books or internet sites to look at can be very vexing and confusing. Often one needs be aware of what one needs to know in order to be able to find it out. This means that guidance is necessary.

A similar point applies more forcefully to skills. As we saw in Chapter 2, academic learning involves understanding principles and key concepts, which requires reapplying them in different contexts. For instance, one learns to apply the concept of gravity in different kinds of physical problems. Or, for example, one learns to make comparisons between the developments of characters in different novels. Such practices require guidance. Likewise, one needs to know what counts as relevant similarities and differences in different contexts, ignoring distractions. Without guidance, this may not be possible. Think of how one might get stuck in details in the study of history, for instance. In short, the development of skills also requires a strong sense of what counts in different contexts as doing badly and doing well. Without the idea of what counts as making a mistake or ignoring a relevant factor, or without an idea of what would count as an improvement and why, it is impossible to develop higher-level skills. All of this requires guidance and feedback rather than mere facilitation. Indeed, one of our criticisms of traditional schooling was that students often do not understand what counts as progress and why, a pertinent point for alternative schools that offer only facilitation.

Cognition aims to be truthful, and it also aims to be appropriately complete. For this reason, cognitive acts can be evaluated as, for instance, accurate, misleading, truthful, incomplete, boring, insightful and distorted. Likewise, cognitive development needs standards and values that require the training of sensibilities that go beyond the individual. For example, there are rules of argumentation, guidelines for good written communication, criteria for what counts as good evidence in physics, history, literary interpretation, etc., which have been kneaded and revised over many generations. Cognitive development involves the assimilation of these standards or values. One has to make them one's own. Although this process of assimilation cannot be conceived as the acquisition of knowledge, nevertheless it is not the flowering of what is contained within either. Due to the need to be sensitive to these (epistemological)

---

[2] This is similar to Plato's *Meno* paradox, according to which 'a man cannot inquire either about what he knows or about what he does not know – for he cannot inquire about what he knows, because he knows it, and in that case is in no need of inquiry; nor again can he inquire about what he does not know, since he does not know about what he is to inquire'.

values, a pedagogy that merely facilitates and which therefore eschews providing guidance will tend to be weak in these aspects of cognition. It is not a question of lacking knowledge and being unaware of what one does not know, but rather of not having a good understanding of what constitutes an improvement, what the relevant values are and how they operate in the context. We will come to this in more detail in the next chapter.

A similar point applies even more forcefully to the nurturing of qualities. Going deeper into an academic field requires cultivating qualities or virtues. As we argued in Chapter 2, such virtues involve appreciating the relevant values. More broadly, an education concerned with the holistic development of the person would require a very personal guiding hand. It requires a mentor. The role of the mentor is really a key to the curriculum we proposed in the previous chapter.

There is an additional point. As we discussed in Chapter 5, adolescence is a time of self-discovery and most adolescents wrestle with questions such as 'What do I want to become?' and 'What kind of work should I engage in?' Answers to such questions require time and space for searching, experimenting and exploring as an ongoing complex process, which in turn needs the input of a mentor as we have discussed.

While a young person is learning more about him/herself, the guidance of a mentor can be crucial. The mentor will exercise some degree of authority in providing significant directional support to the young person. A young person may not always know clearly where his/her interests lie and may be confused about his/her goals. Furthermore, a young person may limit his/her horizons because of a lack in self-confidence or ignorance of the possibilities. The mentor can challenge the student to undergo processes that broaden these horizons. Of course, this mentoring role requires a tremendous amount of trust on the part of the young person and this indicates the need for a relationship that goes beyond teaching both as transmission and as facilitation.

Diagnosis

Let us focus our discussion on the conception of teaching as facilitation that Beth advocates here. The key principle in the idea of teaching as facilitation is that students should learn according to their own interests and inner motivations. Goodson (2006) apparently supports this point, namely that it is only what interests the child that is 'of intrinsic value'. Because of their inner drive to learn, students should direct themselves and manage their own learning. Any directive action by an adult would interfere with this natural growth of following one's interests, and such an imposition might distort and damage the natural learning process. Beth and her colleagues would argue that young people are able to manage their own learning and the role of the adults should be limited to providing some facilitation to help the young people work towards their own personal goals.

As we have touched upon briefly in earlier chapters, such ideas have their origin in the work of the French philosopher Jean Jacques Rousseau, which is an important source of much alternative thinking about education today, albeit sometimes implicitly. Much of Rousseau's philosophy is contained in the contrast between an optimistic view of human nature and a pessimistic view of social history. On the one hand, like Voltaire and other French Enlightenment philosophers, Rousseau rejects much of the teaching of the Church, especially the concept of original sin, claiming that humans are by nature fundamentally good. On the other hand, Rousseau subscribes to a pessimistic view of human social history, according to which human civilisation has caused us to degenerate. He denies the standard Enlightenment view advanced by Voltaire that more civilisation and learning brings progress to humankind. Whereas Voltaire argued in favour of reason and progress, Rousseau praised spontaneous feeling and nature (Kolak and Thomson, 2006).

This contrast between nature and society highlights how Rousseau's thought conflicted with both the conservative and the radical thinking of his day. Much of Rousseau's work praises nature and ways of life that are naturally simple. He idealises the noble savage, who naturally loves the good and who lives freely. In contrast, Rousseau's writings condemn cosmopolitan civilisation and corrupt commercial culture.

We can also find this general contrast in Rousseau's views on education: children have a natural ability to learn and develop, but normally educational institutions thwart these natural tendencies by imposing adult expectations on children. Rousseau's idea is that the child develops like an oak tree from an acorn when left to grow naturally without outside interference (Forbes, 2003). His sharp dichotomy between the natural and the social shapes his view that the responsibility of the teacher is to stand out of the way of the natural process of development, which would unfold on its own.

Many alternative educators, such as Beth, often think in ways that are reminiscent of Rousseau. They reject teaching as imparting knowledge so that the students can align their activities with their 'true goals' and their 'true inner nature'. According to this view, the facilitator has a very limited role. The young person is free to explore and choose what he/she wishes to learn, rather than being coerced to study something that is imposed externally. Additionally, there should be no teacher-centred monologue, or teacher-led group discussions. Furthermore, there should be no centrally planned group activities, such as laboratory sessions or discussion groups. The student must always take the lead and drive the process, not the teacher.

Beth's learning centre is not an atypical example. In fact, in most alternative models of education, the teacher, as a facilitator, does not actively guide students in their search for the focus of study. Instead, the facilitator trusts in the young person's innate capacity to be self-directed. Thus the facilitator's work is underpinned by a profound confidence in the ability of young people to lead themselves on a complex journey of growing and maturation, even if this takes time. For example, in Summerhill School, children attend classes and other school activities by their own choice, when they feel the need to and are ready. As a result of this, the teacher acts in a way similar to an external consultant, but without attempting to mould the goals of the student.

In conclusion, the idea of teaching as facilitating respects a young person as an autonomous being, and trusts his/her capacity to identify his/her own goals. This contrasts sharply with a traditional or mainstream view of teaching. However, such a view is problematic. First, facilitation provides no criteria for the young person's progress, except what interests him/her (Egan, 1975). Second, mere facilitation is not sufficient to challenge the student. Finally, it is not the case that all teaching in alternative schools consists of mere facilitation. Many alternative schools would affirm the need for adult guidance, and others would practise such guidance in a subtle and implicit way. Yet the point remains: there is a philosophical current, with its source in Rousseau, which implies that teaching should remain as facilitation, and that more would count as interference.

Teaching in a human-centred way

So far, we have analysed the role of the teacher from both the mainstream and alternative perspectives, and discussed the strengths and weaknesses of these polarised views of teaching. Even if we accept such simplifications, so-called 'mainstream' and 'alternative' approaches have much in common: both approaches have much to offer, and elements of both may be appropriate in different contexts. We can also see that they are complementary with one being strong where the other is weak. For instance, growth from within is good, but so too is rising to meet external challenges and standards.

This indicates that we need a different approach to both Rousseau's idea that children will learn best when left alone without interference, and the imposition from adult teachers. We can avoid the idea that young people need to learn principally by being taught or lectured to in a classroom setting, without thinking that guidance is interference. Clearly, there are many alternatives to, on the one hand, the idea that teaching consists mainly of telling young people certain truths and facts, and on the other, the idea that children learn best by following their own interests, with no interference from an adult. Individuals of all ages need guidance in their learning. However, we should *not* simply assume that the best way forward is to combine them, or to find the middle path between them.

There is no such a thing as '*the role*' of a teacher

According to the General Teaching Council for England (GTCE), the teacher's professional role is multi-faceted and in addition to subject/academic teaching includes pastoral and other duties, such as general administration; liaising and collaborating with different professional parties, colleagues and parents; participating in the development of the school; and catering for their own growth and professional development. The state usually expects teachers to fulfil a number of duties. However, this does not help clarify the ways teachers should support the young person's learning and growth.

To define this, let us return to the outline of the curriculum we constructed in the previous chapter. This curriculum requires a fundamental shift in the conception of teaching. In contrast to the English national curriculum, the vision of a human-centred curriculum rejects imparting prescribed knowledge, and teacher's tuition as instruction in order to achieve a pre-determined outcome. So what are the responsibilities that teachers ought to assume in order to help students embark on the various activities sketched in our curriculum that has the development of the whole person at its core?

Broadly, in such a curriculum there are at least four different pedagogical roles:

Mentors – As we have seen, mentors are primarily responsible for helping the young person construct their own individualised curriculum or study plan and goals, during direction time. The mentor will know the young person well, develop a trusting relationship with him or her, and serve as a guide in all aspects of his or her development.

Counsellors – Counsellors are adults who facilitate the students' interactions during group time. In particular, they help young people explore their feelings and emotions. Counsellors can also be mentors, but unlike mentors, they must be trained in psychology and counselling and have experience in therapeutic work.

Specialist tutors – Specialist tutors will work closely with the mentor and provide support to the students during individual project time, general knowledge time, and speciality time. They have expert knowledge in a particular subject field, such as science or humanities.

Academic tutors – Academic tutors are responsible for students' cognitive development, but also provide more specific support to their academic needs during project time and specialty time.

At first glance, it may appear that our proposal risks separating teachers' responsibilities, in contrast to the GTCE's more integral conception of a teacher's professional role. The proposal may seem to create a new kind of 'silo' (silos are often said to exist in current mainstream schools as the result of subject division). In reply, we would say that, because these curriculum components are mutually interdependent, they require that the four pedagogical roles outlined above need to be intertwined. Moreover, a curriculum that focuses on developing qualities or virtues further makes close interaction, communication and collaboration between these types of teachers a key to good pedagogical practice.

In effect, we replace the traditional monolithic conception of teacher with different kinds of educational professionals, who require different kinds of qualities and skills, and hence different types of training. Instead of expecting a teacher to be a specialist *and* generalist, we split the role into different functions. To show this, we shall discuss the differing qualities most desirable in each of these four groups of educational professionals.

The art of teaching

What are the qualities needed for each of these four kinds of educational professionals?

Personal mentors

Upon entering the secondary school, each student will be assigned a personal mentor who will support the adolescent and oversee his/her holistic development throughout his/her time in secondary education. The mentor helps the student construct a personalised curriculum for each term, and an accompanying set of goals, which includes all the curricular elements outlined in Chapter 7. The mentor and the mentee will work together to develop a tailor-made learning plan over the short, medium and long term, and will continue to adjust these learning plans. These collaborative and self-reflective planning activities will enable the young person to become more aware of his/her needs, talents, shortcomings and character. It will enable him/her to connect more fully to other people, to the meaning of the various learning activities and to the content of what he/she is learning (cf. Chapter 2).

What kind of qualities should the mentors have? Mentors need to have a good understanding of the challenges and opportunities that adolescents face at this exciting time of life. They will be aware that young people embrace this transitional time differently. This means that mentors must be caring, patient and empathetic towards young people, and sensitive to their needs. They must be able to get along with very different kinds of people. The mentor will have a good understanding of the student as an individual.

Mentors should be genuine and authentic in their efforts to build a close relationship with their mentees. As we have seen, such relationships enable the young person to open up so that he/she can more readily accept support and guidance. Through such trusting relationships, young people can be helped to recognise their own talents and limitations. However, such trusting relationships take time and effort to establish. The mentor would need to visit the mentee in their home environment and get to know his/her family, allowing the mentor to place the adolescent's talents, interests and aspirations in context. To a certain extent, a mentor should be like a friend or family to the adolescent within the learning institution.

To help students develop self-understanding, it is part of the mentor's task to create opportunities for the young person to learn, understand and develop, and then reflect on those experiences constructively. The mentor must challenge the young person personally in ways that he/she might not challenge him/herself. Nevertheless, such challenges would need to make sense in terms of what the student can relate to or understand. They cannot be alien. Since education is finally about developing qualities, and this means changing one's character, these challenges cannot be superficial. For example, he/she might challenge the student to be more confident or more independent in very specific ways. All this requires that the mentor is someone who deeply respects the young person as an individual. This means that the mentor must have both the student's current well-being, and his/her long-term development at heart.

It also requires that the mentor must have the capacity to understand what counts as progress in many different academic disciplines, as well as more broadly in terms of personal and cognitive development. Of course, mentors will consult colleagues to understand what learning, progress and development mean practically for the student at any time. Mentors have the responsibility to ensure that all efforts to support the young person's learning are well co-ordinated and integral to his/her developmental needs.

Finally, mentors will help the student prepare learning portfolios (more on this in Chapter 9), which represent the young person's progress. This not only provides an overview of the student's passage in growth, but is also a celebration of his/her learning. This personalised track-record of the student's progress could then be shown to higher educational institutions and potential employers.

Counsellors

The work of Pattison *et al.* (2007) suggests that young people don't want their subject teachers to provide counselling to them. This is understandable as counselling is personal and private and requires skills and qualities that one would not expect of a normal teacher. For these reasons, we propose that the person responsible for coordinating and facilitating group time should be a counsellor, with a professional qualification in counselling and psychotherapy, who is trained to facilitate the group interactions and activities, which includes supporting the young people in sharing their experiences and feelings with their peers. One central task of the counsellor would be to help young people learn how to relate to each other better, including romantic relations, within the context of an agreed code of ethics.

The most important quality that a counsellor ought to have is the ability to listen with care. During adolescence, young people often find it difficult to talk to anyone about how they feel. Counsellors should be sensitive enough to 'hear' the young person's frustration, and offer the student the opportunity to feel 'listened to' either during group time, or in a one-to-one situation. Although in many English state schools, counselling is currently offered to students who suffer mental health problems or learning disabilities, the counsellor's work that we are proposing here is not remedial, rather it is part of the process of development for all young people.

It is also very important that counsellors create safe group spaces in which the young people can open up. The counsellor has to be expert in managing group dynamics, and defusing potential violent and emotionally intense outbursts between the students.

Like mentors, counsellors should be individuals who really care for young people; they should be friendly and patient, approachable and personable, and their manner and attitudes towards the adolescent must encourage safe and trusting relationships. When the need arises, the counsellor will provide individual therapeutic counselling.

Ideally, the counsellor would have some training in arts therapy. Some of the group activities may include the expressive arts, such as drama, dance, playing music, and drawing. Art is really important for adolescents. For instance, many young people find that they can easily relate to the rhythms, melodies and lyrics of pop songs, rap and other modern forms of music. Songs can help them express frustrations in their life. Counsellors should be able to offer the opportunity for young people to participate in music, drama and arts together and discuss their feelings and experiences during artistic activities.

Specialist tutors

A specialist tutor is someone who is trained in a particular academic discipline, such as one of the natural sciences, humanities, business studies, literature, and so on. Specialist tutors guide students in their individual projects so that each project has the necessary quality, depth and breadth. The specialist tutor also runs seminars and classes related to students' speciality time. In short, teaching for the specialist tutor can take a number of forms:

- Lectures to introduce a general knowledge within a particular field, and help equip the students with appropriate knowledge about certain subject(s). These lectures would be part of the young person's exploration process. Other lecture or classroom interactions would be for students' speciality time.
- Seminars for discussion, reflection and questioning on specific topics within the subject areas. These sessions would also relate to the students' speciality time and perhaps to some individual projects.
- One-to-one supervision on the student's project progress.

Throughout these different teaching activities, it is vital that the specialist tutor cultivates in the student care for the content of the discipline, as well as for its methodology and values. A good specialist tutor is not only a knowledge specialist, but also an expert in helping students understand the need to make connections between different concepts, to adopt appropriate approaches to inquiries within a particular field, and to develop the epistemological virtues required to pursue learning within the field.

For individual projects, the specialist tutor should question the student's ideas, and challenge his/her project design or approach in a constructive and supportive manner. This might include facilitating discussions about the subject topic or the problems encountered, as well as provoking debates with other students who are studying the same course or who are working on projects within a similar field. When students are stuck, the specialist tutor will be at hand to help solve the problem, offering a one-to-one tutorial or a three-way conversation between the student, mentor and specialist tutor.

Academic tutor

In some mainstream secondary schools, it is usually the English and maths teachers who teach study skills. In our outline curriculum design, we have specifically allocated time for cognitive development in order for the young person to focus explicitly on this aspect of his/her growth. We see this as a necessary foundation for all subject studies and project work, and would assign an academic tutor for this specific role.

Many secondary schools tend to classify the relevant capacities under two broad categories: numeracy and literacy. However, as we discussed in Chapter 2, the required qualities are more than skills. They form part of the person because they require the internalisation of epistemological values. The person who thinks deeply, reads critically, reasons logically, articulates artfully and imagines creatively, sees the world anew. The work of an academic tutor is very much at the centre of nurturing the whole person.

Academic tutors will work with the students in smaller groups and individually. The tutor would be able to design a tailor-made programme for the young person and work with him/her on a one-to-one basis. Therefore, the role requires some of the trusting qualities associated with the personal mentor. We suggest that academic tutors work with specific young persons throughout their secondary education.

Conclusion

In this chapter, we have contrasted two conceptions of what a teacher is: from a mainstream and from an alternative perspective. We argued that neither of these two conceptions is entirely adequate.

After that we tried to understand teaching from a more human-centred perspective. As we have seen, the art of teaching requires caring for the whole person, within a trusting relationship between the teacher and the student. This also implies that teaching is a moral act (Palmer, 1998). The central concern of teaching must be the well-being and development of the student as a human being.

Human-centred education respects the young person as an autonomous being, but does not reject caring guidance. It recognises the adolescent's need for independence. However, at the same time, it acknowledges the need for guidance and nurturing based on values and challenges that do not come from the student alone. Growth needs both internal push and external pull. By focusing on the well-being and holistic development of the person, teaching can avoid both the obsessive pursuit of academic subject knowledge, and the romantic idea of no-interference.

The mainstream multi-faceted role of the monolithic teacher needs to be deconstructed for the human-centred curriculum. No one person can perform so many different roles well. Instead we conceive teaching as a partnership and collaboration amongst many professionals, who together can facilitate and guide learning. Common amongst all the teaching staff is genuine care for the young person, a willingness and capacity to build positive human relations with their students; professional qualifications and knowledge; profound understanding of what learning is and love for learning for oneself. Of course, there are other qualities that research has identified as belonging to all great teachers, such as a sense of humour, patience, friendliness, firmness, and the ability to make learning an engaging experience for all (Onwuegbuzie *et al.*, 2007).

In this book, we have insisted that the conception of teaching cannot be detached from the aims of education. These aims and the nature of learning underpin the curriculum and pedagogy, which in turn require a framework of learning feedback. It is to the third aspect that we now turn.

Further reading

Fisher, R. (1995) *Teaching Children to Learn*. Cheltenham: Stanley Thornes.

Freire, P. (1993) *Pedagogy of the Oppressed*. New York: Continuum Books.

Marshall, L. and Rowland, F. (1993) *A Guide to Learning Independently*. Buckingham: Addison Wesley Longman.

Palmer, J. (1998) *The Courage to Teach. Exploring the Inner Landscape of a Teacher's Life*. San Francisco, CA: Jossey-Bass.

9
Assessing assessment

Introduction

In 1977, Rowntree wrote: 'If we want to discover the truth about an educational system, look into its assessment and procedures. What student qualities and achievements are actively valued and rewarded by the system?' (Rowntree, 1977). Here are some more recent quotes from students about exams:

> When you are in primary school everything is geared towards SATs, then when you get to secondary everything is geared to your GCSEs . . . but I think that education should not be driven by exams and sort of . . . run by exams . . . because that sort of dominates it . . . which I think shouldn't be the point of education. Education should be about learning . . . achieving things.
>
> (Merriam, aged 14)

> [Exams] it's not about how you understand a subject, it's about how you can say exactly what they want you to say. Like in Chemistry at the moment you have to give an exact definition, you have to quote the ones out of the book, even if you may understand it and you can write it a different way, then you only get two grades. I know I didn't have a very good exam technique last year and I was getting Us and stuff. So I inspected absolutely every single past exam paper and I got loads of As – just because I knew how to answer the exam questions . . .
>
> (Sally, aged 16)

▶

> Like you could get an A without actually having any understanding of the subject, which is a bit irritating.
>
> (George, aged 17)

> I hate exams. They are so stressful. They make my life miserable. I would have loved my school and education if there were no exams.
>
> (Steve, aged 16)

Potentially enriching educational processes can easily become reduced to preparation for exams and tests. There is nothing fundamentally wrong in preparation for tests, but the problem is that it easily absorbs everything else, and exam preparation is not the same as education. As we discussed in the previous two chapters, when the curriculum is aimed at the development and growth of the whole person, pedagogy and assessment must be conceived accordingly. So far, we have seen the art of teaching from a human-centred perspective; now we will focus our attention on Bernstein's third pillar of schooling – assessment.

As pointed out by the students above, it is easy to slip into viewing the whole educative process as simply a means to achieving better grades, especially since the advent of performance-linked league tables and performance targets in recent decades. There is increased pressure on students to view their time at school in this manner, and teachers and schools are compelled to reinforce that view. Ultimately, this is deeply self-defeating, as well as unnecessary and harmful. This is one of the major themes of this chapter.

Given the strong influence that tests and qualifications have on young people and their learning, and on the culture of learning institutions, we need to reassess the very idea of assessment. We will do this by challenging some of the theoretical assumptions that are built into the current use of performance targets and tests. After the theory, we will examine the purposes that educational assessments serve, and argue that these functions can be better served in a more human-centred way.

The assessment of students has four basic purposes:

- to help students improve the quality of their learning
- to help teachers improve the quality of their teaching
- to act as an indicator of students abilities for further studies, work, etc.
- to help the government and prospective parents assess the work of the school (to ensure public accountability)

Of these four, the second is really a subsidiary of the first. Even though it involves processes that are different, let us ignore that for the moment. The problem is that the word 'assessment' covers such a wide multitude of different processes and products, and fails to separate the three main aims above. Of course, writers on education typically make some important distinctions such as: 'formative' vs. 'summative' assessment; 'assessment *for* learning' and 'assessment *of* learning'; external vs. internal; and criteria vs. norm assessment methods. So it is one of our tasks to examine these distinctions, especially the first (formative vs. summative).

The word 'assess' has its origin in the medieval Latin word for assessing for the purposes of tax collection, and etymologically has roots in the idea of the assizes, a court, where the tax assessor sat next to the judge. Hence the word 'assess' also has links to the Latin word for sitting, 'sessio'. The meaning of 'assess' is similar to 'estimate', which originally means to judge a person as good or bad, which is why it is cousin to 'esteem'. Clearly, at least in the origins of the word, either we assess something for a purpose and assessing involves judging the instrumental value of the thing in question in terms of fulfilling that purpose, or else we assess a person in moral terms, like passing judgment in a court, to see if he/she is worthy of esteem.

The two prominent models for assessment are: estimating the instrumental value for a purpose, and sitting in judgment in a court. In contemporary education, the word 'assessment' still has the flavour of its roots. When we think of education from a human-centred viewpoint, these two connotations make the idea of assessment seem problematic and inappropriate. We ought to avoid assessing young people like judges in a court, passing judgment on their character and condemning them

▶

for being too immature or too lazy, and we also ought to avoid treating them as mere tools that might be useful for some company or for GNP or for society generally. Let us see what happens when we try to decompose the concept, and remove these connotations by re-examining it in terms of the various separate feedback needs.

The debate about testing and assessment tends to be dominated by issues about fairness and reliability, which of course are important. Nevertheless, any assessment has to be carried out relative to a set of standards that embody principles of value. It is these that we will dig out and discuss in this chapter.

Theory of assessment

A major contention of this chapter is that the current insistence on the assessment of pupils, teaching and school performance is – in part – based on a general misunderstanding of what assessment and measurement are. However, at the same time, we will try to isolate and specify in what ways assessment can be appropriate, as well as useful, from a human-centred viewpoint.

In effect, the British government has an implicit theory about assessment, which, since 1988, has become the orthodoxy. According to the QCA:

> Assessment is at the heart of a successful curriculum and is a fundamental part of good teaching and learning. It enables learners to recognise achievement and make progress, and teachers to shape and adapt their teaching to individual needs and aspirations. Effective assessment enables learners to make smooth progress throughout their time at school.
>
> (www.qca.org.uk)

The main theoretical challenge to this orthodoxy comes from those writers who distinguish formative and summative assessment and argue for the former as assessment for learning (Torrance and Pryor, 1998; Black and Wiliam, 2005; Clarke, 2005). Black and Wiliam (1998a, 1998b) conducted a famous study that showed that constructive feedback led to significant improvement in learning and thereby launched the idea of formative assessment (Beck and Earl, 2003: 31). This research was focused on the evidence for the claim that 'improving formative assessment raises standards'. We shall argue that this challenge tends to accept too much of the orthodoxy, although we agree with the spirit of much of it.

Separating measurement and value

There is a strong tendency in management sciences to identify measurement with what is measured. This predisposition arises from the philosophy of science of the early twentieth century. The idea was to operationalise all scientific concepts by identifying the meaning of the concept with the relevant method of measurement. Operationalism states that a procedure of measurement *defines* the relevant theoretical term. The physicist P.W. Bridgman (1927) argued that all scientific concepts are synonymous with the operations or procedures that are used to measure them, and that science should not postulate the existence of entities or qualities that cannot be measured by clear procedures. This view, which is similar to some forms of logical positivism, was influential in the development of behavioural psychology as well as economics. It became an implicit part of management thinking, and has since, we suspect, crept increasingly into the field of education.

The operationalist idea is unsound. The measurement of value cannot logically be identified with the value that is measured. The main problem with operational *definitions* becomes apparent when we consider the question: 'What are we trying to measure?' For example, suppose we define behaviour as 'nothing more than the sum total of the measures and operations that are used to measure it' (Uttal, 2000: 165). In fact, the definition is viciously circular; it implies that behaviour is *no more than* a measure of behaviour, which is no more than a measure of behaviour, which is . . . In other words, what we are attempting to measure is simply a measurement of something, which is a measurement . . . Given operational definitions like this, there is nothing to measure. To escape this problem, the thing that is being measured must have some specification apart from the way we measure it. It cannot be *defined* semantically solely in terms of the measurement. In conclusion, we have to separate what is measured from the measurement of it; otherwise there is nothing to measure.

This is an important conclusion for educational thinking because it permits questions such as: 'Why do we want to measure X?' or 'Is the way we are measuring X a good way to do so?' Operational definitions render these kinds of question logically impossible because they identify what is measured with the way it is measured. Making these questions meaningless reinforces the educationally pernicious idea that only something quantifiable is real. Yet, as we all know, what we count is not necessarily what counts.

By way of a technical qualification, the above points do not mean that natural and social scientists cannot or should not seek ways to measure a phenomenon (or operationalise a concept); rather they imply that these do not constitute a definition of the term's meaning. In this sense, there has to be a logical separation between what is measured and the measurement of it. In this way, we can refer to a quality through the way it is measured without identifying the two because the measurement does not provide the sole and complete *definition* of the term. For this reason, value cannot be defined solely in terms of its performance measurement.

The dangers of assessment

Given this separation, we will examine how the management thinking that identifies or confuses the two can be harmful, especially in an educational context.

The danger is in how we conceive of the measurement of the value of activities. Consider the following statement (which we invented), which superficially appears innocuous:

> To assert that something is valuable is roughly to say that it has character-
> istics that provide a reason for action or choice. The activities that we
> engage in always have aims, goals or ends. In the case of educational activ-
> ities, these goals are that we want students to learn and develop. So in order
> to see what the most effective ways of achieving these goals are, we measure
> the value and effectiveness of different learning processes, and these mea-
> surements can be used as targets for students and teachers, and as a basis
> for assessing individual and school performance.

This statement is far from innocuous; in fact, it is harmfully misleading. In it, the way in which we measure a value has subtly become a substitute for the value that is supposed to be measured, and this constitutes a grave misunder-standing of the role of values in education. The upshot, though, is that the measurement becomes a target. In brief, getting the measurement figures right becomes identified with the value of the learning activity. This is about as absurd as thinking that one has warmed up a room because we have changed the thermometer reading. The seduction occurs in two all-too-easy steps, which the reader may have spotted.

The first step has already been charted in Chapter 1. There is a lived process that is potentially valuable in itself, as part of life, such as finding out about the history of the Industrial Revolution. This activity is directed by goals, without being only instrumentally valuable to them. So in the first error, one assumes that the non-instrumental value of the process lies entirely in these goals or intended results. This assumption or identification has the logical consequence that the activity becomes purely of instrumental value, which in turn implies that it is only a cost that should be minimised in the name of efficiency. This destroys the non-instrumental value of the process, thereby rendering impossible the idea that the activity itself has value. Thereby, it also erodes the possibility of appreciating what is learned. As we saw in Chapter 3, to appreciate what one learns is to attend to the valuable or interesting aspects of what one discovers. This requires regarding the activity as more than just an instrument for something else, and necessitates feeling that the activity is valuable for itself.

In summary, the first error has damaging implications: it renders that part of a person's life into a mere tool, and in this regard, treats the person as an object. Children become the assets of the future. Furthermore, insofar as one treats the activity instrumentally, one no longer connects to the value or interesting features of what is learned. In short, it reduces learning to a chore done purely as a means to an end.

The second mistake is perhaps worse: the goal (of, say, learning about the Industrial Revolution) becomes identified with the measurement of the achievement of the goal (passing the relevant test). This identification is apparently justified by the idea of operationalising a concept. In this case, to operationalise the concept would be to claim that to have learned about the Industrial Revolution is equivalent to being able to perform well on the relevant test or exam. Because of this operationalisation, the measurement becomes the goal. In other words, the goal of the educational process becomes identified with passing various tests and exams, or achieving well according to the relevant performance targets.

This second error is comparable to mistaking the word 'rose' for the flower itself, or the thermometer reading for warmth. It is the gaffe inherent in the kind of quasi-scientific and management-style operationalism we discussed and dismissed earlier. The sign is not the thing signified. In fact, a measurement (such as a grade) acts like a sign or indicator of the value or qualities that it is supposed to measure. For this reason, the indicator and the value cannot be identified.

Through this false identification, one's goal becomes to get a B on the test, achieve an 80 per cent literacy scoring at level 4, or improve effectiveness by 10 per cent. A set of activities that could be appreciated for themselves has thus become a target-led task. They are performed for the sake of getting the numbers right.

The net effect of these two errors combined is that educational activities become drained of value. In combination, these views suggest that learning is merely an instrument to achieve measurement targets. This view is problematic in a practically important way, because when we perform an activity, we need to be sensitive to the underlying non-instrumental value (say, the development of children or the enjoyable features of the activity). However, if we devise a way or a measurement and make that our goal, then we are no longer responsive and connected to the original value, but rather to the measurement targets. We are connecting to the appearances of value rather than to the values themselves.

In this way, confusing measurement and value is hollow. This is apparent when we consider more efficient ways of attaining the measurement targets but without connecting to the relevant values at all. For instance, one can reduce unemployment figures by altering what counts as employment in a variety of ways. This 'playing with the figures' is often some form of cheating, but it needn't be. For example, in order to maintain a high rank in the league tables, schools might try to avoid admitting students who might not perform well on exam results. This is a bit like a hospital turning away fatally sick patients in order to keep its mortality rate lower. The absurdity results from confusing the measurement with the value measured.

None of this means that things of value cannot or should not be measured, but it does imply the fundamentally important conclusion that the measurement must not and cannot become a substitute for the real, valuable qualities themselves.

Performance targets

The idea that goals and measurement are identical looks unproblematic because our language often persuades us to identify the two by referring to measurement scores (or other signs of value) as 'targets' and 'standards', which implies that they should become goals. However, this identification is dangerously problematic for the reasons that we have already given, but most of all, because it implies pursuing a representation or measurement of something valuable rather than the valuable thing itself.

One might be persuaded to measure learning outcomes and performance rather than student capabilities on the grounds that the former is much more precise than the latter. It says: *'Outcomes and performance can be measured; abilities (and qualities) cannot'*. Fiddlesticks! This is the wrong way around. Learning outcomes are already supposed to be a measurement; in fact they already are a way of measuring certain abilities. They are like an indicator of capabilities. For argument's sake, suppose, on the contrary, that they weren't. We would not be interested in learning outcomes if we thought that they were not at all indicative of some underlying student abilities. They are important precisely because they indicate the capabilities that we expect will result in similar performances on other future occasions in different circumstances. In other words, they are thought to be reliable for prediction. Without this assumption, they would be worthless. This does not mean that learning outcomes are a bad idea. However, it does mean that they are *not* a substitute for the underlying values they measure or they are supposed to be indicative of, which pertain to the development of the student.

We might say the same about IQ tests. What do IQ test scores measure? At the most general level, there are two possible answers: either such scores only measure one's performance on a specific IQ test on a particular day, or else such scores measure roughly and approximately something that is only vaguely defined, namely intelligence (or certain kinds of intelligence). The second is vague, and the first looks very precise. Therefore, we might be tempted to opt for the first in order to be more scientific. With a little thought, however, one can see that it is a completely empty option. Suppose we made up a test, call it the YZ test. If someone were to ask 'What does the score on this test measure?' then it would be an empty response to reply: 'The test score measures one's performance on that specific YZ test.' Back to the obfuscations of operationalism! To avoid such muddles, we need to accept that what we are trying to measure may be vague because it is open-textured.

Management words such as 'achievement', 'performance', 'target' and 'attainment' all threaten to fall foul of this crucial central point, i.e. confusing the means of measurement with the underlying valuable learning process. Likewise, the term 'standard' has a similar ambiguity. 'Standards are falling' can mean that what counts as a good piece of work is lower in quality than before. It can also mean that fewer people are reaching a fixed measurement or benchmark of quality. The two are different because one concerns value and the other their measurement. In the wish to be more precise, management language can blur the two.

Let us return to the main point: the pursuit of good scores or the achievement of performance targets per se constitutes a gross misunderstanding of value because it implies that one has connected to the measurement or the sign of a value rather than the valuable state itself. It is a bit like wearing expensive clothes as a sign that you are rich. If one made expensive clothes one's goal then one would not have connected to wealth-making at all. Likewise, a diet of performance targets does not feed the need for educational transformation.

Who needs what assessment and why?

Assessment serves three main purposes: (1) the learning needs of students; (2) the informational needs of other institutions and employers; and (3) the informational needs of the government. In this section, we will sketch an argument to the effect that these three types of informational needs should be kept apart. In other words, there should not be one grand process called 'assessment' that attempts to serve all three purposes at once, which is, of course, what happens now with SATs and GCSEs and other general grading, especially in secondary education. The three needs are different and should be served by different procedures. Furthermore, we shall argue that the nature of the learning feedback needs of students is such that it should not be regarded as, or even called, 'assessment' (even so-called 'formative assessment').

Lumping together the three kinds of purposes that so-called 'assessment' serves is, we shall argue, a form of failing to respect young people because it involves testing them for the sake of ends that are not theirs. Furthermore, it does so in a way that damages their ends and harms the educational process. Basically, the educational system assesses students and allows them to suffer any negative consequences of this in order that the government can exercise control over the quality of schools and teachers. It makes student needs and students themselves subsidiary or subservient to public accountability. For example, if teachers' pay rises and professional reputations are made conditional on SATs results then teachers will, even unknowingly, tend to teach for the sake of the results, and will tend to put the results before the students' intrinsic learning. Students, too, will tend to conceive of their education mainly as a means for exam results. If a school's funding also depends on those results, then there will be increased pressure to make education a tool for results. But note! The word 'results' here does not refer to the consequences in terms of the underlying value; it refers to exam results that are supposed to measure the real value (the development of the young person). In other words, the measurement has become the goal. So, we have an absurdly costly way to make teachers more accountable (by ruining the students or making education hollow)!

Of course, there is a clear logic to the idea of public accountability: taxpayers pay the government to provide public services, and the government has the responsibility for ensuring those services are of good quality, and it can only do that by making sure that schools are accountable, which requires measurement figures. This train of reasoning makes sense, even though the contortions it produces do not. There ought to be a way of making schools accountable that does not involve treating children as numbers and misshaping their education. This way requires separating out the needs that so-called 'assessment' is sup-posed to serve. The idea that the three purposes of assessment can, and ought to be, kept separate should strike one as a liberating idea, because it allows each requirement to be considered on its own merits. The learning needs of students do not have to be mixed up with those of employers and muddled up with those of the state. Let us treat each of the three purposes according to their own requirements rather than devising tests and other grading mechanisms that lump them together in one soup or glutinous mess.

The student's needs for feedback

We will perform a thought-experiment in order to address one issue at a time. Let us imagine, for a while, an informational heaven where teachers, institutions, employers, parents and governments have all their information needs regarding students and schools satisfied as if by magic or by telepathy. In this fictional land, there is no need to grade and test students for the sake of qualifications and direct needs external to those of the students. This imaginative fiction will allow us to concentrate exclusively on the students and their learning processes. Under these conditions, do students still need exams and grades? What feedback does each student need under these idealised hypothetical conditions? Let us make a list in answer to this question.

Learning in order to improve

Clearly the student needs constructive feedback on how to improve his/her work, and also a deeper understanding of what counts as improvement and why. This last point is super-important because such understanding helps to build the character traits and develop the qualities that we discussed in the chapters on learning (cf. Chapter 2). The young person has to undergo a process of internalising the epistemological and other values inherent in what he/she is studying or learning. Internalising these values or standards involves connecting the learning activity back to his/her development.

Understanding what constitutes an improvement and why it counts is the most neglected area of student feedback. In this sense, students need more models of good work and to understand why they have been selected as models. However, under current educational conditions, models may have a limited value for the depressing reason that students tend to merely copy models because insofar as the implicit aim of education is good grades, there will be only a superficial connection to the underlying values or standards. To recap, the student needs feedback to know what constitutes improvement.

Learning 'how to learn'

The student will need to be able to critically evaluate his/her own learning and development processes. This is essential to the fostering of self-responsibility.

For a student to be responsible for his/her own motivation, he/she needs space to self-evaluate reflectively and with care in terms of his/her own goals on a regular basis. He/she needs the opportunity to ask questions such as 'How have I improved as a learner in the last two months?' 'How have I developed as a person in the last month?'

As discussed in the previous two chapters, this process will also require guidance because it is easy to be too hard or too easy on oneself, to be too self-judgmental and self-blaming, or too quick at self-praise or satisfied with very little. In addition, it is difficult to identify clearly how one needs to improve. For example, students sometimes accuse themselves of being lazy when it is more a question that they do not give themselves the right kind of space (free from distractions) and preparation for work. This general kind of self-reflection requires some kind of framework, which, in the main, might be provided by the student but which may require guidance.

Leaning about the subject

The student will also need feedback on how well he/she has learned in terms of the concepts, principles and knowledge of a subject. Again, this is a normal part of the learning process. Of course, there is a strong tendency for teachers to interpret this feedback requirement as the need for tests that result in a score, grade or mark. However, this does not count as substantial feedback because it does not tell the student how to improve or what improvement consists of. Despite this, it might be argued that students need exams because they bring specific purpose and clearer structure to schooling. Student attitudes to exams vary; some respond well to the challenge of exams, others less well. However, this is not a clear argument for examinations because there might be other forms of review and indeed other kinds of purpose (more learning oriented) that might play a similar psychological role. Nevertheless, the point remains that students (like everyone else) need a sense of purpose in their work, as we stressed in Chapter 1 and in Chapter 7 on curriculum.

Learning to know one's talents

The student will also need feedback in order to know what kinds of activities he/she is temperamentally good at. By 'good', we do *not* mean good in terms of exams!

A young person will obtain some feedback on what he/she is good at from his/her own likes and dislikes. Often we dislike doing things that we are less good at. Alternative educational philosophies based on Rousseau insist on this point.

However, tastes are a good guide to talents, only up to a point. There are many caveats. First, a person can like or dislike something for extraneous reasons, such as image, misconceptions and past associations. For example, a young person may dislike medicine because he/she assumes that medicine is for middle-class people and 'I am not snob' (in a different area, Billy Elliot the dancer overcame this particular bias). Second, people cannot always identify what they like about an activity or what features of the activity make it likeable. This is an important point because if one knows what aspects of the activity one really likes, say constructing the big picture, helping another person, etc., then one can find similar kinds of activities in other fields that one might also enjoy. For example, the kinds of mental activities that a person might enjoy as an architect could also be applied to some activities in software design. By identifying the kinds of activities that a person really appreciates and knowing why, the person can build up a portrait of his/her own talents and character within other areas of work. Feedback is needed to strengthen this process of self-discovery.

In summary, if someone is very good at something then there is usually a tendency for that person to love that activity (apart from extraneous reasons that can cause the person to reject it). In this sense, despite the caveats, likes and dislikes can serve as a guide for what one is good at. They suggest, but they don't define it. In other words, such temperamental dispositions need to be informed and shaped by external appreciation and criticism. As a young person, one needs to have opportunities to check one's likes and dislikes against one's abilities as defined by standards that are initially external to oneself. I may be attracted to activities that I am not especially good at, and I may be very good at activities that I am not especially attracted to. This anti-Rousseau point indicates the need for a dialogue between internal talents and external standards. This dialogue is feedback. In short, a young person needs feedback in order to understand better his/her talents and working disposition within particular areas of work.

Formative assessment

By reviewing a wide range of previous research and developing their own project with teachers from Oxfordshire and Medway, Black and Wiliam identified four broad areas for formative practices which have become the major tenets of the current government's Assessment for Learning (AfL) initiative. Black *et al.* (2003) summarise the four areas as follows:

- *Questioning* – This involves a process whereby teachers ask oral questions in order to discover more about students' understanding of the subject instead of merely their mastery of facts.

- *Feedback through written comments* – Along with oral questioning, written comments and feedback are given on the student's work, which include how well the student has done and how they can improve, and what action is necessary in order to follow up the suggestions.

- *Peer and self-assessment by the student* – This includes making assessment criteria transparent to students, as well as an overview of both the aims of their work and what it means to complete it successfully; this also has the aim of encouraging students to own their learning and to become independent learners.

- *The formative use of summative assessment* – The idea is that exams can be used to improve learning directly. Exams are perceived as a positive part of the learning process insofar as they involve cultivating an understanding of the criteria against which test papers are marked. Occasional exams help to chart students' learning but ought not to dominate the entire assessment process.

Based on this work, among others, many educators claim that there is a fundamental distinction between formative and summative assessment, and maintain that formative assessment escapes the problems associated with summative assessment. There is an allied distinction between assessment for learning (formative) and learning for assessment (summative) (Clarke, 2005; CERI, 2008).

However, we want to point out that formative assessment continues to be situated within a narrow conception of learning. It also fails to distinguish the need for feedback of the student and the teacher from the need for accountability and the need for knowing more about a student's capacity for further learning or for employment. It does not separate the informational needs we distinguished.

The dangers of formative assessment

We will briefly criticise one aspect of the above view by arguing for a distinction between feedback and assessment. The various learning-related feedback needs of students should not be characterised as 'assessment'. It can be misleading even to call them 'formative *assessment*' or '*assessment* for learning'. We might better call them 'formative feedback'. It is important to distinguish between feedback and assessment. There are three reasons for this distinction.

First, as we said earlier, the root of 'assessment' involves passing judgement on a person's character and/or estimating the instrumental worth of that person's capacities. The term 'assessment' retains this quality of passing judgement even when we refer to assessing pieces of work. It concerns merit. For this reason, assessment, like measurement, has to be accurate and truthful;

by the very nature of the concept, this is necessarily a major dimension of the act of assessing. Merit has to be deserved. This is why assessment has related notions, such as evaluation, statement of value, estimation and calculation of value. In contrast, however, the feedback needs of the students mentioned above do not have to involve such judgements of worth or merit. Indeed, feedback does not necessarily have to be accurate and truthful in order to reinforce (or feed back) into a process. For example, the very idea of encouragement does not necessarily imply truthfulness or accuracy. Indeed, the concept of feedback keeps company with usefulness (rather than truth). This means that the feedback needs of students do not really count as assessment. (Note: this does not mean that feedback should be false! It simply means that accuracy is not part of the concept of feedback. In contrast, assessment necessarily includes that idea. So, the two concepts are distinct.)

Second, the feedback needs of students should not automatically be regarded as formative *assessment* because 'How well are you doing?' is a very different question from 'What needs to change?' The assessment question 'How well?' looks for an evaluation and for some kind of measurement, whether quantitative or not. 'Excellent', 'very good', 'good', 'satisfactory' and 'poor' are the same as letter grades A, B, C, D, E and not substantially different from percentage points. Therefore, verbal cues that implicitly send the message 'good but not very good', etc. are not much different from scores. In sharp contrast, the feedback question 'What needs to change?' does not have the connotations of assessment. It does not pass on judgement. This appears to be in line with what Black *et al.* (2003) suggest in connection with written comments on students' work, namely that such comments do not have any judgemental or evaluative marks such as 'good' or 'poor'. According to Black *et al.*, such comments ought to offer ways for the student to examine the qualities of their work, and guide the student towards improvement. In this way, what Black *et al.* call 'formative assessment' ought to be called 'formative feedback'.

The third reason for not regarding the feedback needs of students as formative *assessment* is that these feedback processes are an absolutely integral part of any learning or teaching, especially given the view of learning outlined in Chapter 2. They are not different from learning/teaching. They do not constitute a separate process of assessment, even if it is called 'formative assessment'. They form part of the continuing dialogue between teachers and students rather than a distinct activity of assessment.

Here is a possible objection to what we are saying:

> Writers who distinguish formative and summative assessment and initiatives such as Assessment for Learning agree fundamentally with many of

the points that you are making in this chapter. Like you, writers on the topic regard formative assessment as fundamentally different from summative, which they criticise for being judgemental and for not serving directly the learning needs of students. You call the process 'formative feedback'. If they call it 'formative assessment', or 'assessment for learning' then there is no problem. Consequently, your insistence that a distinction should be drawn between formative feedback and assessment is purely semantic and a bit pedantic.

In essence we agree with the points in this objection except the very last. For the reasons just outlined, we think that there is a distinction between feedback and assessment, even formative. Maintaining this distinction is important for practical reasons, which we will now discuss.

First, it is important because the distinction between assessment and pedagogy needs to be maintained. The term 'formative assessment' tends to mix the two up. What is called formative assessment is really an integral part of teaching and not a distinct activity of assessing. This is important practically because, as we saw, the concept of assessment has built into it the idea of assessing whether a person has met certain standards. According to the mainstream conception, standards have to be operationalised, and so the concept of a standard becomes linked to the idea of measurable performance outcomes. In this way, the term 'formative assessment' has built into it a pedagogical approach based on measurable learning outcomes, which in fact are conducive to summative assessment. In other words, formative assessment is the rival sibling of summative assessment. They may be rivals, but nevertheless they are siblings born of the idea that learning must be directed towards outcomes that can be understood as measurable performance targets. Of course, this point in itself does not constitute a criticism of formative assessment as a methodology, and certainly, it does negate the fact that formative assessment and AfL are to be sharply contrasted with summative assessment and learning for assessment. However, we are arguing that this contrast needs to be made even more sharply because so-called 'formative assessment' is really part of pedagogy and is not part of assessment. We are insisting on this point because the term 'formative assessment' carries with it the idea of a specific pedagogical approach. This approach defines the value of education in terms of goals or outcomes and specifies that outcomes can be made into performance targets. In contrast, what we call 'formative feedback' is not linked to any particular pedagogical model.

Second, regarding student learning feedback needs as a form of assessment implies a negation of a principle that we tried to establish as fundamental at the beginning of this chapter. This was that we should not lump together the learning feedback needs of students with the accountability demands of a government and the informational needs of outsiders, such as employers and other institutions. These three requirements need to be met separately. Mainstream examination and school ranking practices unite them because it is convenient and less expensive but, as we have seen, the combination instrumentalises the student and can destroy the value of learning.

For this reason, we need to separate the learning-related feedback needs of students from assessment that responds primarily to the informational needs of outsiders, such as a higher education institution, an employer or a government. Of course, the principles of formative assessment and AfL constitute a very welcome move towards this separation and towards a more human-centred approach. However, 'formative assessment' is located in a broader culture of testing. AfL is akin to a group of islands in a sea of summative assessment. For example, the idea of improving learning is set alongside concepts such as improved *performance* and raising standards of *attainment*, which conflate value with its measurement in the way we discussed earlier.

The distinction between formative and summative assessment can be difficult to make. In reality, formative assessment can sometimes be a continuing or ongoing summative assessment (Clarke, 2005: 1). Likewise, summative assessment can be used for educational purposes. Rather like Black and Wiliam, Clarke (2005) tries to distinguish between formative and summative assessment. She says that summative assessment is a measurement of attainment, and includes any assessment method that 'aims to establish whether learning has taken place or a target has been met' (p. 2). In contrast, she says, formative assessment enables achievement.

Unfortunately, the latter definition does not succeed in marking the distinction. This is because even summative assessment can enable achievement and so might a million other things, such as good school meals and a charming teacher. Anything that comes under the wide umbrella of 'teaching' aims to enable student achievement. We could amend Clarke's definition to say that formative assessment is *a form of assessment* or measurement that aims to enable achievement. However, the problem is that summative assessment methods can do that too. For example, the teacher can assign students' final grades and exams in the hope that this will help them to improve in the next academic year.

Furthermore, one might question the term 'achievement' in the definition of formative assessment because this word indicates a willingness to accept the orthodox theory and a state system of measurement in which achievement is constituted by reaching performance targets set by the national curriculum, and which are measured by exams that test how well the curriculum contents are delivered to and mastered by the students. In brief, Clarke has not drawn a clear distinction between the two kinds of assessment.

Once again, the danger is that 'formative assessment' is similar to summative despite protestations to the contrary. The key is how learning is conceived and how progress is understood. When the goal of formative assessment is claimed to be learning, the result, unfortunately, often turns out to be attainment, rather than learning. As clearly stated in Black *et al.* (2003: 2): 'There is ample evidence that the changes involved will raise the scores of students on normal conventional tests.' This is dangerous for two related reasons. First, it accepts the idea that student learning feedback needs are a form of assessment, contrary to the three points that we made at the beginning of the section. Second, as a crucial result, it buys into the process of lumping together the learning feedback needs of students with the accountability demands of the government and the informational needs of outsiders.

What is wrong with grades?

Given the list of general feedback needs of students discussed above (see pages 215–17), then it seems that students do not need grades (in this fictional world). In other words, it seems that (outside of this heaven) grades primarily serve needs other than those of the students. This should not be a surprise, perhaps, because usually students are not in a position to understand what a grade really means. For example, the grade reflects a certain level of performance relative to the standards established in a national curriculum. To know what this means requires a good understanding of the subject itself as well as the curriculum. A student is likely to understand a poor grade as meaning 'I am not good at studying Y', 'I am not intelligent', or 'I am lazy', or even 'I am not middle-class'. Poor grades often encourage students to devalue themselves, and hence to have low expectations of themselves. Students understand them in personal and judgemental terms, and can use them to label themselves. This labelling can easily become a damaging self-fulfilling prophecy: the feeling that one cannot do well usually leaves a person unmotivated and thus unable to do well.

Therefore, we can tentatively conclude that grades on their own do not give the student adequate informational feedback, and may have damaging personal effects. Additionally, grades are comparative (e.g. to another student), and thus foster the false idea that learning well is a question of outperforming someone else. In combination with the previous point about personalisation, this necessarily sends a negative message to most students. Since the top places are by definition available to only a select few, the majority of students are sent the message that they have not succeeded. It is a short psychological step from that feeling to the judgement that one has failed, and therefore that one is a failure. 'Success' is a judgemental term because it implies 'failure'. If only the select few can succeed, the majority must fail.

Even the thought 'I am not the best' is not appropriate because learning is not a comparative achievement, i.e. not a question of doing better than someone else, unlike say perhaps tennis or chess. Despite the fact that it is not as heavily self-condemning as 'I am a failure', the judgement 'I am not best' still carries the ideas of comparative league tables, and subsequent self-devaluation that are not apposite in the context of human-centred learning and self-development. No one thinks 'I am the best at taking a bath in my family' or 'I am best at watching television'. It is not only that the relevant standards are unclear; it is also that such comparisons are simply absurd in terms of their point within the context. It is not a competition. Likewises, there is no need to encourage turning the school into a race with winners and losers. We do this when we make a classroom into a place where judgemental comparatives such as 'I am better than . . .' 'he is best . . .' and 'I am worse than . . .' find a natural home and an appropriate context. Teachers themselves may not do this directly, but grades unavoidably do.

At their time of life, young people need to be in a social environment that encourages them to have self-respect and dignity. This is more than just having self-confidence. Self-confidence is roughly either the feeling that one can complete a task or job or the feeling that one is better than a comparable group of other people in relation to some task or standard. Self-respect is the appreciation of oneself as a person.

Although self-respect perhaps cannot be directly taught, nevertheless it can be facilitated. It requires a nurturing environment in which someone is treated as a person however badly he/she performs. However, teachers tend to view students who perform poorly implicitly as lazy, or immature, or rebellious or unintelligent (Pye, 1988). The words used on any specific occasion may be different, but the categories will remain fundamentally the same. This means that teachers sometimes refer to students in a judgemental way.

Negative judgements about a person can be very harmful. For instance, in most state secondary schools, students are taught in different ability groups. Here 'ability' refers to students' ability to do well within a subject as perceived by the teacher or in accordance with their attainments on standard tests. 'Ability grouping' refers to any of a variety of forms of homogeneous classroom ability groupings or settings. In English secondary schools, students are often grouped and taught according to their abilities in certain subjects. Research has identified that ability grouping or setting is a way of judging or labelling students. Often the students in the top groups or top sets benefit from the label, and appear to be more motivated and to develop more self-confidence, whereas students in low-ability groups suffer from such labelling, which results in low expectations, rote learning, loss of motivation and positive self-image (Braddock and Slavin, 1995; Boaler *et al.*, 2000; Boaler and William, 2001).

Given all this, feedback that essentially compares a student's work to the work of other students needs to be reduced to a minimum. This claim needs two qualifications. First, of course, students need feedback that relates to external standards and, as we have seen, such feedback ought to help them internalise and understand the relevant academic standards, and how these relate to more basic epistemological values. Second, prospective institutions, employers and the government, and the public may need comparative evaluations. So far, we have confined ourselves to the needs of the students and their learning process rather than those of society or external agencies.

One might object (against what we say here) that judging is a necessary good that is part and parcel of teaching. However, in reply, there are different kinds of judgement, some of which are harmless, others potentially very pernicious. To *make* a judgement is not to *pass* judgement on something. Judgements may be necessary but passing judgement is not. First, we can distinguish making a judgement about a person from judging his/her actions: 'John did not understand so well' is quite different from 'John is stupid'. Second, we need to distinguish the content of the judgement from its tone – friendly vs. impersonal; caring vs. dismissive; respectful vs. authoritarian. The content of a judgement can be entirely different from its tone. At the extreme, it is possible to make a judgement about a student's work that is positive in its content (semantically) ('This is a good piece of work because . . .') but which is delivered in a negative tone. For example, one's facial expression and body movements can give quite the opposite message to what one says. Students will usually pick up on the tone.

In this sense, grades do have a (perceived) tone. They are final, impersonal, objective and dismissive. They are final because they have no nuances or qualifications. They are impersonal because they ignore history and context. Even when they are good grades, such as George's 'A' grade, they do not necessarily provide the kind of feedback the student needs. In George's case, he hadn't a clue why he was awarded an 'A' in psychology. Grades, especially bad grades, are dismissive because they cannot carry any message of hope. Grades are, well, degrading! If they are degrading, they fail to treat a person with respect.

Learning feedback: alternatives to grades

We are in broad agreement with Hattie and Timperley (2007) that learning feedback addresses the four kinds of need of the student in order to improve: (1) feedback on the task/project and how well one is doing in achieving the goal(s) of the project; (2) feedback on the process of learning and approaches to learning; (3) feedback on one's self-regulation including commitment, self-control and confidence; and (4) feedback on the overall development of oneself as a person. To a certain extent, much of these four aspects of feedback has been discussed in Chapter 7, so we shall not repeat that here.

If students do require comparative feedback on their work, then we might try alternative tacks. For example, suppose that students have written a paper and now they receive detailed comments on what aspects of their work could be improved, how and why. The feedback function that grades are supposed to play (for the student) is to give him/her a general comparative idea of how well he/she has done, not in relation to other students, but rather in relation to certain standards. This feedback needs to be given in a manner that is less judgemental and more informative (not one-dimensional) than a simple single grade. One might, for example, provide students with anonymous high-quality essays written by other students on a similar topic, which could then be analysed with the group. In this way, students learn more about the qualities that they need to develop, and about what counts as improvement and why.

An alternative approach is to encourage more active self-evaluation in terms of the student's own past, ipsative feedback. How have I improved since last month? How could I improve more? This has four very important features to recommend it. First, it requires understanding the relevant standards well. Second, it embodies the idea that students are responsible for their own learning and promotes a more proactive motivation. Third, it embodies and requires critical self-reflection. Fourth, it hits a better comparison in the sense that it encourages the student to improve relative to his/her own past rather than being better than someone else.

We are not reviving the old chestnut that grades are unfair. Rather the point is that, at least in the form that they are currently administered, grades are discouraging and unkind and do not send the correct learning message. Indeed, in the Danish system, students do not realise that they are being assessed. Their grades are not shared (White, 2000: 170). Another example of an alternative is portfolio-based records as opposed to grade-based exams. Many schools in North America have begun to use student portfolios of selected work to represent the student's progress over time. We introduced the idea of portfolios in Chapter 8; it is a systematic collection of students' narratives, learning plans and project work, the selection of which is agreed by both the teacher and the student in order to reflect his/her progress in one or more areas of development. In this way, portfolios serve the purposes of both feedback and self-reflection. The portfolio can benefit the student and the teacher, and offer the student the opportunity to understand the learning process and the transformation in themselves.

A learning portfolio is a record of the student's educational and learning journeys and his/her progress over a period of time. It contains significant evidence of the young person's learning, such as the following:

- Personal statement (e.g. interests and hobbies, personal strengths and characteristics, values and worldviews, dreams and ideal work or occupation as an adult, etc.).
- Research questions, hands-on projects and reports (over a specific period of time, such as a year, a term, or a week, etc.).
- Books and other literature and information read over time, and reviews written about the reading.
- Learning journals which record significant experiences and memorable moments over time and also reflect on questions such as 'What have I enjoyed in doing the project?' and 'What makes me feel confident?'.
- Formal training or cognitive development programmes (e.g. maths topics, reading skills, etc.).
- Personal narratives, website, social network sites, CV, and other autobiographical information, and so forth.

Teachers can use students' portfolios as a diagnostic tool for the individual or the class as a whole. These portfolios can feed back into the teacher's ongoing engagement with the student. Such a portfolio can become an integral part of the student's learning. Students can set their own learning goals and understand the relevance of the programme of studies to their personal development. When they are well integrated with learning, portfolios can also help students understand their talents, strengths and needs, and see their own learning journeys over time.

Learning and exams

We now need to reinforce the main point about the harmful nature of exams. This is that they tend to become the main goal of the student (and increasingly the teacher and school, and hence part of the learning culture of the school). This is as a result of the two-step process discussed at the start of this chapter, whereby first learning becomes instrumentalised, and second, the real goal becomes substituted or replaced by its measurement. This is the most pernicious aspect of grades because, insofar as this occurs, the students cannot appreciate the intrinsic value of the processes that they are engaged in. Testing drains the value from learning. Learning becomes for the sake of a score.

On the other hand, exams or written tests provide an excellent opportunity for students to learn a lot in a focused way. The problem is that preparation for exams tends to be focused on learning at the knowledge level; the priority of the other levels is *ipso facto* ignored. This is a severe limitation. To see this, suppose that we explicitly made our goal to achieve the set performance targets very efficiently. There would be a seductive simplicity to this. Imagine: we establish an extremely strong system of rewards and punishments for the students, and an army-like discipline to attain the targets. We teach the students explicitly how to please examiners. We teach memorising techniques and tips for answering questions. We treat school like the most intensive crammers for three months while the students take three GCSEs. We then repeat the process for three more exams, and so on. At the end of a year, the students will come away with good qualifications, but of course, perhaps little else.

The problem is that good exam results easily become regarded like money, and in this sense, they become transformed from a representation to something real, from a measurement to an instrumental value. They become a real goal of instrumental value, but merely because they are perceived as such by society at large. It is an unfortunate self-fulfilling prophecy.

The assessment structure combines several purposes in one: exams and tests serve as a basis for grades; they give the student and teacher informational feedback; the results serve to punish the student who is lazy and reward the conscientious; they can motivate the student; and exams function as focal points and grades as targets for study.

Teachers' need for feedback

Teachers need information about how their students are progressing in order to be able to adjust what and how they teach and to better understand the learning needs of their students, individually and as a group. The trouble is that we tend to think of these needs mainly in terms of 'Have they [the students] learned the facts well?', i.e. at the level of knowledge rather than those of concepts, skills and qualities. This is due to the word 'teach'. It is understandable that teachers, especially secondary teachers, who are trained in a specific subject area, should assume that teaching is imparting knowledge within the subject domain. It may *seem* obvious that the job of a history teacher is primarily to impart knowledge of history (i.e. to teach). However, the reflection we went through in Chapter 2, and the discussion we had in Chapter 8, suggest that this is not so. Well-motivated students with a reasonable dose of common sense can acquire knowledge without needing a teacher to deliver it. A historian engages with the past and has different ways of understanding the past. Therefore, as we have argued, teaching does not necessarily mean imparting knowledge, but rather helping students develop qualities or virtues in order to learn better (and learn to learn better).

As we discussed in the previous two chapters, it is necessary that the teacher is caring and sensitive to young people's needs to explore and identify their interests (and what they are good at). Once the students feel motivated and connected with what they are doing, they are more likely to take the responsibility for their own learning. To be motivated intrinsically, the student needs to understand the value of what he/she is doing in the school and how it connects with his/her overall development as a person and be involved more directly in identifying his/her own trajectories in learning. When the student understands what he/she doing and why, ongoing feedback enables him/her to reflect on the experience and use the reflection to guide further learning.

So, given human-centred education, the feedback that a teacher needs is not confined to whether John or Jody has learned such and such set of facts. Nor is it restricted to the student's ability to perform certain intellectual tasks such as answering questions about a text or solving an equation. It includes these, but these make best sense in the context of the wider development of the student. As we have seen, the teacher's needs for feedback are connected to those of the students, and from what we discussed in Chapter 8, the teachers in their different capacities (of mentor, counsellor, specialist tutor, academic tutor and other supporting staff) will have different feedback needs, and we pointed out that teachers ought to work together in providing addressing the students' feedback needs.

The key is that such feedback is always about the overall development of a student. In the example of the portfolio, an accumulation of the student's work is more useful than a stack of exam papers completed one Thursday morning when students vary in their moods, nerves and abilities to respond to the stress.

Needs of institutions and employers

Let us now leave the hypothetical constraints of the first section. While it is difficult to generalise the needs of potential employers, which may be very varied, some generalisations can nevertheless be made.

In this context, people often assume that society has increasingly become knowledge-based, and that schools must prepare young people for the so-called 'knowledge economy' and this 'new world' of work (Taylor and Lehmann, 2002; Lehmann and Taylor, 2003). This assumption, as we shall see, avoids debates about the nature and meaning of work, thereby making employment the main end of education (Kincheloe, 1999). The assumption implies that, for instance, students will take as many GCSEs and A levels as they can in order to prove their educational attainment, which is needed for entering higher education and by employers.

Against this assumption, however, employers do not need to know that such and such applicant has a grade C in history and a B in geography. The information that the employer usually needs will not be specific in this way (Johnson, 2007). The potential employer is more likely to want to know the following: will the candidate be able to do the work well? In practical terms, this means, for instance, that the employer wants to know about the capacity of the person to be persistent and systematic in achieving a goal. Is the candidate well motivated, and does she have a generally positive attitude? Can she work well in a team? Can she communicate well both in writing and orally? Is she sensitive to the needs of others? How well can she relate to the demands to be professional? Can she understand a request and solve problems? Is she intelligent? Can she set priorities? Many employers would regard these qualities as 'soft skills' that are necessary regardless of the type of job and regardless of the technical skills or professional knowledge that a particular job might require.

Even for the latter (the technical skills, etc.), usually, the potential employer does not have very detailed needs about what the students ought to study at GCSE, and even A level. Of course, there will be some basic skills and knowledge that any employer will want, and some will be looking for persons who are computer literate and competent in mathematics and have general scientific knowledge. Some employers may require specific training and relevant professional qualifications, such as in accountancy, nursing or tiling. But such exact demands apply to job candidates with qualifications beyond secondary schooling.

Given that this is the case, then it is evident that there is a mismatch between the three types of aims of education that we discussed in Chapter 1. It indicates that we do not have the three general aims in the correct relationship in two ways. First, potential employers do not request the specifics of the GCSE, A level or other forms of assessment. Instead, these specifics are driven by academic standards, and the employers adapt to these. Second, these academic standards ought to be responsive to the development of the young person rather than standing alone. For instance, we are concerned primarily with the intellectual development of the young person, which cannot be divorced from his/her general motivational and emotional development. The academic standards are subsidiary to, and are supposed to reflect, the development of abilities such as the capacity to think critically, ask investigative questions, look for evidence and argumentation, solve a problem constructively, and communicate systematically and persuasively.

On the basis of these points, we can argue that there ought to be other forms of information that potential employers and educational institutions might find more useful than the standard public exams. Such alternatives could liberate acres of the curriculum from the supposed need to learn facts in order to test knowledge retention. For example, Instead of exams, the suitability of candidates for various kinds of work can be recorded through psychological testing so that institutions and employers can learn about the characteristics, personalities and qualities of the candidates, and about their capacities in relation to work, and whether they are suited to do the work the employer has to offer. Such testing would not require more than minimal preparation.

Potential employers could learn about the student through attending annual or graduation exhibitions organised by the schools. These are occasions when students invite parents and other members of the community to see their work for comment and discussion (see Chapter 11). However, potential employees will usually want pre-packaged information about the student that is less costly to obtain, and standard personality and intelligence tests might perform this kind of function without hijacking the curriculum. Furthermore, the community fairs should not be turned into job markets. This would eventually destroy their community-building function.

A similar point applies to learning portfolios. These should *not* be turned into vehicles for students to sell themselves to potential employers and other institutions. For if we did so then we would be combining so-called 'assessment purposes' in a way that threatens the integrity of pure learning feedback and of learning processes themselves. In this chapter, we have argued for the separation of these purposes. Learning portfolios are ipsative feedback; they are not badges.

One of the major aims of human-centred education is to help each student identify work that is meaningful for them and in which they can excel. Institutions and employers may need to know this kind of information about potential candidates. They need to have standardised as well as the more personalised information in order to be able to make comparisons between candidates based on common and clear standards. However, such standardised information need not consist of GCSEs and A levels, which tend to dominate and direct the curriculum, and thereby make learning a means to employment. Standardised information can include CVs, personal statements, letters of recommendation (from the teachers and the school leaders), personal aptitude tests, intelligence tests and personality maps that do not require such a lengthy and all-consuming preparation.

Clearly, employers do require detailed and personal information about individuals. If someone were to examine those needs strictly on their own terms, without mixing these with academic standards, parental expectations and government dictates, then we would be able to find much more effective ways of providing for those needs that do not involve teaching to test and, worse, forming a curriculum of targets.

Needs of government and the general public for schools' accountability

Public accountability in education needs to be reconceived for three reasons. First, the values that schools and other educational institutions cultivate are primarily non-economic, and therefore, not properly accounted for in terms of cost–benefit analysis. One could try to quantify in monetary terms the value of someone living a better life, but it will inevitably distort and misrepresent the nature of the value because it involves the categorical mistake of confusing instrumental and non-instrumental values.

Second, framing accountability in purely cost–benefit terms fosters the idea that the rational course of action is only the one that maximises net benefit. In other words, it makes maximisation the key concept. This is severely problematic and potentially dangerous because, however much benefit one derives from a process, there could always be more. So, the idea of maximisation leads policy-makers to look at the additional units of benefit that could have been obtained, and never to be satisfied with the good that they already have.

Third, the need for public accountability cannot demand that we turn the education of young people into an exercise for trying to raise scores and to improve one's standing in various league tables. This would undermine the very value of learning. For, as we argued earlier, such a change involves two frightening errors regarding values: first it instrumentalises the process, and second, it substitutes the end-results for their measurement. In other words, it turns a living valuable process into a mere tool for results, and degrades those results into mere measurements. It destroys value. The need for public accountability must not fail to respect the value of what one is supposed to be accountable for! Accountability cannot destroy what it is accounting.

It is difficult to frame correctly the requirements of public accountability in this area. For example, one might state that many students are not developing their full potential and thus imply or suggest that the taxpayers' money is being wasted or not used well. However, this implication presupposes that money has priority over the students and thus, we end up with the idea that students need to be motivated, so they don't waste taxpayers' money. Clearly, this puts the cart before the horse. On the other hand, we cannot ignore economic considerations; we do not want to waste money.

One way of ensuring public accountability is for the students and parents themselves to rate the school's teaching based on the learning and other experiences of the students. In some Nordic countries, the government allocates funds to each individual student based on the young person's (and their parents') decision to choose a particular school. Indeed, students' experiences and parents' feedback on their children's experience can serve as an indication of how well the school has provided for the students' needs for learning and development. Another way to safeguard the school's accountability is through a review carried out by a board of reviewers consisting in external consultants, school governors, teachers, students, parents and members of the community.

Governments need reliable information that is standardised in order to help ensure that the comparative measurement judgements are based on the same scale. However, if such information is gained through student testing, it is not necessary to turn that potentially impersonal information into personalised exam results, which would then become the instrumentalising learning goal: better exam results.

Conclusion

An analysis of exam questions shows that the majority of them test the memorisation of subject knowledge. Of course, this does not mean that students who can analyse, argue, make connections and write well do not perform better than students who cannot do this. These intellectual skills are awarded points. Nevertheless, it remains true that exams generally focus on knowledge retention, and that for most students and teachers to prepare for an exam means to revise, which means to garner knowledge.

In Chapter 2 on learning, we argued that the development of relevant qualities was more important than that of relevant skills, which was more important than the acquisition of the relevant knowledge and information. This is because having the relevant qualities would entail having the motivation and capacity for the value-sensitive judgements that the subject matter requires. For example, it would involve being cautious but decisive in the appropriate way, being attentive to detail but having an overview, or being sceptical in a strategic way. Of course, these qualities cannot be developed without the requisite skills and knowledge, but the point is that, because the qualities are states of being of a person in a way that knowledge and skills are not, the development of the student's qualities is more important for helping a person to grow.

As we saw in Chapter 7, a curriculum built in part around these qualities will look quite different from one that is built on knowledge. This may appear to be a question of emphasis, because existing structures and institutions do not ignore qualities and the person. Many of the themes that we touch on are already present in existing institutions, practices and thought. At root, however, the difference between human-centred and mainstream education is not merely one of emphasis, it is a question of principle and priority.

As we discussed in Chapter 8, focusing on qualities will change pedagogy. Currently, the domination of standardised tests dictates that teaching be focused on imparting knowledge rather than cultivating qualities. As we have seen, pedagogy that is intended for developing the whole person will determine a very different conception of what teaching is.

Noddings (2003) reminds us that the kind of evaluation process to be seriously encouraged in schools should include an ongoing review and examination of questions such as: 'Is education aimed at the student's development as a whole person?', 'Are the goals of curriculum logically derived from such aims?', 'Are our pedagogical methods likely to promote the goals and aims?' and 'How do our routines stack up under this sort of evaluation?' These fundamental questions are ways to reflect on the educational process from a wider perspective. They are essential antidotes to assessment that attends to details in ways that threaten to erode learning. Standardised exams take the joy out of learning. They tend to make students the slaves of a production line mentality. They make many adolescents live in fear of failure, of inadequacy, of being judged by the grades they receive. Such fears make our young persons feel miserable and alienated.

Further reading

Davis, A. (1998) *The Limits of Educational Assessment*. Oxford: Blackwell Publishing.

Hattie, J. and Timperley, H. (2007) The power of feedback. *Review of Educational Research*, (77)1, 81–112.

Kohn, A. (1993) *Punished by Rewards: The Trouble with Gold Stars, Incentive Plans, A's, Praise, and other Bribes*. Boston, MA: Houghton Mifflin Company.

Race, P., and Pickford, R. (2007) *Making Teaching Work*. London: Sage Publications.

10
Young people's experiences of secondary schooling

Introduction

The extended argument of this book has been to support a human-centred approach to education and to examine some of the implications of such an approach for practice in the context of state secondary education in the UK and other parts of the world. Now we would like to start a new thread by supplementing the argument with a review of the perspectives of some young people about some of these issues. In this chapter, we will summarise the views of some young people about secondary schooling, which includes areas that we have already covered, such as the curriculum, teaching and exams.

For this research, we employed the methodology described in Chapter 4. As in that chapter, the principles of selection for the quotes are simple: we have picked out comments for their forcefulness and clarity, and we have avoided repetitive comments. At the same time, we have tried to be as comprehensive as we can in this informal summary by incorporating all comments of significance, including those that conflict with our own views. These interviews were conducted in 2008 and there have been many interesting governmental reforms since then. However, we have tried to select student comments that would still be relevant today.

▶

We undertook this research in order to help us amplify the significance of the human-centred approach in practice. To understand how the approach might best be implemented, it is essential to incorporate students' views about their schooling and education into the deliberations. Such views might agree with the broad conclusions of our argumentation. However, the two might also conflict. Additionally, students' comments can help us understand how the approach can be put into practice. In this light, we read the 50 interviews carefully in order to flag up all the major themes mentioned by the students. We then tried to identify ideas and themes that had not been covered in our previous discussions, so that we could employ these to construct a more complete conclusion. The results of these interviews have helped build a more comprehensive picture of a human-centred learning community in the final chapter.

There are two preliminary observations worth noting here. First, there is a stark difference between the comments we received when interviewing students from different backgrounds and in different educational institutions. Broadly, the young people we interviewed came from three institutions: a group of 14–16-year-olds from a community school in a deprived urban area (group A); a group of 14–16-year-olds from a school in a relatively affluent urban area (group B); and a group of 16–18-year-olds from several sixth-form colleges in a city in south-east England (group C).

In general, students from group A tended to say very little, and were more inclined to respond with short bursts of words, compared to the two other groups. For instance, answers from a group A student to questions such as 'Can you tell me about your experience of secondary education?' would be 'It's pretty all right . . . it's just the breaks and stuff are quite short', or 'Boring. Some of it's OK you know, yeah boring.' In contrast, compare this answer to one from a group B student:

> Boring. I think it's quite long . . . every day is the same . . . or similar . . . or like every week is the same . . . with the same timetable, the same sort of teachers, the same people . . . it just gets boring.

Both of these comments can be contrasted with a response from a young person from group C:

Well...I enjoyed it. Umm...I found it quite difficult at times because I think teachers get a lot of hassle at secondary schools, so maybe you don't get the attention that you should because they are so busy dealing with kids that are disrupting. Also...I think that at secondary school, because I...well I was always really, really shy, until I came to secondary school, but you know, you need to speak out – stuff goes on – I think that's where I learnt to be assertive and that's where I learnt to like get my point of view across – not at the expense of other people but, you know, I'm gonna be myself...and muddle through this...or like telling a teacher that I need help with this...Before, I would have just sat there and thought well, I've got to do this by myself, but it's OK to ask for help.

The differences are very striking especially in terms of their assertiveness and articulation. In general, young people in group C appeared to be more open-minded, and receptive to learning. They also showed more willingness or capacity to enter into the points of view of others. The reasons for such contrast are varied, but here we would speculate that it is partly because of their different social and family backgrounds; partly due to the fact that an age gap of even just 2–3 years would make a difference (see Chapter 5 for more on adolescence).

The second observation from the research is that although the majority of the young people interviewed had complaints about the current system, they didn't often have matching views about educational reforms. When they were prompted with questions asking for alternative ideas of education, many students did not say much. A few suggested improvements. Fewer advocated reforms or innovations, possibly because their own experience is framed within the current educational model.

In this chapter, we report these comments under four headings: (1) the overall experience of secondary schooling; (2) the experiences of exams; (3) young people's perceptions of their teachers; (4) young people's experiences of pedagogy in secondary schools.

The overall experience of secondary schooling

Most young people interviewed said that secondary schools were *boring* because what takes place is too predictable, 'because you know what is going to happen and all of that', as Kai put it. Extracts from the extended comments of Bob and Claire (who were both in sixth-form college at the time of the research) recalling their secondary school experience summarise the point well:

[Bob] . . . well in my experience of secondary school . . . I went to school, did my work, had a few friends there and came away at the end of the day and that was it. It wasn't that exciting. Well, I wouldn't say I didn't enjoy it, but I wouldn't say I specifically enjoyed it. It was something that I had to do. I made some very good friends there, I had a good time at times, I had a bad time at others, but I'm not sure if it could have been much different really . . . it's school isn't it? For school it [my experience] wasn't bad.

[Claire] Oh God . . . it felt like a struggle all the way through . . . it is being under attack and kind of having to like shove your way through every day in like . . . just thinking . . . oh God, I can't wait until I can go home. I mean, there were good times, there were definitely good times, like funny things happened and obviously it's where I met all of my friends – well not all of them – but a lot of people and I suppose it's a major growing period for your life. It's like where you go from being a child to an adult . . . so it's a massive, massive experience. I feel . . . a lot of my time spent there . . . I just felt really resentful against all of the things . . . It felt like the school really didn't give a damn about what we thought, it was almost like this great big meat processor . . . it felt like you were put through a machine, so that you're kind of ground out as this end product and it doesn't really matter what happens to you on the way and it doesn't really matter how you feel and I think it's not necessarily the teachers' fault because they are having to stick to the rules and the policies the school makes. But I don't know who the hell makes a lot of the rules there . . . it's like the Governors . . . who the hell are they? . . . It's like a few weird parents who don't actually come into the school . . .

Some students regarded schooling as 'training you to be obedient', 'to stop questioning' and 'how to put up with things'. Here is an extended quote from a 17-year-old:

[*in schools, you learn*] how to put up with things, shut up and be docile basically [laughter]. I think a lot of state learning, a lot of learning is training you to be obedient and training you to stop questioning why you are doing things and to just do them . . . because, I mean there probably is a lot of that in life . . . but at the same time I kind of miss that part of myself which kind of used to question things. These days I just kind of just go 'oh yes, whatever' and just do things because it makes it simpler to just go through the system, but . . . I remember being really . . . angry . . . with having to jump through hoops rather than learning actual skills for later life.

A few of the students articulated how schools might be less dull and more inspiring:

It would be good if education can make our life at school interesting. Lessons are often quite boring and dull. Make it fun and hands-on and experiential, so people don't get bored with just like looking up at the board.

Despite the fact that most of our interviewees found school boring, some reported that school days 'can be exciting', especially when there were the subjects that they enjoyed. Students seemed to be most willing to engage in a class if they loved the subject or liked the teacher.

Overall, the adolescents interviewed in our research were least satisfied with education between 14 and 16 years of age – Years 9–11 at an English secondary school. They felt that schooling was a struggle, and merely something they are forced to do. The pressure of taking their GCSEs seemed to have contributed to their feeling of dissatisfaction.

In general, most of the secondary school students (aged 14–16) interviewed felt that the institutions they were in were very impersonal. Some said that students were considered merely as numbers in an institution rather than as individuals. They felt that they were not listened to, or respected for their opinions.

Young people didn't seem to like the culture of conformity at secondary schools. They said that there were unnecessary rules, such as the insistence on the type of trainers to wear at school. Several of the adolescents in our research described the experience of secondary school as being expected to behave like an adult (by the rules and disciplines) but being treated like a child (because they were not listened to or allowed to take real responsibilities).

Sadly, when we asked the young people to describe good and bad experiences in their lives, none of them identified their school experiences as good. The participants connected 'good experience' exclusively with events outside school, such as holidays, family gatherings and outings with friends. Such events were described as 'joyful', 'fun', when 'everyone was happy'. School was not associated with having a good time together. One student mentioned that one good experience was 'a ski trip with the school . . . that was just a chance to forget about the school'. In contrast, many interviewees identified bad experiences, such as being bullied, with school.

Nearly all participants mentioned their relationships and friendship with peers as the most important aspect of their school life. Young people articulated a need to be with others, and they saw school as the one of the few places where they could spend time with their friends. Yet, many of the young people we interviewed reported that having close relationships and friendships at school could be at the same time stressful. The girls in particular confirmed having difficulties with friendship groups, especially between the ages of 14 and 16. Rowena explained:

> I'd say that secondary school is the time when you are just starting to get an insight into this life after being sheltered by parents for the last 14 years. So, there's a lot of insecurities there.

The notion that *the world is a tougher and darker place* seemed to be accepted by many of the young people. Rosa, aged 17, told us that the difficulties in her social life at secondary school helped her learn how to cope with the toughness of life.

> I think all secondary schools, well at least most secondary schools, are really rough, but I think that's good, because it helps you get strong in yourself and learn how to deal with the world and its rough sides really . . . I think it kind of breaks you down, your self-esteem. I think a lot of people go downhill and it takes quite a while to build back up. But also you, um, I don't know, it helps, it helped me, like, being able to think of 'come-backs' and like have experience with, . . . um . . . really confrontational people and become a lot more confident in that area. So if I was just brought up in say a civic community where everyone was really lovely to each other, then I would be a lot more sensitive and I would just, it would just be really horrible to have to go into quite a darker world.

A few of the adolescents in our research expressed the view that it was *character-building* to endure the negative aspects of their social experience at secondary school. Especially in large schools, students can be affected negatively by peer pressure and bullying, but some also saw this as a learning process. Students' views of peer pressure vary; some thought it was positive: 'it makes you want to be as clever as friends, and you then put more effort into work', said one 15-year-old. Even sitting in a class with disruptive students was an important experience for some. Such experiences are not available if one is at home or in a very small school environment. One student had been home-schooled for part of her secondary education. She told us that it was not fruitful for her at that age because of the lack of society and companionship of others.

Training to become tougher through secondary education was accompanied by a lack of emotional support within secondary schools. One student recalled how she became angry at the age of 14/15 and rebelled against her family. She was drinking a lot of alcohol and was in danger from drug abuse. However, no help came from her school, despite her cries for support.

According to some students, PSHE (personal, social and health education) was a very important aspect of secondary education for them, especially when it was well designed and programmed. They thought that it could help them learn about themselves, relationships and emotions, and about taking responsibilities. Many of the young people reported that they were interested in understanding their emotions such as anger and anxiety and would appreciate the opportunity to talk about these with someone whom they could trust.

In addition to schools being perceived as places for socialising with peers and developing friendships and bonds with other young people, these adolescents realised that, through schooling experience, they could begin to develop broader interests, find out more about the world, and about themselves, and above all, learn to become more confident and independent individuals.

Overall, from the comments of the young people interviewed, they seemed to feel that there was a stereotypical and unhelpful attitude against learning from which they were unable to escape. Some young people said that it was generally considered 'uncool' to learn in secondary schools. The idea of 'uncool' consists of working hard or trying to please the teachers. One girl said that she was called the 'teacher's pet' when she showed enthusiasm in lessons.

Although learning was perceived 'uncool', many of the students stressed the importance of personal achievement in schools as a way to build self-confidence and boost self-esteem. Personal achievement was not limited to academic attainment in these youngsters' eyes. They listed a number of things such as winning at sports, being in a band, putting on a play, winning the school's version of *The Apprentice*, etc. They emphasised the importance of feeling that one is good at something and of having accomplished something well.

The young people also felt that it was very significant to have these achievements acknowledged by parents, teachers and peers. On this note, some young people mentioned that more could be done through the 'Gifted and Talented' programme run in some schools, such as through a talent show. As we shall see, some students recognised that, with more self-confidence, they had been more able to resist the peer-pressure to be cool, and because of this, they could find value in their studies.

As mentioned earlier, there were several students from FE colleges or sixth-form colleges. From what these young people said, it seemed that in such institutions, education 'felt like more about the students learning rather than the teachers teaching' (while in the state secondary school it was the reverse, as these young people recalled their prior experience). They reported that, in colleges, the young people were more willing to participate in academic learning and that there tended to be a 'better class environment and atmosphere'.

The sixth-formers also pointed out that, at college, they were more likely to be respected, to be allowed to make decisions for themselves, and to be trusted in their independence. They felt more like adults than children.

A few students who had been to alternative schools, such as a Steiner School, found that they were freer to develop and learn at their own pace in those institutions; and that teaching and learning was more creative and more centred on each individual student. A student summarised that, in the alternative school, 'it didn't feel like school, rather it was a place for learning'. George was the only person we interviewed who had been to three kinds of school: alternative, independent and state schools. Here, he summarises the differences:

> The Steiner School is the kind for creativity and they sort of allow you to develop at your own speed. They sort of don't push academic work onto you too early, but then, as I got older, I started to find that I didn't feel that I was being challenged, so then I went to the prep school which was really good in terms of getting a lot of individual tutoring from the teachers. I learnt a lot because I was being catered for individually because the classes were so small, which is really good. I suppose the negative aspect of being in that school was the lack of diversity of the students. Everyone was from a similar background and I don't really agree with the whole idea behind private schooling. So, I mean, there's that negative aspect. But there's no doubt that the education I got there was much better than what I had at the state school I went to afterwards, which was sort of, you just sort of . . . they want to put you in a box with everyone else, you don't really get taught as an individual, or treated like an individual.
>
> I suppose each establishment I've been in has taught me different things, so the Steiner School gave me a good sort of creative ability to express myself creatively I suppose. When I went to prep school, that kind of gave me confidence in my sort of academic ability and then when I went to state school, because it was such a mixture of a variety of people, I sort of . . . socially that was good for me to sort of meet a lot of different sorts of people.

The experiences of exams

The young people interviewed singled out exams as the main reason why they did not enjoy schooling. 'Exams are so stressful', 'unfair evaluation', 'testing your ability to answer exam questions and not testing your knowledge' and 'I think if I didn't have exams I'd be fine' were common remarks.

Many of the young people criticised exams as unfair. For instance, a sixth-former talked about how ridiculous it was to have long exams, sometimes on the same day:

> I think it's a fault – not only of the education system, but the governing system. That's where I see the problem. You know, it's so intense and it's too difficult, there's too much – something that has really frustrated me is that they put some exams on the same day. So, for example, one of my friends does politics and philosophy – both of which are three-hour exams, three hours of essay writing exams on the same day. That's six hours of essay writing.

Additionally, students pointed out that grades based on exams are not equivalent to learning. They may reveal only that one has learned how to pass exams. Here Sally (16 years old) explains:

> It's not about how you understand a subject; it's about how you can say exactly what they want you to say. Like in chemistry at the moment, you have to give an exact definition, you have to quote the ones out of the book, even if you understand it and you can write it a different way, then you only get two grades. I know I didn't have a very good exam technique last year and I was getting Us and stuff. So I inspected absolutely every single past exam paper and I (now) got loads of As – just because I knew how to answer the exam questions.

Sally can see clearly that this kind of exam does not encourage learning.

> I don't think it is really learning. I think it kind of doesn't make you stand on your own two feet and learn yourself. They kind of spoon-feed you as well. It doesn't give you the skills of how to learn and how to use knowledge. You need to be analytical, which I think is useful, but you have to know how to play the exam game and if you don't then . . .

Merriam pointed out that schooling should not be driven by exams, and this should change so that education is about learning:

> When you are in primary school everything is geared towards SATs, then when you get to secondary, everything is geared to your GCSEs . . . But I

think that education should not be driven by exams and sort of . . . run by exams . . . because that sort of dominates it . . . which I think shouldn't be the point of education. Education should be about learning . . . achieving things.

Many felt that they were put under tremendous pressure by exams and tests. Grace's (17) comments here capture the feeling well:

I think the exam system that we have to go through is way too strenuous and I don't think it works with everyone. . . . I don't always think that just, like, rigid three-hour essay-writing exams are the right way to test actually people's intelligence, or maybe that . . . does people's intelligencc really need to be tested to such a level? Maybe some people aren't interested in politics and history – maybe some people want to demonstrate their understanding of the world in different ways . . . I think the whole thing . . . it's too set . . . I think we have to find different ways of assessing, you know, how everyone sees the world and how everyone wants to learn in their own way.

However, quite a number of the young people expressed the need for some kind of evaluation and measurement of their learning, which would allow them to feel that they had accomplished something. Although they thought that a more accurate assessment or evaluation was done by their teachers, at the same time, they concluded that assessment conducted purely by the class or subject teacher would be problematic. This was because, they pointed out, some subject teachers only saw the group of students once every fortnight. This makes the students truly mere 'numbers on the school register book'. Therefore, the young people simply didn't believe that these teachers were able to mark their work according to their knowledge of the student as a person.

Many of the students expressed an ambivalent attitude towards exams, such as this 15-year-old, who was preparing for her GCSEs. She first said that exams were too stressful, that one's mind could go blank at such pressure. Then she explained that exams could sometimes show a person's learning even if not very accurately:

Sometimes in exams you get a bit nervous or you can't remember something because your mind goes blank. But it does sometimes show your learning, or it does represent your learning, but not accurately. I think, maybe, the only way you could possibly measure it is, like, through your teacher really, because they know everything that you can do, like, when it's not a test . . . so I don't know . . . it's quite hard really to do that.

Such ambivalence is not uncommon amongst students who are preparing for GCSEs perhaps because of the messages their parents and teachers had given them about the importance of acquiring good GCSEs. For example, Sally (17 years old) said:

> To go to University you need to have A levels. If you don't, you can't get in and to get a good job nowadays, yes you need to have qualifications. So it's, like, if you don't go to secondary school your life goes downhill – that's what we are taught.

In general, nearly all the young people we interviewed had complaints against exams and many expressed criticisms of the exam system. However, only a few could suggest alternatives approaches, despite the fact that many articulated the need for measurements. Some of the alternatives mentioned were: coursework, portfolios of artwork, oral examinations and completing practical tasks.

Young people's perception of their teachers

Young people confirmed that the quality of their experiences at school was dependent on the teachers they worked with. The students reported that a good teacher who was caring and passionate about the subject he/she was teaching would often make their own experiences good and make them love studying the subject too. Tina (17 years old) explained why she loved her sixth-form college so much:

> The teachers are stunning – they are really genuine and they care. They are so passionate about their subject, which makes you so passionate about what you are studying, which I absolutely love . . .

The students' choice of subjects for GCSEs and A levels was sometimes determined by their impression of the teachers of these subjects. Some said that they worked hard because they liked a particular teacher, and that if the teacher was not a nice person, they would not choose a subject even if they might have liked it.

They also reported that the quality of their learning was dependent on how well they thought their teacher taught. For example, Kate (17) said that Spanish should have been one of her favourite subjects because her family had spent many holidays in Spain, and she was motivated to learn the language. Nevertheless, Kate said that she was not doing well in Spanish because of a 'bad' teacher:

> It usually doesn't just boil down to the subject itself, I think the teacher has the greatest impact on how you feel about that subject. I like Spanish but I

am not doing very well at the moment . . . I don't know, but I think my teacher is really bad . . . I suppose I could try harder, but it just doesn't work that way . . . I'm not motivated to try harder . . . because the teacher isn't very good. I mean . . . I know he tries . . .

Many students remarked that teachers need to give their students more individual guidance and support. For instance, 15-year-old Marcus expressed this with respect to his coursework:

I would prefer to get more time to complete course work . . . in English for example . . . we would have had, like, two lessons to start our coursework and then we would have to finish it at home . . . so maybe, like, a bit more time in school to, like, sort of start our coursework and [the teacher] put us in the right direction and all that, and then we can go home and talk about it and finish it off. I think it's good [to do the course work at school] because you've always got the teacher there in class and all that. Otherwise it's hopeless, like . . . [at home] I'll just, like, go on the internet and muck around on MSN or whatever, go and get some food and watch TV, but not actually do my homework.

Rowena (17) linked this need for individual attention to the question of teachers' respect for their students:

Teachers should be much more respectful of the children – really listening to them. But because a lot of the time the teachers are really stressed, so they don't have time, or can't be bothered to listen to the children, or students. This is another cycle really . . .

Another young person (15) suggested that such respect was reciprocal: if a teacher showed respect to the students, then he/she would receive it too:

I really got on well with my art teacher – actually, yes, my art teacher was the only person that I really felt I could connect with as a person and not just as a teacher. She was a lot more jokey than other teachers. Um . . . I don't know, I guess that art is so important to me and we both shared that, that was sort of like a connection; so I wasn't disrespectful to her, and I listened to her, and therefore she respected me and that was kind of positive reinforcement sort of thing.

Rowena also mentioned a cycle of disrespect that she thought was caused by the strict disciplinary approach that many teachers adopt:

Well, I would completely change the way student teachers are taught how to approach children who are disrespectful to the teachers. At the moment, apparently, when you are training to be a teacher in state education, you are taught to be really firm and really strict at the beginning, and then slowly regain people's trust, which I think is really bad and it makes you not respect the teacher at all and then you'll be more rebellious and that leads down to a cycle of not working because you don't care.

If teachers can respect the individual as a person then this might create more of a learning culture. Kate recalls her experience here:

What I noticed . . . what really hit me when I moved to college . . . was that I was respected as a person, as a young person. Yes like I said, not just like another figure in the classroom, which was amazing. I'm really good friends with some of my teachers and there is so much more an atmosphere of wanting to learn, partly because students are respected so that makes them want to learn.

Like the previous ones, this comment suggests that teachers can improve the learning environment by seeing beyond the student-teacher roles that often define the classroom setting, and instead perceiving themselves and the young people more often as persons, who potentially share an interest in a subject or a field of knowledge.

Interestingly, only sixth-formers mentioned their experience of being respected by their teachers, whereas none of the adolescents in the secondary schools mentioned such experiences.

Young people's experiences of pedagogy in secondary schools

As one might expect, the comments about pedagogy tended to echo those regarding teachers. For example, Claire criticised teaching that followed pre-ordained scripts and treated students like robots without attending to their individual needs:

Teachers are trained to do one certain script and if people are acting up or being difficult, then they are trained to act in this way . . . Do this, this and this and it doesn't work and people just get more and more frustrated . . . they should respond to people more and listen to what students need, rather than kind of just following a script all the time . . . because people aren't robots . . .

Several students emphasised this point but from different angles: for instance, by stressing the need to acknowledge the different abilities and preferences students have in their approach to learning. Several commented that they would appreciate more differentiation in the way they are taught and encouraged to learn. George said that if there were one thing that could be changed in secondary education, it would be for teaching to be 'more based around the individual':

> I think everyone has got different abilities, everyone's good at different things and you can't really just put everyone in the same box and say 'you should be able to do this at this age' or 'you should be learning this at that age' . . .

Others made a similar comment about learning styles, such as this quote from Mimi (15):

> I think it would be better if there was a much more individual to the student's needs approach in education. . . . some students learn very well the sort of facts being bombarded at them and then go and sit an exam at the end stuff. Some prefer practical learning and some maybe the course work sort of style things – yeah.

Grace pinpointed another facet of the lack of individual attention in the classroom: there are many quiet students, who are usually ignored, who may end up not feeling worthy of attention and who lose the opportunity to develop:

> I know that there are some people that will go through the whole of secondary school thinking they are not worthy of that attention, or that they are not the people that that help is designated for – like those quiet kids that just sit there and try and do it by themselves . . . and I think that's wrong because everyone deserves the same opportunity, but they're not getting it.

Several students linked the lack of respect and care for the individual to the highly controlled or disciplined environment of secondary schools. The following comment from a 16-year-old may remind us of Rowena's earlier observations about the cycle of discipline and disrespect:

> The thing I most disliked, especially in P School – is that there is a lot of control. We used to call it P Prison Camp. It had this massive fence going round the whole of the school with barbed wire on top . . . and they installed lots of security cameras . . . and they were really strict on uniform and stuff like that, so I used to get quite told off and have loads of detentions and stuff because I just didn't want to be controlled in that way and

it was just so disrespectful in some ways, but I guess they had to otherwise the really disruptive people would just go overboard. So I didn't like how they kind of had to clamp down on you.

Many students expressed the desire for more freedom to choose what and when to learn. Claire articulated this view clearly:

I think it [secondary education] would have been much better if we had been allowed to make more of our own choices . . . and sort of . . . I mean . . . I don't mean that it should be tailor-made to every single person because obviously, it's too much work and everyone's individual, but I think that one of the things that frustrated me most and therefore one of the things that I would change was the way that they didn't make any allowance for people's sort of individual . . . like way of learning . . . or something . . .

In a similar vein, Rowena reported that college education was more motivating because she was able to choose topics connected with what she wanted to do in the future:

If you choose subjects at college that you feel are going to be really bene-ficial to your future, because you really feel passionately about them, then you are surrounded by that and you can really talk and relate to your teachers about them and they can help you follow that course. 'Being cool' has kind of dissolved because people are a lot more confident about themselves and being who they want to be, so pressure – peer pressure – doesn't get in the way as much . . . um . . . and kind of you know that you want an education and that's going to help you in your future. It's amazing; it's so refreshing.

It is interesting how she links this choice to an increased feeling of self-confidence, which allows her to transcend counterproductive peer pressure. Many students mentioned the need to strengthen self-confidence: here is a comment from 16-year-old Peter:

We should be taught how to talk to other people and express our ideas . . . we sort of only feel we can talk to people in our group . . . so I think . . . and another thing is confidence . . . schools and education should give us enough confidence and sort of . . . you need to . . . give people confidence in what they are doing, then they will feel like they can do things.

This was also the main concern that the students expressed about ability-setting (or streaming). Although streaming may be good for those in higher sets, students pointed out that it was not so good for those in the lower ones because it destroyed their confidence. Generally, the lower-ability students get the worse teachers, lack motivation in class, and often do not make good progress. Once streamed, students are labelled, put into a box throughout their schooling. Here are one student's (15) comments:

> Putting students in sets of their ability, I just think . . . I don't know, it's a bit rubbishy. I started in a low set for . . . maths or something and you do realise that if you are in a low set for one subject you are not going to get better because you are with all the students who aren't good and you get the worst teacher . . . and it's such a bad way of doing things.

Grace shared a similar concern about the problems of streaming:

> I don't think it's right that kids should be sort of set into categories – you're the clever people, you're the alrightish people and you're, you're just thick. I think that's wrong because how are you supposed to motivate children when they are banded like that?

Some adolescents we interviewed seemed to be dissatisfied with learning that was geared primarily towards remembering facts. They appeared to want to understand more. Here are George's comments:

> I thought that a lot of what you had to do, well in psychology anyway, wasn't really about understanding the subject, it was more sort of about learning a lot of facts, but you didn't have to understand anything. Like you could get an A without actually having any understanding of the subject, which is a bit irritating.

In a similar vein, 16-year-old Kane felt that the syllabus was adhered to too rigidly. This did not allow for questions, and as a result, much of the time, what he was told to learn did not make sense to him:

> It means that . . . the important thing is learning what's on the syllabus, rather than learning what's useful. Like you learn something, but then you won't learn the other half of it, you'll just learn half truths just because it's on the syllabus – even if you question the teacher like 'that doesn't make any sense'. It's like well 'that's what you're meant to learn'. But it doesn't actually make any sense.

Several students wanted a much broader range of activities at school, as 15-year-old Matt pointed out:

> Schools should offer a range of activities which while they are educational are motivating. I wouldn't have anything like this, too boring, and that's because it can affect their [the students'] behaviour.

Several students mentioned non-academic subjects and extra-curriculum activities as more motivating. However, the reasons were varied – some students felt that learning should be 'relaxing' and 'enjoyable' and only the non-academic qualified; others said that they needed breaks from the routine of academic classroom learning. According to Sally:

> My drama classes in Years 10 and 11 – they were fantastic. I loved them! . . . The breaks from the routine were often the best bits and that's why drama was always good, because you weren't sitting behind a desk . . . you were kind of running around and doing crazy things and having warm-up games and what have you . . .

Similarly, Tessa felt that drama engaged all students, even the usually disruptive ones:

> Drama is fun because they get you actively involved in it – it's enjoyable and also because it's enjoyable and active the usually badly behaved kids won't behave badly because they are enjoying the lesson.

Some students linked these activities to the discovery of what they were good at. For example, Nathan (15) talked enthusiastically about sports as an extra-curriculum activity, because through participating in tennis training, he discovered that he was really good at it. Nathan said that the best experience he had at school was 'winning my tennis tournament because it made me proud and I felt I was good at something'.

In a similar vein, students mentioned that work placements and visits to universities had left a lasting impression, sometimes inspiring and usually confidence-building. Millie (15) said that she was the first person in her extended family to want to go to college for further education and thereafter university for higher education:

> Yeah it has influenced me because they organise trips where you go to university . . . it just helps you get experience of what it's like, and makes you think that you can do it too.

Pat (15), who considered herself shy and timid, found that role-playing during English lessons had given her the confidence to want to become a journalist:

> You got to do your own newspaper reports . . . I had to go round to interview people, and acted like a news reporter, and things like that . . . and since then I've always wanted to be a journalist . . . it was really good fun and I think it will help me lots in the future . . .

Students also commented that a broad programme would allow them to organise themselves, make discoveries as they explored and identify their interests and focus. George talked about his experience of sorting out his own ideas within a broad framework:

> I am doing Fine Art, which is quite . . . well it's really broad . . . you can do anything you want really. It's more about sorting out your own ideas, what you are interested in, and then you can think up whatever you want to do really within that. It's challenging to start with, 'cause you really need to think hard, and make up your mind about it. It is hard 'cause you were never told to think for yourself before . . .

This kind of comment can be contrasted fruitfully with Claire's reflections on her graphics course. She had no idea what to expect from the subject, what she was supposed to learn and why. It took two years before Claire felt she could understand what graphics was about:

> Sadly, I didn't realise that graphics was a lot more than just doodling and colouring in . . . which is why I kind of felt like I was a bit . . . was completely directionless for almost two years in graphics . . . it was like being dumped in the middle of the ocean and being told to swim to land . . . we didn't know what to expect at all . . .

These last two observations diverge: the first wants free space to explore in and the second a set of expectations. However, their combination echoes a theme central to Chapters 7 and 8, namely that making autonomous choices requires a background of good understanding, and thus when necessary, guidance.

Some of the students emphasised the importance of novel approaches towards more academic studies. First, a few students mentioned the importance of experiential learning. Alex, a Year 10 student, gave the example of how a demonstration in a science lesson enlivened a topic for him:

> I remember a lesson in Mr W's class. We were learning about the digestive system and he did like a little experiment where he put food in a bag and then he put acid in the bag and mixed it all up and then he showed like all the process of digestion and I thought it was really interesting.

Second, several students mentioned the need for integrating different areas of knowledge. 14-year-old Merriam regarded 'theme days' as 'a stroke of genius':

> Themed days . . . I thought that was just a stroke of genius because I think it would be really cool to have all the subjects sort of rolled into one . . . having a theme. I think it would help it become more interesting in . . . like our subjects because it would be about something . . . it wouldn't just be blankly staring at a book for the sake of getting it down . . .

In a similar spirit, Rowena explained that the connection between different concepts and areas of the curriculum should be made more explicit so that students don't just learn 'parts of things which weren't linked and therefore they just didn't make sense'.

Third, several students commented on the value of active group discussions, which encourage participation and independent thinking. Students also see such discussions as good for entering into other people's points of view. Grace said how much she benefited from discussions:

> Well something that has been really good at college is that there is a lot of discussion and so you get to learn a lot of different people's points of view and their interpretations of things. And when I've had trouble grasping things, you know, a friend that has understood has been really helpful and good at communicating something that I haven't understood and that's . . . that didn't really happen in secondary school – like it was all about the teacher . . . but at college . . . yeah there is a lot of discussion and that's really impacted on my learning.

In general, the young people we interviewed from college felt that there was a huge gap between their classroom experiences at secondary school and at sixth-form college. Here Grace describes college as:

> A really nice change from secondary school I'd say – because it was a lot more about the students rather than just about the teacher teaching something. It was about everyone participating – everyone getting their point of view across, like regardless of how broadly people thought about an issue . . . like everything was important; and like I always felt listened to in my classes and that I could say things like whenever I felt something important needed to be said or something like that and also the whole environment of the class, like the walls . . . just the way they're decorated. Like the teachers have really made an effort and it sort of enthuses the way you feel about the subject – like you are really in a real good learning environment, and it is fun to learn, if you know what I mean . . .

Grace's brief account above summarises the views of some of the young people being interviewed. In addition, they pointed out four important assumptions that should underpin all classroom practices:

1. The focus of classroom practice should be students' learning rather than teacher's teaching, or the delivery of the curriculum content.

2. Students are not empty vessels to be filled; they are active participants in the process of their own learning – they need to be listened to, respected for their

ideas, and encouraged to work in collaboration with one another and with the teacher.

3. The environment where students find themselves should be conducive to their learning – a warm atmosphere to make students feel relaxed and comfortable, visual stimulation to enthuse the students, and so forth.

4. Learning should be fun, exciting and enriching. Hence the importance of 'having a laugh during school time'.

Conclusions

As we said at the beginning of the chapter, we reviewed the interviews carefully in order to identify the major themes that emerged from the young people's experience of schools. These major themes were as follows:

1. Many young people feel bored with their experience of secondary education. Some of this boredom seems to be due to a lack of variety in their daily activities. However, some of the boredom seems to have a deeper root: a feeling of estrangement or disengagement with the learning processes at school.

2. Many of the students whom we interviewed felt that they were a part of a mechanical and impersonal system that did not care for them as individuals or even regard them as such. Some reported that this environment fostered feelings of disaffection with the school and unruly behaviour patterns, which bolster the apparent need for an impersonal system. Students reported a similar cycle of disrespect with regard to discipline and control. However, in theory the solution is simple: many of the students reiterated their desire to be treated as individuals.

3. Several young people mentioned that they felt controlled at school, and that they lacked independence and choice.

4. Quite a few students mentioned the need for feeling accomplished.

5. The young people stressed the importance of relationships.

For some of them, in particular the ones who had moved on to sixth-form and were studying in colleges, a reflection on their 14–16 education provided clearer insights into the inherent problems existing in state secondary schools.

11
Building learning communities – humanising schools

Introduction

We think that a clear argument has emerged throughout this book in terms of the meaning of human-centred education, the relevant concepts and a set of principles pertaining to curriculum, pedagogy and feedback for learning. We have drawn on some interviews to illustrate these insights by referring to young people's perceptions of their experience of adolescence and of secondary education in the UK. In this chapter, we shall characterise what a human-centred learning community (as opposed to a school) might look like. This provides another opportunity to discuss how the different aspects of educational endeavours interact within an institution designed to nurture learning and human flourishing.

As we explained earlier, this book strives to integrate the strengths of both mainstream education and its alternative counterpart into a human-centred vision. In this final chapter, we shall continue to do so through the following three steps:

1. We take a critical view of mainstream schooling. As part of this process, we will also analyse possible reasons why the mainstream schooling system is so 'seductive' by taking a closer look at the non-educational practical benefits it offers.

▶

2. We examine the institutional structure of radical alternative schools, and explore their strengths, but also analyse why radical alternative institutions have never truly succeeded in replacing mainstream schooling.

3. We propose a third option with the intention to combine the strengths of both mainstream and alternative/progressive schools. This will constitute our vision of a human-centred learning community. In the process, we will revisit some of the main points already developed in previous chapters and integrate them in this idea of a learning community. We will also use examples of educational projects in the UK and other parts of the world to illustrate how our ideas of curriculum, pedagogy and feedback can be incorporated in the day-to-day practice of a learning community.

Education and schooling

Let's take a brief look at the differences between education and schooling. In Chapter 1 we pointed out that there are three broad types of educational aim: social, academic and personal. We maintain that the third, the personal, ought to have priority over the other two, and can be used to adjudicate between the requirements and recommendations of the others. Embedded in this position is the rejection of the theory of instrumental rationality, and its dominant position in influencing the conception of education (such as that elaborated in a business model of education – see, for example, Greene, 2002). We have argued that education should not simply be a means to different ends, but rather, various forms of activity engaged in for their own sake (see Chapter 1). Such educative activities include the process of cultivating values, virtues and other qualities that make us more fully human, as well as connecting to knowledge beyond us.

The question is: how does an educational institution meet such aims? Undoubtedly, schooling is not equivalent to education. We do not reject training and other processes associated with human development, provided that human beings are not being treated merely as a means to an end. However, schooling as it is currently conceived and structured in mainstream education serves mostly as a means to social, political and economic ends. Even when the human development agenda is brought in, as we have already seen, it tends to instrumentalise learning as a means to the development of the individual.

Understandably, schooling must address other very complex concerns, such as providing the young person with the means necessary to continue studying, and to work well. Although these concerns don't have to instrumentalise the person or learning, nevertheless, when schooling focuses on external goals, it usually fails to respect the students as persons or encourage them to appreciate more deeply the valuable aspects of living.

What are the possible reasons why schooling has been perceived as merely instrumental? David Carr characterises a (state) school as 'a social institution that is provided for out of public funds, and is to that extent accountable to the desires of taxpayers and their democratically elected political representatives' (Carr, 2003: 15). This description details the state school's obligations of accountability including those of meeting parents' wishes for their children's future and policy-makers' social, economic and political agendas. This implies that schooling is a means to an end.

In the context of schooling, accountability is concerned with the kind of checks democratic societies ought to use to ensure that children and young people have been provided with the opportunity to receive a good education. The school's responsibility is to be accountable to the communities and institutions that support and fund it, including parents, employers and the state, as well as specialist professionals. This underpins the school's overriding emphasis on measurable results and outcomes, and its narrow approach to learning (see our critique on this conception in Chapters 2 and 3). School inspections, exams and, most recently, school report cards are important measures to ensure accountability. The school's goals are often motivated by its concern for students' measurable attainment, hence the concentration of effort on improving the performance of teachers and students. Under these assumptions, leadership is mostly about ensuring that the school maintains and improves students' academic performances. In the present educational climate, schools failing to achieve good exam results face being put into 'special measures' and ultimately closure.

Schools juggle between parents' desires and policy-makers' agendas. What parents want for their children does not always coincide with what government needs. Take the example of the James Dyson Foundation's plan to build a Dyson School of Design Innovation.[1] According to an article entitled 'James Dyson on his fight to build a design school' (*Guardian*, 23 September 2008), the new school was meant to cater for the next generation of inventors, engineers and designers. It would teach young people of 14–16 years of age on a part-time basis through day-release from school, and 16–19-year-olds full time. The curriculum would largely be project-based, stressing hands-on learning and problem-solving. Successful projects could be marketed commercially.

---

[1] The Dyson proposal for the Academy did not come to fruition because of a dispute over land use for the proposed site.

The motivation for sponsoring a new school like this is manifold. Apart from encouraging innovative design, creativity and entrepreneurship, the Dyson School's rationale was also that there are vacancies for trained engineers, and that the British education system needs to produce what its economy needs. Obviously, this satisfies the policy-makers' agenda of not losing 'British competitiveness' in the international market of design, technology and engineering. The government certainly sees the potential of such a school in helping maintain the key role that British engineering plays in the world economy. What about parents? According to the *Guardian* article, the debates on the pros and cons of the school were fierce. Many parents do not regard engineering and design technology as 'serious' A level subjects, and more parents would like their children to prepare for a professional life rather than a vocational training. No doubt the parents' desire is linked to their concern that some jobs (such as manufacturing and product design) might not provide their children with a sufficient livelihood or social status.

In this example, we can see that both policy-makers' and parents' concerns are thoroughly instrumental, and hence presuppose the view that schooling is supposed to cater for aims other than purely educational ones. Perhaps it is not an exaggeration to suggest that schooling has not been able to lead to individuals' flourishing because what is happening in school is conceived of in mostly instrumental terms, as training and moulding instead of educating. In this spirit, teaching is about instructing and delivering fixed curriculum content, and learning is narrowly conceptualised as acquiring knowledge and skills.

The question we need to address is this: can structured schooling be truly educational?

Mainstream approaches to schooling

Mainstream secondary schools operate as institutions whose aims are mostly instrumental. The main purpose of education in the current schooling system is to prepare the young person for adult life in both a civic and an economic sense, including, in particular, cultivating economically useful skills for one's own livelihood and for strengthening the nation's competitiveness in the global economy. Indeed, the marketisation of education has made authors such as Michael Fielding and Peter Moss claim that 'Today in England, we have the worst kind of school system' (Fielding and Moss, 2010: 134). So it might seem at odds with this, if we make a few positive points about the current endeavour.

One of the strengths of mainstream schooling is its insistence on academic rigour. This is reflected in the ongoing search for diverse approaches to raising academic standards. Although many have critiqued the relentless reforms in the mainstream schooling system, which have become part of a wider political agenda, such efforts nevertheless give people hope for improvement. (As we pointed out, the rigour can only be a service to education when it steps out of the vicious cycle of standardising what is taught in schools, monitored by statistical outputs, as apparent evidence of the success or failure of students, teachers and education itself.)

Another significant strength of the mainstream state system is its commitment to making the same high quality of education available to all, regardless of their backgrounds, abilities, aptitudes and needs. Given the great diversity, this is a hugely laudable task, which may seem to require a detailed centralised curriculum and standardised testing and evaluation, which we disagreed in Chapter 9.

Furthermore, most mainstream schools are supposed to be non-selective, and are intended to be inclusive and to embrace diversity among students. For adolescents, such diversity provides an opportunity to encounter people from different cultures and backgrounds. This can be enriching for the individual. It also helps keeps society multicultural.

In addition to making schooling accessible to students from all backgrounds, mainstream schools also offer free meals for students from poorer families. These efforts to narrow the social gap through education are honourable and praiseworthy. Furthermore, mainstream schools are often equipped to provide specialist care and support to those students who have special educational needs.

However, there are other aspects of mainstream secondary schools that are disservices to adolescents. First, as we saw from the interviews in Chapter 10, mainstream secondary schools tend to be impersonal, and often show little respect for the students as individual persons (Wallace, 2009). As impersonal institutions, schools are governed by a set of externally imposed rules, such as uniforms and timetables. One comment from Riley and Docking's (2004) study expressed frustration about such disciplines: 'As long as we're learning, what does it matter what colour hair band we wear?' (p. 176). Yet young people are often sent home because they have come to school in the wrong clothing or hairstyle. These rules are supplemented by a reward and punishment system that encourages conformity. Some have argued that all these constitute part of a larger form of social control (Harris, 1977; Dornbusch et al., 1996).

Second, within such a highly structured and controlled environment, it is easy to conceive learning as the acquisition of knowledge and skills. Given this definition, the whole package that we have been criticising throughout this book apparently follows: young people are empty vessels to be filled with content imposed externally through a curriculum; teaching consists of 'delivering' the curriculum in order to produce outcomes that are measurable through the standard attainment tests. Sadly, this transmutes the concern for equality into coercion: all students must be proficient at algebra; they must memorise certain facts about the Second World War; they must be able to do persuasive writing according to set guidelines; and so on.

Third, another feature of large impersonal institutions is that students cannot easily form meaningful and long-lasting relationships with their teachers. The size of schools (especially those with over 1,500 students) makes it impossible for teachers and other staff to have a deep knowledge of any individual student. There is little opportunity for teachers and students to build relationships and trust. Yet, as we have seen, the relationship between adolescents and their teachers is a key to their learning and growth. This makes the current state school culture particularly detrimental for the young person's holistic development. No wonder the youngsters we interviewed said that they felt like a number within a system, rather than a person whom their teachers knew.

Finally, a well-acknowledged weakness of the mainstream institution is that young people have little opportunity to play an active part in determining their own learning trajectories or in school decisions that affect their well-being. In recent years there have been new initiatives to engage students, such as school councils and other 'student voice' projects; however, without a genuine transformation of the whole system, student voice merely pays lip service to democratic values in schools (Fielding, 2004b). Student voice becomes a means to an end in a 'grades-obsessed society' rather than a way to acknowledge the autonomy of young people (Rudduck and Flutter, 2000).

In short, mainstream schooling is permeated by a culture of coercion. The young people we talked to did not perceive schools as *cool* places perhaps mainly because they are forced. Indeed, coercion makes students resistant and unhappy (Noddings, 2003). It fails to respect the student as a person. Many adolescents appear to be lacking in motivation because a school for them is a place of disengagement and boredom. Many are labelled *underachievers*, which reinforces the message that they are failures. There is a prevailing distrust between disaffected young people and their teachers, and many such students suffer emotional distress (Riley and Docking, 2004). Schools therefore also serve as *barracks* to keep youngsters in check and to manage their behaviours.

Riley and Docking's study also uncovered some teacher disaffections. They found that there are few opportunities for relationship building at school, and when they are under stress because of disaffected students, some teachers resort to humiliating students who present behaviour difficulties, exacerbating rather than reducing problems of disrespect and disaffection and contributing towards the creation of a group of young people who become disenfranchised from education.

(Riley and Docking, 2004: 177)

Carl Rogers described the instrumental approach to learning as 'lifeless, sterile, futile, quickly forgotten stuff, which is crammed into the mind of the poor helpless individual tied into his seat by ironclad bonds of conformity' (Rogers 1979: 3). It is impossible for schools to foster a culture of caring when their main concern is for students' recordable attainment rather than their development as persons. Yet, as we have seen, adolescence is a time of personal exploration. The state's demand for measurable attainment makes it difficult for a school to create safe and caring spaces and opportunities outside school for the young person to explore.

Ironically, these features of state schooling tend to favour children from well-off families and disfavour those from less privileged backgrounds. This in turn defeats the honourable aim of making schooling and education inclusive and equally accessible for all (Goodson, 1990).

Given all these negatives, why is the mainstream system of schooling so robust? One of the reasons is that schools serve other important social purposes, such as child-minding, socialising, and basic healthcare such as free school meals. For example, the child-minding function allows parents to work so that the workforce can contribute more fully to the nation's economy. Over the years, many theorists have criticised curricula established for political rather than educational purposes (Stenhouse, 1975) and have questioned whether the state should have this level of control over the culture of schools (O'Connor, 1990).

Alternative approaches to schooling

Over the last few decades, alternative schools have allowed educational researchers to investigate education that takes the person seriously. We use the term 'alternative' to refer to non-mainstream institutions, but not to those independent private schools that emphasise students' academic attainments and national league tables. Alternative schools include the free school movement pioneered by A.S. Neill's Summerhill School; Sands School in England; free or democratic schools worldwide described by David Gribble (1998) in his book *Real Education*; the schools that are part of the Human Scale Education movement in the UK; as well as other schools dedicated to the student's holistic development, including Waldorf Steiner schools and the Krishnamurti school. Although each of these schools has a distinct ethos and approach to learning, they all share some fundamental values, such as: respect for the student as a whole person; prioritising human relationships; seeing teachers as facilitators; a commitment to democratic values and non-coercion; and viewing the main aim of education as human development (self-actualisation for Maslow or becoming fully human for Carl Rogers).

Rather than review each of these alternative models, we will choose the democratic/free schools as a paradigm example to illustrate the institutional features of these alternative approaches. According to Gribble (1998), free schools, such as Summerhill or Sands School, believe in the goodness of every child, and that one's innate goodness can only flower through a happy, open and free environment, which includes close human relationships. The emphasis is on encouraging the young person's autonomy and free will. Yet freedom is not equivalent to permissiveness; it must be balanced by an appropriate understanding of an individual's responsibilities. In such an environment, both children and adults can respect each other, be authentic and truthful, and become self-disciplined, self-motivated and independent in society.

In contrast with the state school, which is part of a larger system of social control, free schools strive to offer an environment that is intended to provide children and young people with freedom and responsibility.

As we saw in Chapter 1, A.S. Neill's idea was to 'make the school fit the child' rather than the other way around. The school's website quotes Neill:

> I magine a school where kids have freedom to be themselves, where success is not defined by academic achievement, but by the child's own definition of success, where the whole school deals democratically with issues, with each individual having an equal right to be heard, where you can play all day if you want to, and there is time and space to sit and dream. Could there be such a school?
>
> (Summerhill website, www.summerhillschool.co.uk)

Let's visit some of the key features of free schools.

First, education in free schools gives priority to non-coercive values and mutual respect. Individuals are valued for who they are. The school is, generally speaking, small and human-scale, and feels more homely, which is conducive to warm relations. The school is regarded as a community of human beings who live and learn together. There are no externally imposed disciplines; rules are negotiated and agreed upon by all members of the community. In free schools, the young person's opinion is respected and listened to. In both Summerhill and Sands, the key governing body of the school consists of students and staff. All decisions are made in school meetings, and each individual has an equal right to vote. In his book, Neill notes that his own vote counted as one, which was the same as a 7-year-old's.

The second key feature is that both schools also promote individual responsibilities, which are key to living together in a community. For example, in Sands, each person is expected to clean the school, take part in preparing the food, eat together and wash up afterwards. A young person must attend the lessons to which he/she has signed up. The school explains:

> Whenever a person does not take responsibility for their actions, there may be repercussions for the rest of the school. It is only in this case that the school may ask that person to make amends. Having a tie done up incorrectly affects no-one; missing your washing up means the rest of the washing-up team has more to do.
>
> (Sands School website, www.sands-school.co.uk/about-sands/
> rights-and-responsibilities)

With this simple approach, the few rules at Sands are beneficial and supportive to all. Furthermore, taking such responsibilities means that life skills such as cooking and cleaning are developed by doing the actual work rather than by being taught.

The third key feature is that free exploration is regarded as an important part of a young person's education. Neill envisaged the exploration to include playing at will and having space to dream. Exploration is connected to one's psychological health, motivation, and finding one's life passions. Neill insisted that 'if the emotions are free, the intellect will look after itself'. Indeed, most alternative schools dwell on this separation between the emotion and the intellect (for our critique of this, see Chapters 3, 6 and 7). Neill regarded the cultivation of sincerity, balance, tolerance, happiness and love as more important than single-minded intellectual pursuits, such as learning about maths.

Finally, alternative institutions generally respect individual needs and choices, and see cultivating relationships as important, but have a less rigorous approach to academic studies. There is a tendency to neglect the fact that academic qualities and virtues are very much part of the whole person. This is in part due to the false dichotomy between the cognitive and non-cognitive aspects of human development (see Chapter 3). In contrast to the mainstream obsession with academic attainment, alternative education tends to devalue academic learning. One obvious difference between mainstream and free schools is whether lessons are compulsory or not. In Summerhill and Sands, students can exercise their autonomy by deciding what and when to study. Paradoxically, however, once they step into the classroom, the teaching is often not dissimilar from a mainstream class, the curriculum is subject-based and students' progress will be assessed through the standard attainment tests. In other words, there is no alternative curricular vision of academic learning.

It is clear that alternative schools reject any kind of coercion. However, this trust in young people's ability to choose independently can be problematic. This is because free choice must be coupled with an understanding of the criteria for choosing (see Chapter 3). Criteria are always concerned with values, and yet children and adolescents may not always be best at judging what their needs are or understanding the appropriate values as a basis for choosing. For example, they may have limited perception of the possibilities before them. This is especially important when there are external standards involved, as there are in perhaps all learning processes. One needs to understand the standards to make wise learning choices. One needs that understanding to know what counts as an appropriate challenge. Therefore, educational activities may risk becoming restricted and less challenging, when left to young people's own perceptions. Yet this point must not be used to deny their autonomy. They may need support, but certainly not coercion. As discussed earlier, well-trained and experienced mentors can help the young person understand the valuable aspects of an activity and better appreciate the range of possibilities open to them (see Chapters 8 and 9). The student decides with the help of a mentor. In their idea of unrestricted freedom, alternative schools may have overlooked the importance of such guidance. For instance, A.S. Neill stopped providing therapeutic counselling to children, believing that the environment alone would heal the child.

This links to how alternative schools view their curriculum and teaching. In the examples we gave above, both schools have a curriculum and teaching methods that tend to be similar to formal classroom instruction, and which is largely indistinguishable from what is happening in the mainstream classroom. There also tends to be a lack of innovation in such teaching. Indeed, Summerhill has proudly claimed that what is happening there hasn't changed much since 1921.

Human-centred learning community

Our aim in this chapter is to sketch a human-centred learning organisation, by first examining the merits of both mainstream and alternative models of learning institutions. We will start with a summary of their respective strengths.

The mainstream school-system:

- aims to provide an equally good education for all students regardless of background
- strives for academic rigour
- is open to innovation and reform
- provides for students with special learning needs
- has a diverse student body

In contrast, alternative schools tend to foster a more caring culture, conducive to students' social and emotional development through close personal relationships.

An alternative school tends to:

- treat the students as individuals and with respect and without coercion
- allow more time and space for young people to explore their own interests and develop self-awareness
- make it possible for students to learn and grow according to their own pace
- enable the student to participate in the school's decision-making processes
- be human in scale and provide an environment in which the student can form close relationships with adults

These lists are not exhaustive, but rather highlight the fact that, because they sit at different ends of the spectrum in terms of schooling practice, mainstream and alternative education each have important ingredients to offer to a truly human-centred educational vision. A human-centred approach to the learning institution ought to integrate the strengths of both.

In the following, we want to show how a human-centred education and the accompanying ideas of curriculum, pedagogy and learning feedback can work synergetically within a caring learning community. The heart of this project has led us to reconsider many aspects of current educational practice. For example, it has required us to rethink the design of the curriculum, the relationship between teachers and students, and the engagement of the young person in his/her own education. It will also necessitate rethinking the institution, especially its culture and its environment, including the function and size of classrooms. What should be the school's values and ethos in order to enable the flourishing of humanity through education? A human-centred education, as we have developed in this book, requires a radical reframing and reconceptualising of schooling. Despite recent policy shifts in English secondary education, the general dehumanising culture often prevails, and despite the fact that transforming this may be a key to educational reform (Louis *et al.*, 1996). So, humanising the school is our starting point.

Humanising the school

Fielding (2001) reminds us that 'respect' means appreciating each other as persons rather than as role occupants within an institution. First and foremost, a school ought to be established as a learning community rather than an institution, because only a community can embody care, respect and trust, which is a human way of living and learning together (Segiovanni, 1994a). All learning communities and institutions embody an implicit understanding of what constitutes human flourishing, how individuals pursue a flourishing life, and how education enables this (cf. Chapter 6).

A school does not automatically becoming a community of humans by merely having an ethos of caring and respect. It needs processes whereby teachers and staff interrogate the meanings, aims and value of their practices. The ethos needs to be built and rebuilt. A well-thought-out whole-school approach requires sharing. It is a communal project of constructing a culture. Once there are commitments from the staff, parents and students towards an emerging shared vision, the next step would be to establish some 'institutional architecture', which would include the governing principles of the community. For example, to have a deeper understanding of each young person, the school may need to provide training to teachers to develop such capacities, or employ those who have already had such training. Within the school there ought to be processes that facilitate relationships and listening, and participation and responsibility.

A culture of respect and care is not instilled piecemeal. Nor can it be taught through lessons. It must be practised in the way that adults and young people learn and work together, and in the manner that they relate to each other. The more a school community and its members live and embody the values of respect and care, the more such values become the very fabric of the community. The school must create a context in which there is no fear: no fear of failure, of teachers, of punishment, of bullying or of speaking one's mind. Instead, there ought to be friendship, love and kindness at all levels. This applies to the relationships between the adults and between the young people themselves. In short, a caring culture must be a deliberate and joint humanising effort.

The case of Colegio Amor

Good schools are often places where there is a strong sense of community (Segiovanni, 1994b). We now turn to an example of such a school in Colombia that has been considered as a good school by UNICEF, in order to illustrate how a school culture based on love, respect and care can be created and sustained.

Colegio Amor is located in a satellite town outside of Bogotá, Colombia. Most of its inhabitants are migrant families and individuals who were victims of the Colombian civil wars and consequent violent displacement. Founded in the 1980s, the school has on average 450 children. Colegio Amor, namely the school of love, regards personal relations as 'a transforming agent, a door to a better world'. It conceives of human relationships as simultaneously emotional, social and spiritual. The heart of the school's ethos consists of the commitment to creating a safe and caring learning community, and building an awareness of the needs of others. The school takes a number of approaches to achieving and living this ethos.

First, the leadership team offer camaraderie to each other, and make new staff members feel fully accepted. The school employs individuals who share this ethos. Among the staff, there is a strong sense of solidarity, and a common expectation to show warmth towards and reach out for each other. In short, the school creates a space that encourages all to treat each other positively. It strives to create an environment that mirrors the warmth and closeness of a home (where ironically for the majority of the children in the school such warmth and closeness is often missing). For example, children and young people from poorer families are provided with food and clothing (in the form of school uniform). The young people support each other.

Second, an important practice in Colegio Amor is that teachers visit the children in their homes, which helps the teacher get to know the young person and understand his/her hopes and the problems he/she might be experiencing outside the school. Domestic violence, street gangs, drug abuse and child negligence are not uncommon in poverty-stricken communities in Colombia. Home visits thus provide a good opportunity for teachers to become more sensitive to the young person's needs. Teachers, psychologists and/or social workers visit the student's home once a term, and more frequently when there are concerns about the student's well-being at home.

Third, the school also encourages mutual support amongst the students themselves. Older children are encouraged to help the younger ones as well as each other. For instance, meals are shared, and each student's birthday is celebrated at the school. In this way, children and young people learn about responsibilities towards oneself to maintain one's dignity, and to others to help them feel cared for.

Fourth, the curriculum is also designed around these principles. It prioritises the capabilities and qualities of the student, such as initiative and the capacity to complete tasks on one's own and in a group. For instance, the curriculum incorporates a Prevention Programme, which helps students become aware of the causes of the social problems in Soacha and the country at large. The programme is organised through a series of workshops that educate young people about violence, drugs, poverty and unemployment; it also encourages young people to discuss sexual diseases. These participatory workshops help young people to feel empowered to make changes in their own lives and their communities. As a result, most graduates of the school have a healthy self-esteem.

Finally, the school has a rich non-academic curricular programme, designed to help enhance young people's self-respect, which includes workshops in art, music, dance and theatre. It is considered important for children from displaced families to reconnect with their own cultural roots. In addition, the school also offers hands-on courses in 'micro-enterprises' that aim at cultivating the young people's initiative, and at preparing them to run their own small businesses after leaving the school. The pedagogy of these courses consists of experiential learning and hands-on workshops, which culminate in each student writing their own business proposals.

Despite horrendous social problems in Soacha, young people in Colegio Amor are growing to become self-respecting individuals, capable and willing to care for others due to the way they have been loved and cared for. This captures the essence of humanising schools, and a fundamentally human way of being in the world (Noddings, 1984).

Creating a culture of engagement

Within a caring culture, students are more likely to engage fully in learning and the school's life. From a human-centred perspective, respect for the student as a person requires the kind of democratic practices exemplified by schools such as Summerhill and Sands, where school meetings are forms of self-government. Such respect also demands that the student has an important say in what projects he/she works on, and what programmes he/she will follow. We propose a step further: a kind of deep listening that allows 'the innermost voice' of the young person to be heard, that which guides a young person's fundamental choices regarding his/her direction in life, potential, and human becoming. For a young person to own his/her learning requires a rejection of passivity. It needs a non-coercive environment but also depends on the capacity of teaching professionals to provide empowering guidance to the students. With the support of their mentors, young people can sit firmly in the driving seat of their learning.

In English mainstream schools, there are some examples of pedagogical approaches that encourage student engagement; these are often educational experiments to engage disaffected young people, who are likely to become drop-outs. Let us briefly visit such a project.

The 'Basement Project'

A few years ago, in an inner city secondary school, a group of thirty young people aged 15–16 who were labelled 'at risk' (of permanent exclusion) took part in an innovative educational programme aimed at providing an engaging learning experience. The project team included a full-time key teacher a learning mentor, and various part-time teachers for arts, English and drama, science and IT specialists, and an educational counsellor. This group worked in a number of classrooms in the school's basement, and the project was thus nicknamed the 'Basement Project'.

In order to involve the young people in the design of the curriculum activities, the team began with a self-introduction where each student explained what they thought they were good at and what they wanted to do in the future. Students also had several in-depth one-to-one conversations with a learning mentor. These sharing sessions helped the teaching staff to get to know the students better, and fostered student self-knowledge.

It then occurred to the team that the students seemed to regard themselves as different persons within the school environment from outside it. For instance, a 16-year-old student, who had never passed maths and science at school, had a passion for motor engines, and was already a skilled mechanic who spent most of his truant days helping out at a local garage. Another 16-year-old, who had persistently failed all her subjects, had been caring for two younger siblings as their mother had cancer, and had been selling her hand-made crafts in a local market at the weekends. She was already a young carer and entrepreneur.

The group discussed how to spend the twelve weeks of the project, and the upshot was that the young people decided to write a play about being adolescents and perform it to other students in the school. The idea of the play emerged because these young people felt that no one understood them, and that they wanted to express their frustration and alienation. In addition, the group discovered that they were a pool of talent – singers, a guitarist, a drummer, a lyrics writer, several actors and actresses, organisers, promoters, and an artist who was responsible for most of the local graffiti.

The adults in the team believed that a creative outlet such as a drama might allow the students to bring out the best in themselves, and could serve as a platform upon which to build other elements of the curriculum. Being a small project, the team had to maximise the use of resources in and outside of the school, such as the local library, museums and charity shops (for stage props and costumes), and all help that friends and families could bring.

Within weeks, the young people from the 'Basement Project' had written a fully fledged play addressing the personal issues confronting them on a daily basis, including the risk of drug and alcohol abuse, bullying, teenage pregnancy, and social issues, such as class and racial discrimination. Although the play centred on these negative experiences, nevertheless, the play was full of humour and optimism. Through writing and producing it, the young people were beginning to find their own paths out of frustration, feelings of failure, and, for some, self-loathing.

Why were these students' experiences of education transformed from disaffection to active engagement? It is because they co-constructed their learning experience. The students reported that they had learned more about themselves, their peers and the teachers who worked with them in these months. The boundaries between studying and learning as 'the way we are' collapsed because of three ingredients: (1) the play allowed the group to own the learning activities involved; (2) it gave the students an opportunity to explore issues that they cared about deeply; (3) it offered a platform where each student could follow individual lines of inquiry. Within three months, the 'Basement Project' witnessed an unimaginable transformation in the students. They wrote and rewrote the play scripts, composed music for it, designed and made most of the stage sets and costumes, and used computer programs to make advertising flyers. The young people worked individually and collaboratively. Everyone said that they had learned how to listen and the team was able to help individual students with their emotional difficulties. One student, who wrote about being trapped in a gang culture for the play, said that he had found a 'bigger purpose' in life, and found the courage to leave the street gang. With the support of the teachers, he started a new life at a music college after receiving a scholarship. The young man with the mechanical talent decided to take an apprenticeship that would eventually lead to a national diploma in mechanical engineering; and the young entrepreneur went on to take business management and design courses at an FE college. At the end of the twelve weeks, the students gave performances to other students, parents and members of the local community. The 'Basement Project' illustrates the potential power of providing a co-constructed curriculum that also enables them to participate in activities in a deeply engaging manner.

Community events

Our examples illustrate two aspects of the human-centred learning community: care and engagement. To imagine a realistic alternative to the current state schooling, it is necessary to start with a robust and holistic proposal for reform, which must include so-called 'assessment'. In Chapter 9, we argued that grade-based exams tend to devalue students as persons. Grades label the person and encourage low expectations. We also pointed out that the current system of accountability for secondary schools through single measurement of GCSEs is a one-size-fits-all solution that is damaging and unnecessary because it does not separate the different needs for assessment. So we suggested that the following could be met separately: students have a continual need for feedback as part of their learning processes and professional staff need to be involved directly in that process. However, this is quite different from the information needs of potential employees. Furthermore, impersonal governmental informational needs are quite different again.

We proposed some possible approaches to these different feedback needs. For example, learning portfolios can enable students to understand their learning journeys and progress holistically. We would now like to take this idea a step further because some elements of the first feedback needs can be integrated into the life of the community. One can imagine that different pathways can serve to satisfy the internal needs for feedback, review and evaluation:

1. A daily meeting where the young person meets with their mentor to discuss experience of activities or project work, and receive feedback from the mentor and/or from their peers.

2. A weekly review with the mentor on a one-to-one basis. This would be an occasion to discuss progress over time, readjust goals and deal with the challenges experienced.

3. A bi-weekly student 'lecture' where the young people take turns to give talks on a topic that they have been investigating. This could be about developing middle-game in chess, a presentation on the river Gambia, showing refraction through a prism, or an analysis of one of Bach's Fugues. Student lectures give an opportunity for peers and teaching staff to see how well the young person is doing in his/her research work, and offer feedback on the topic.

4. A monthly meeting with teachers (mentor, counsellor and tutors) where parents are invited to discuss the young person's work progress, meeting their needs, and how all parties can work together to support the young person's learning.

5. A half-termly open day/evening organised by the young people themselves where parents, teachers, school administrators and other staff are invited. Students take turns to report on their learning, and take the opportunity to showcase their work, present projects and discuss their experience of the curriculum activities. At the end of the report, students can give performances,

or stage a talent show. This is an occasion to take stock, review the young person's learning experience and celebrate progress.

6. A termly exhibition co-organised by the teaching staff and the students. Each student will be able to present their learning portfolio to peers, teachers and families. School administrators, governors, trustees and other members in the wider community will be invited to this occasion. The student will be expected to explain how they have identified the questions and worked through the projects, and the audience will provide feedback, show appreciation and have other engaging conversations with the young people.

7. A yearly student conference organised by the staff where the participants (students and adults from within and without the school) will come together to explore in depth a theme of common interest. This is an occasion for papers to be written and presented, debates organised, or individual research on a topic shared.

With proposals like these, we can see that the learning community can have some sense of how the students are doing through events that bring the community together, without the need for grades and exams.

A human-centred leadership

A culture that is conducive to flourishing cannot be imposed like a set of rules. Rather, it has to be nurtured through the practices of the community. It needs leaders capable of human-centred thinking.

First, such thinking will avoid instrumentalising the person, as it attempts to create a culture of care. Otherwise, relationships and learning activities and initiatives such as 'student voice' can easily become merely a means to the end of raising attainment.

Second, human-centred thinking will define leadership as collaborative rather than authoritarian. A learning institution's ethos and values need to be co-constructed, and such processes provide an opportunity for individuals to confront each other directly, resulting in a closer human relationship (Bernstein, 1971: 166). In this way, leadership should not be confined to just one person. The human-centred approach makes leadership a communal process. A learning community that survives and prevails often has a strong educational philosophy and sense of values, and this means that, although the process of reaching agreement can be long and exhausting, nevertheless, it is most worthwhile (Rogoff *et al.*, 2001).

In his analysis of the work of Alex Bloom, one of the best-known educationalists in the UK, Fielding (2005) postulates that, as an outstanding educational leader, Bloom's insistence on negotiated values and innovative practices in St George-in-the-East secondary school was crucial in transforming the lives of 260 boys and girls there in the 1940s. Bloom's vision as the leader of the learning community was to create a culture of what Bernstein regarded as organic solidarity.

Third, human-centred leadership prioritises mutual learning. It sets a tone that fosters the teachers' commitment to their area of work and a renewal of its inherent values and and good practices. The staff's learning is not only limited to continuing professional development and learning more about one's area or subject, but also includes their own flourishing as persons.

Fourth, human-centred leadership includes nurturing young people's self-responsibility by providing space for them to participate in dialogue about schools' decisions that affect them. In our interviews with adolescents, students seem to desire broader experience and encounters as part of their education. School leaders ought to include in the community-design and the curriculum, the explicit intention for students to initiate and participate in community-based projects.

Human-centred leadership thinking would re-examine the part that parents can play in the learning community. Their input and sense of belonging can be of crucial importance. Although adolescents may not be so eager to see their parents at school, it might be less awkward for them if they see parental involvement as integral to the school's learning activities. For instance, parents with expertise might offer specialist or exploratory classes; or they might help organise programmes for experiential learning, such as film-making, cooking, rock climbing and so forth. Similarly, parents from various professions and occupations can run regular workshops about the nature of different kinds of work, and how each occupation contributes to society and the well-being of people. Widening the community can bring variety. The example of the 'Open Classroom' (in Rogoff et al., 2001) shows that if parents are expected to be part of the school's teaching activities, then these adults are more willing to make a positive contribution to the school life as a whole. In the case of Colegio Amor, parents also learn and grow through such participation. A note of caution: of course, many parents are not available to make such contributions, although this doesn't negate the valuable aspects of parental involvement in a learning community.

In summary, human-centred leadership encourages the learning institution to foster a culture or a way of being and flourishing together. The learning community is renewed and recreated collaboratively through the learning, growth and transformation of its members.

A nurturing physical environment

For the learning community to be a home-from-home, it needs a relaxed and casual atmosphere. The physical space ought to be exciting, attractive, safe and responsive to diverse needs. This space breaks the boundaries between school and home, making it both a formal place for studying and an informal space for hanging out – a leisure and a cultural centre. Informal and inviting spaces can foster significant and informal encounters between the students and staff, for instance, in the canteen or the library.

Building Schools for the Future (BSF) aimed to renew all 3,500 English secondary schools over a 15-year period starting in 2005. The project claimed that redesigning spaces could help schools to make a vital contribution to the community, including adult learning, return to work schemes, community sports, arts and music experiences, libraries, community festivals, holiday clubs, and health and social care. Although BSF ended abruptly due to a change in government and a lack of funding, the human-centred approach would share this optimism. The diverse spaces provide more options for when, where and how the students learn. For example, in the BSF project the seating of some rooms was horseshoe shaped so that all participants could face each other and a speaker at the same time. Paying attention to the design of spaces can help create a sense of community in which an adolescent is not automatically labelled as a student, but rather as a person.

Bishop Park School in Clacton-on-Sea, Essex was a tailor-made learning community. The founders had the vision of a person-centred learning community, and translated it into a physical learning environment where the boundaries between the school and the community were minimised. In the school's compound there was a nursery, a care home for older people and a public library open to all. The students and staff used the same cafeteria for lunch and refreshments, giving many opportunities for informal meetings.

The United World Colleges (UWCs) are another example. There are thirteen UWCs around the world, sharing a vision based on German educationalist Kurt Hahn's belief in the unity of people from diverse backgrounds who live and learn together. The UWC vision brings together young people from different nations, races and religions to live communally and to learn and share intensely. Following this pattern, each UWC intentionally creates a global learning community.

In recent years, technological innovations have transformed the physical spaces of learning communities. For instance, a VLE (virtual learning environment) can allow students to study and learn at any time and anywhere they choose, such as their own homes, a public library, the school premises, and so on. ICT can make systematic learning possible without classrooms. We would still need designated group spaces such as seminar rooms, resource centres, libraries, science labs, centres for creative activities, VLE terminals, quiet rooms, private facilities for counselling, public spaces for relaxation and so on (for more examples see Davies *et al.*, 2006).

The reconception of learning and teaching combined with new technology changes the way that time (or the timetable) is perceived within a learning community. As we saw in Chapter 7, each person's timetable is determined on an individual basis with the mentor. The institution may have a common timetable for cognitive training and speciality courses to which individuals could sign up. For instance, the institution might provide a six-week training programme in critical thinking, and students of different ages (14–19) who are working on individual projects might participate. Cognitive development therefore could occupy a common space in the institution's timetable, and might require an important physical space too.

Similar points apply to courses related to specialties and to exploratory lectures or discussions. In this regard, outstanding or unusual members of the community, such as astronauts, politicians, poets and sports personalities, could share their life stories to help the young appreciate better what it means to aspire to a more meaningful or full life. Other outside speakers such as physicists, university professors and researchers can offer lectures to help broaden their horizons and see a love of learning for its own sake at work.

This depiction of a learning environment supported by technology may seem to resemble a university campus rather than a school. Rightly so. The key difference between a university and a conventional secondary school is autonomy. Secondary schools are coercive and are sometimes perceived like 'prisons' where young people are locked inside and are forced to do things that they don't want to do. The design of a university campus indicates more trust, in which the adult roles in the human-centred learning community pertain to guiding, counselling and tutoring.

Conclusion

In this concluding chapter of the book, we have explored the question of how participation in a learning community can help adolescents to flourish and develop as human beings. We have discussed both the 'software' and the 'hardware' of the community. In doing so, we also revisited a number of core questions such as the aims of education, the nature of learning and the role of teachers.

In summary, in the learning community, individuals ought to be treated as persons rather than objects. This perspective creates an opportunity for a fundamental shift from the dehumanising mechanisms of current schooling to a human-centred learning community. This is imperative if individuals are to relate to each other in a human way, and co-create a culture of care. Very often in a human-centred learning community, it is the closeness between all the people that touches and changes the individual.

In a recent review of Fielding and Moss (2010), Claire Tupling concluded that the prospects for the authors' vision of a democratic school were: 'it won't happen'. According to Tupling, this is because for any vision to become a reality, 'there requires a political will to transform society for the mutual benefit of all'. So we must either wait for wise politicians to adopt a new vision or start to make the shift by inviting young people, teachers and others to join this new movement. The choice is simple.

Further reading

Kohn, A. (1996) *Beyond Discipline: From Compliance to Community*. Alexandria, VA: Association for Supervision and Curriculum Development.

Noddings, N. (1992) *The Challenge to Care in Schools: An Alternative Approach to Education*. New York: Teachers College Press.

Palmer, P. (1998) *The Courage to Teach*. San Francisco, CA: Jossey-Bass.

Sergiovanni, T.J. (1994) *Building Community in Schools*. San Francisco, CA: Jossey-Bass.

References

Adams, G. and Marshall, S. (1996) A developmental social psychology of identity: under-standing the person-in-context. *Journal of Adolescence*, 19, 429–42.

Adams, G., Montermayor, R. and Gullota, T. (eds) (1996) *Psychosocial Development During Adolescence: Progress in Developmental Contextualism*. London: Sage.

Adamson, L. and Lyxell, B. (1996) Self-concept and questions of life: identity develop-ment during late adolescence. *Journal of Adolescence*, 19, 569–82.

Anscombe, G. (1997) Modern moral philosophy, in R. Crisp and M. Slote (eds) *Virtue Ethics*. Oxford: Oxford University Press.

Bailey, C. (1984) *Beyond the Present and the Particular: A Theory of Liberal Education*. London: Routledge & Kegan Paul.

Bandura, A. (1994) Self-efficacy, in V.S. Ramachaudran (ed.) *Encyclopedia of Human Behavior*, Vol. 4. New York: Academic Press, pp. 71–81.

Barro, R. and Lee, J-W. (2000) *International Data on Educational Attainment: Updates and Implications. Centre for International Development, Working Paper No. 42*. Cambridge, MA: Harvard University Press.

Baudrillard, J. (1989) *Selected Writings* (ed. M. Poster). Cambridge: Cambridge University Press.

Baumeister, R., DeWall, C., Ciarocco, N. and Twenge, J. (2005) Social exclusion excludes self-regulation. *Journal of Personality and Social Psychology*, 88, 589–604.

Bearne, E., Dombey, H. and Grainger, T. (2003) *Classroom Interactions in Literacy*. Maidenhead: Open University Press.

Beck, J. (2003) The school curriculum, the National Curriculum and New Labour reforms, in J. Beck and M. Earl (eds) *Key Issues in Secondary Education*, 2nd edn. London: Continuum.

Beck, J. and Earl, M. (eds) (2003) *Key Issues in Secondary Education*, 2nd edn. London: Continuum.

Beckert, T. (2007) Cognitive autonomy and self-evaluation in adolescence: a conceptual investigation and instrument development. *North American Journal of Psychology*, 9(3), 579–94.

Benton, M. and Fox, G. (1985) *Teaching Literature: Nine to Fourteen*. Oxford: Oxford University Press.

Ben-Ze'ev, A. (2000) *The Subtlety of Emotions*. Cambridge, MA: The MIT Press.

Bernstein, B. (1971) *Class, Codes and Control, Vol. 1*. London: Routledge & Kegan Paul.

Bernstein, B. (1977) *Class Codes and Control, Vol. 3: Towards a Theory of Educational Transmissions*. London: Routledge & Kegan Paul.

Black, P. and Wiliam, D. (1998a) Assessment and classroom learning. *Assessment in Education*, March, 7–74.

Black, P. and Wiliam, D. (1998b) *Inside the Black Box*. London: King's College.

Black, P. and Wiliam, D. (2005) Developing a theory of formative assessment, in J. Gardner (ed.) *Assessment and Learning*. London, UK: Sage.

Black, P., C. Harrison, C. Lee, B. Marshall and D. Wiliam (2003) *Assessment for Learning: Putting it into Practice*. Maidenhead: Open University Press.

Blenkin, G., Edwards, G. and Kelly, A. (1992) *Change and the Curriculum*. London: Paul Chapman.

Blos, P. (1967) *The Second Individuation Process of Adolescence: The Psychoanalytic Study of the Child*. New York: International Universities Press.

Boaler, J. and Wiliam, D. (2001) 'We've still got to learn!' Students' perspectives on ability grouping and mathematics achievement, in P. Gates (ed.) *Issues in Mathematics Teaching*. London: Routledge Falmer, pp. 77–92.

Boaler, J., Wiliam, D. and Brown, M. (2000) Students' experiences of ability grouping – disaffection, polarisation and the construction of failure. *British Educational Research Journal*, 26(5), 631–48.

Booth, T. (2011) Curricula for the common school: what shall we tell our children? *Forum*, 53(1), 31–48.

Bouchery, H. and Jurman, W. (2006) Dating and romantic experiences in adolescence, in G. Adams and M. Berzonsky (eds) *Blackwell Handbook of Adolescence*. Malden, MA: Blackwell.

Boyd, D. (2006) *Identity Production in a Networked Culture: Why Youth Heart MySpace*. St Louis, MO: American Association for the Advancement of Science.

Braddock, J. and Slavin, R. (1995) Why ability grouping must end: achieving excellence and equity in American education, in H. Pool and J. Page (eds) *Beyond Tracking: Finding Success in Inclusive Schools*. Bloomington, IN: Phi Delta Kappa Educational Foundation, pp. 7–20.

Brandsford, J.D., Brown A.L. and Cocking, R. (1999) *How People Learn: Brain, Mind, Experience and School*. Washington DC: National Academy Press.

Bridgman, P. (1927) *The Logic of Modern Physics*. New York: Macmillan.

Bronfenbrenner, U. (1989) Ecological systems theory, in R. Vasta (ed.) *Annals of Child Development*. Greenwich, CT: JAI Press, pp. 187–249.

Brooks, V. (2004) Learning to teach and learning about teaching, in V. Brookes, A. Ian and L. Bills (eds) *Preparing to Teach in Secondary Schools: A Student Teacher's Guide to Professional Issues in Secondary Education*. Maidenhead: Open University Press, pp. 7–17.

Brophy, J. (1983) Conceptualizing student motivation. *Educational Psychologist*, 18, 200–15.

Brophy, J. (2004) *Motivating Students to Learn*, 2nd edn. New York & Oxford: Lawrence Erlbaum Associates.

Brown, B.B. and Lohr, M.J. (1987) Peer group affiliation and adolescent self-esteem: an integration of ego identity and symbolic interaction theories. *Journal of Personality and Social Psychology*, 52, 47–55.

Brown, B.B., Classen, D.R. and Eicher, S.A. (1986) Perceptions of peer pressure, peer conformity dispositions and self-reported behaviour among adolescents. *Developmental Psychology*, 22, 521–30.

Buckingham, D. (1999) Turning on the news. *Journal of Adolescent and Adult Literacy*, 43(3), 250–3.

Buhrmester, D. (1990) Intimacy of friendship, interpersonal competence and adjustment during preadolescence and adolescence. *Child Development*, 61, 1101–11.

Bynner, J. and Parsons, S. (2006) *New Light on Literacy and Numeracy*. London: NRDC.

Byrnes, J. (2003) Cognitive development during adolescence, in G. Adams and M. Berzonsky (eds) *Blackwell Handbook of Adolescence*. Malden, MA and Oxford: Blackwell.

Carnie, F., Large, M. and Tasker, M. (eds) (1996) *Freeing Education*. Stroud: Hawthorn Press.

Carr, D. (ed.) (1998) *Education, Knowledge and Truth*. London: Routledge.

Carr, D. (2003) *Making Sense of Education: An Introduction to the Philosophy and Theory of Education and Teaching*. London: Routledge.

Castello-Climent, A. (2008) On the distribution of education and democracy. *Journal of Development Economics*, 87, 179–90.

Cauce, A. (1986) Social networks and social competence: exploring the effects of early adolescent friendships. *American Journal of Community Psychology*, 14, 607–28.

CERI (Centre for Educational Research and Innovation) (2008) Assessment for learning: the case for formative assessment. Paper presented at OECD/CERI International Conference 'Learning in the 21st Century: Research, Innovation and Policy', OECD, Paris, 2008.

Chen, H., Mechanic, D. and Hansell, S. (1998) A longitudinal study of self-awareness and depressed mood in adolescence. *Journal of Youth and Adolescence*, 27(6), 719–34.

Clarke, S. (2005) *Formative Assessment in the Secondary Classroom*. London: Hodder & Stoughton.

Claxton, G. (1984) The psychology of teacher training: inaccuracies and improvements. *Educational Psychology*, 4(2), 167–74.

Cole, D. *et al.* (2001) The development of multiple domains of child and adolescent self-concept: a cohort sequential longitudinal design. *Child Development*, 72(6), 1723–46.

Coleman, J. (1974) *Relationships in Adolescence*. London: Routledge and Kegan Paul.

Coleman, J. (1995) Adolescence, in P. Bryant and A. Colman (eds) *Developmental Psychology*. London: Longman.

Coleman, J. and Hendry, L. (1999) *The Nature of Adolescence*. London: Routledge.

Corden, R. (2000) *Literacy and Learning Through Talk*. Buckingham: Open University Press.

Cornbleth, C. (1990) *Curriculum in Context*, Basingstoke: Falmer Press.

Crain, W. (1985) *Theories of Development*. Upper Saddle River, NJ: Prentice-Hall.

Crane, T. (2001) *Elements of Mind*. Oxford: Oxford University Press.

Dacey, J. and Kenny, M. (1997) *Adolescent Development*, 2nd edn. Boston, MA: McGraw-Hill.

Davies, C., Hayward, G. and Lukman, L. (2006) *14–19 and Digital Technologies: A Review of Research and Projects, Report 13*. FutureLab Series, available at: www.futurelab.org.uk.

Davies, J. and Biesta, G. (2007) Coming to college or getting out of school? The experience of vocational learning of 14–16-year-olds in a further education college. *Research Papers in Education*, 22(1), 23–41.

Day, J. and Tappen, M. (1996) The narrative approach to moral development: from the epistemic subject to dialogical selves. *Human Development*, 39, 67–82.

Dearing, R. (1995) *Skills for Graduates in the 21st Century*. Cambridge: The Association of Graduate Employers.

Deković, M. and Meeus, W. (1997) Peer relations in adolescence: effects of parenting and adolescents' self-concept. *Journal of Adolescence*, 20(2), 163–76.

Dewey, J. (1902) *The Child and the Curriculum*. Chicago, IL: University of Chicago Press.

Dewey, J. (1916) *Democracy and Education: An Introduction to the Philosophy of Education* (1966 edn). New York: Free Press.

Dewey, J. (1938) *Experience and Education*. New York: Collier Books.

DfEE (Department for Education and Employment) (1998) *The National Literacy Strategy: Framework for Teaching*. London: DfEE.

Dillon, J. and Maguire, M. (eds) (2004) *Becoming a Teacher*. Buckingham: Open University Press.

Dixon, P., Bortolussi, M., Twilley, L. and Leung, A. (1993) Literary processing and interpretation: towards empirical foundations. *Poetics*, 22(1–2), 5–33.

Dornbusch, S., Glasgow, K. and Lin, I. (1996) The social structure of schooling. *Annual Review of Psychology*, 47(1), 401–29.

Dreikurs, R., Grunwald, B. and Pepper, F. (1982) *Maintaining Sanity in the Classroom*, 2nd edn. New York: Harper Collins.

Durkin, S. and Paxton, S. (2002) Predictors of vulnerability to reduced body image satisfaction and psychological wellbeing in response to exposure to idealized female media images in adolescent girls. *Journal of Psychosomatic Research*, 53(5), 995–1005.

Eccles, J. and Wigfield, A. (2000) Schooling's influences on motivation and achievement, in S. Danzinger and J. Waldfogel (eds) *Securing the Future: Investing in Children from Birth to College*. New York: Russell Sage Foundation, pp. 153–81.

Eccles, J.S., Wigfield, A. and Schiefele, U. (1998) Motivation to succeed, in N. Eisenberg (ed.) *Handbook of Child Psychology: Vol. 3: Social, Emotional, and Personality Development*, 5th edn. New York: Wiley.

Egan, K. (1975) *The Philosophy of Open Education*. London: Routledge.

Eisenberg, N. and Morris, A. (2004) Moral cognitions and prosocial responding in adolescence, in R. Lerner and L. Steinberg (eds) *Handbook of Adolescent Psychology*. New York: Wiley, pp. 155–88.

Elkind, D. (1980) Strategic interactions in early adolescence, in J. Adelson (ed.) *Handbook of Adolescent Psychology*. New York: Wiley.

Elliott, D., Huizinga, D. and Menard, S. (1989) *Multiple Problem Youth: Delinquency, Substance Use and Mental Health Problems*. New York: Springer-Verlag.

Erikson, E.H. (1962) Reality and actuality. *Journal of the American Psychoanalytic Association*, 10, 451–74.

Erikson, E. (1963) *Childhood and Society*, 2nd edn. New York: Norton.

Erikson, E. (1968) *Identity: Youth and Crisis*. New York: Norton.

Erikson, E. (1980) *Identity and the Life Cycle*. New York: Norton.

Fielding, M. (2001) Beyond the rhetoric of student voice: new departures or new constraints in the transformation of 21st century schooling? *Forum*, 43(2), 100–9.

Fielding, M. (2004a) 'New wave' student voice and the renewal of civic society. *London Review of Education*, Special Issue on Education for Civil Society, 2(3), 197–217.

Fielding, M. (2004b) Transformative approaches to student voice: theoretical underpinnings, recalcitrant realities. *British Educational Research Journal*, 30(2), 295–311.

Fielding, M. (2005) Alex Bloom, pioneer of radical state education. *Forum*, 47(2), 119–34.

Fielding, M. (2007a) On the necessity of radical state education: democracy and the common school. *Journal of Philosophy of Education*, 41(4), 549–57.

Fielding, M. (2007b) Beyond 'voice': new roles, relations, and contexts in researching with young people. *Discourse*, 28(3), 301–10.

Fielding, M. (2009) Public space and educational leadership: reclaiming and renewing our radical traditions. *Educational Management, Administration and Leadership*, 37(4), 497–521.

Fielding, M. and McGregor, J. (2005) Deconstructing student voice: new spaces for dialogue or new opportunities for surveillance? Paper given at the Annual Meeting of the American Educational Research Association, Montreal, Canada.

Fielding, M. and Moss, P. (2010) *Radical Education and the Common Schools: A Democratic Alternative*. Oxford: Routledge.

Flavell, J. (1985) *Cognitive Development*, 2nd edn. Englewood Cliffs, NJ: Prentice-Hall.

Forbes, S. (2003) *Holistic Education: An Analysis of its Ideas and Nature*. Brandon, VT: Foundation for Educational Renewal.

Ford, M. and Forman, E. (2006) Redefining disciplinary learning in classroom contexts, in J. Green and A. Luke (eds) *Rethinking Learning: What Counts as Learning and What Learning Counts. Review of Research in Education*, 30, 1–32.

Friere, P. (1970) *Pedagogy of the Oppressed*. New York: Seabury Press.

Friere, P. (1973) *Education for Critical Consciousness*. New York: Seabury Press.

Frost, L. (2003) Doing bodies differently? Gender, youth, appearance and damage. *Journal of Youth Studies*, 6(1), 53–70.

Furbey, M. and Beyth-Marom, R. (1992) Risk-taking in adolescence: a decision-making perspective. *Developmental Review*, 12(1), 1–44.

Furlong, J., Barton, L., Miles, S., Whiting, C. and Whitty, G. (2000) *Teacher Education in Transition: Re-forming Professionalism?* Buckingham: Open University Press.

Furman, W., Brown, B. and Feiring, C. (eds) (1999) *The Development of Romantic Relationships in Adolescence.* Cambridge: Cambridge University Press.

Gaffney, D. and Roye, C. (eds) (2003) *Adolescent Sexual Development and Sexuality: Assessment and Interventions.* Kingston, NJ: Civic Research Institute.

Gardner, M. and Steinberg, L. (2005) Peer influence on risk-taking, risk preference, and risky decision-making in adolescence and adulthood: an experimental study. *Developmental Psychology*, 4, 625–35.

Geldard, K. and Geldard, G. (1998) *Counselling Adolescents.* London: Sage Publications.

Gilligan, C. (1982) *In a Different Voice: Psychological Theory and Women's Development.* Cambridge, MA: Harvard University Press.

Ginzberg, E., Ginsburg, S., Axelrad, S. and Herma, J. (1951) *Occupational Choice: An Approach to General Theory.* New York: Columbia University Press.

Giroux, H.A. (1989) *Schooling for Democracy: Critical Pedagogy in the Modern Age.* New York: Routledge.

Gladwell, M. (2006) *Blink.* London: Penguin Books.

Glaeser, E., Ponzetto, G. and Shleifer, A. (2007) Why does democracy need education? *Journal of Economic Growth*, 12, 77–99.

Glasser, W. (1985) *Control Theory in Classroom.* New York: Harper and Row.

Goodson, I. (1990) On understanding of curriculum: the alienation of curriculum theory, in I. Goodson and R. Walker (eds) *Biography, Identity and Schooling.* London: Routledge.

Goodson, I. (1991) Teachers' lives and educational research, in I. Goodson and R. Walker (eds) *Biography, Identity and Schooling.* London: Falmer Press, pp. 137–49.

Goodson, I. (1998) Towards an alternative pedagogy, in J. Kincheloe and S. Steinberg (eds) *Unauthorized Methods: Strategies for Critical Teaching.* London: Routledge.

Goodson, I. (ed.) (2005) *Learning Curriculum and Life Politics.* London: Routledge & Kegan Paul.

Goodson, I. (2006) The reformer knows best, destroying the teacher's vocation, *Forum*, 48(3), 253–59.

Goodson, I.F. and Hargreaves, A. (eds) (1996) *Teachers' Professional Lives.* London: Falmer Press.

Grace, G. (1995) *School Leadership: Beyond Education Management: An Essay in Policy Scholarship.* London: Falmer Press.

Greenberger, S. and Steinberg, L. (1981) *Part Time Employment of In-school Youth: An Assessment of Costs and Benefits.* Final report to National Institute of Education.

Greene, J. (2002) The business model. *Education Next*, 2(2), available at: http://educationnext.org/the-business-model/ (accessed July 2011).

Greene, K., Krcmar, M., Waters, L., Rubin, D., Hale, J.L. (2000) Targeting adolescent risk-taking behaviors: the contribtions of egocentrism and sensation-seeking. *Journal of Adolescence*, 23(4), 439–61.

Gribble, D. (1998) *Real Education: Varieties of Freedom*. Bristol: Libertarian Education.

Grundy, S. (1987) *Curriculum: Product or Praxis*. Lewes: Falmer Press.

Gutierrez, K., Raquedano-Lopez, P. and Tejeda, C. (1999) Rethinking diversity: hybridity and hybrid language practice in the third space. *Mind, Culture, and Activity*, 6, 286–303.

Hacking, I. (1975) *Why Does Language Matter to Philosophy?* Cambridge: Cambridge University Press.

Hall, G. (1911) *Educational Problems, Vol. II*. New York: Appleton & Company.

Handelman, R. (1999) Defining and assessing adolescent apathy. *Dissertation Abstracts International*, 60(1), 407B.

Hargreaves, D. (1982) *The Challenge for the Comprehensive School: Culture, Curriculum, and Community*. London: Routledge & Kegan Paul.

Harris, K. (1977) Peters on schooling. *Journal of Educational Philosophy and Theory*, 9, 33–48.

Hartas, D. (2011) Young people's participation: is disaffection another way of having a voice? *Educational Psychology in Practice*, 27(2), 103–15.

Harter, S. (1999) *The Construction of the Self*. New York: Guilford.

Harvard, G. and Hodkinson, P. (1995) *Action and Reflection in Teacher Education*. Norwood, NJ: Ablex Publishing.

Heron, J. (1992) *Feeling and Personhood: Psychology in Another Key*. London: Sage.

Herzberg, F. (1959) *The Motivation to Work*. New York: Wiley.

Hidi, S. (2000) An interest researcher's perspective: the effects of extrinsic and intrinsic factors on motivation, in C. Sansone and J.M. Harackiewicz (eds) *Intrinsic and Extrinsic Motivation: The Search for Optimal Motivation and Performance*. New York: Academic.

Hidi, S. and Ainley, M. (2002) Interest and adolescence, in F. Pajares and T. Urdan (eds) *Academic Motivation of Adolescence*. Greenwich, CT: Information Age Publishing Inc.

Hill, T. (1991) *Autonomy and Self Respect*. Cambridge: Cambridge University Press.

Hirst, P. (1971) What is teaching? *Journal of Curriculum Studies*, 3.

Hirst, P. and Peters, R. (1970) *Logic of Education*. London: Routledge & Kegan Paul.

Holland, J., Daiger, D. and Power, P. (1980) *My Vocational Situation: Description of an Experimental Diagnostic Form for the Selection of Vocational Assistance*. Palo Alto, CA: Consulting Psychologists Press.

Holt, J. (1964) *How Children Fail*. New York: Pitman. Revised edition 1982, New York: Merloyd Lawrence, Delta/Seymour Lawrence.

Hope, T. (2006) Are schools in tune with disaffected youth? *International Journal on School Disaffection*, 4(2), 28–34.

Hoy, W.K. (2003) An analysis of enabling and mindful school structures: some theoretical, research and practical considerations. *Journal of Educational Administration*, 41(1), 87.

IBO, available at: www.ibo.org.

Illich, I. (1971) *Deschooling Society*. New York, NY: Harpers & Row.

James, W. (1950) *The Principles of Psychology*. New York: Dover (first published 1890).

Jeffs, T. and Smith, M. (eds) (1999) *Informal Education – Conversation, Democracy and Learning*. Ticknall: Education Now.

Johnson, M. (2007) *Subject to Change: New Thinking of the Curriculum*. London: Association of Teachers and Lecturers.

Kant, I., Gregor, M. and Korsgaard, C.M. (1998) *Groundwork of the Metaphysics of Morals*. Cambridge: Cambridge University Press.

Keating, D. (1980) Thinking processes in adolescence, in J. Adelson (ed.) *Handbook of Adolescent Psychology*. New York: Wiley.

Keating, D. (2004) Cognitive and brain development, in R. Lerner and L. Steinberg (eds) *Handbook of Adolescent Psychology*, 2nd edn. New York: Guilford Press, pp. 45–84.

Keeffe, D. (1989) The National Curriculum critique. *Educational Notes*, No. 4. Libertarian Alliance.

Kelder, R. (1996) Rethinking literary studies, from the past to the present. *Proceedings of the World Conference on Literacy*, Philadelphia, 1996.

Keys, W. and Fernandes, C. (2004) What do Students Think About School? in B. Moon and A. Sherton Mayes (eds) Teaching and Learning in the Secondary School, Abingdon, Oxon and New York, NY: Routledge Falmer.

Kieran, E. (1975) *The Philosophy of Open Education*. London: Routledge.

Kiesner, J., Cadinu, M., Poulin, F. and Bucci, M. (2002) Group identification in early adolescence: its relation with peer adjustment and its moderating effect on peer influence. *Child Development*, 73, 196–208.

Kimberly, H. (2010) Skipping school and using drugs: a brief report. *Drugs: Education, Prevention & Policy*, 17(5), 650–7.

Kincheloe, J. (1999) *How Do We Tell the Workers? The Socioeconomic Foundations of Work and Vocational Education*. Boulder, CO: Westview.

Klein, R. (1999) *Defying Disaffection: How Schools are Winning the Hearts and Minds of Reluctant Students*. Stoke on Trent: Trentham Books.

Kliebard, H. (1999) *Schooled to Work: Vocationalism and the American Curriculum 1876–1946*. New York: Teachers College Press.

Kohlberg, L. (1958) The development of modes of thinking and choices in years 10 to 16. Unpublished doctoral thesis, University of Chicago.

Kohlberg, L. (1980) Stages of moral development as a basis for moral education, in B. Munsey (ed.) *Moral Development, Moral Education, and Kohlberg*. Birmingham, AL: Religious Education Press, pp. 15–100.

Kohlberg, L. (1981) *Essays in Moral Development, Vol. 1: The Philosophy of Moral Development*. San Francisco, CA: Harper and Row.

Kohlberg, L. (1984) *Essays in Moral Development, Vol. 2: The Psychology of Moral Development*. San Francisco, CA: Harper and Row.

Kohlberg, L. and Wasserman, E. (1980) The cognitive-developmental approach and the practicing counsellor: an opportunity for counsellors to rethink their roles. *The Personnel and Guidance Journal*, 58, 559–67.

Kolak, D. and Thomson, G. (2006) *Longman Standard History of Philosophy*. New York: Pearson/Longman.

Kostanski, M. and Gullone, E. (1998) Adolescent body image dissatisfaction: relationships with self-esteem, anxiety, and depression controlling for body mass. *Journal of Child Psychology and Psychiatry*, 39, 255–62.

Kostiuk, L. and Fouts, G. (2002) Understanding of emotions and emotion regulation in adolescent females with conduct problems: a qualitative analysis. *The Qualitative Report*, 7(1), available at: www.nova.edu/ssss/QR/QR7-1/kostiuk.html (accessed January 2010).

Kroger, J. (2004) *Identity in Adolescence: The Balance between Self and Other*. London, New York: Routledge.

Kroger, J. (2007) *Identity Development: Adolescence Through Adulthood*, 2nd edn. Newbury Park, CA: Sage.

La Greca, A. and Harrison, H. (2005) Adolescent peer relations, friendships, and romantic relationships: do they predict social anxiety and depression? *Journal of Clinical Child & Adolescent Psychology*, 34(1), 49–61.

Larson, R. and Richards, M. (1994) *Divergent Realities: The Emotional Lives of Mothers, Fathers, and Adolescents*. New York: Basic Books.

Lave, J. and Wenger, E. (1991) *Situated Learning: Legitimate Peripheral Participation*. Cambridge: Cambridge University Press.

Lehmann, W. and Taylor, A. (2003) Giving employers what they want? New vocationalism in Alberta. *Journal of Education and Work*, 16(1), 45–67.

Lerner, R. and Steinberg, L. (eds) (2009) *Handbook of Adolescent Psychology: Individual Bases of Adolescent Development*, 3rd edn. Hoboken, NJ: Wiley.

Locke, J. (1979) An essay concerning human understanding, in P.H. Nidditch (ed.), *Clarendon Edition of the Works of John Locke*. USA: Oxford University Press.

Louis, K.S., Kruse, S.D. and Masks, H.M. (1996) Schoolwide Professional Community. In F.M. Newmann & Associates (eds), *Authentic Achievement: Restructuring Schools for Intellectual Quality*. San Francisco: Jossey-Bass.

Lumby, J. (2011) Disengaged and disaffected young people: surviving the system. *British Educational Research Journal*, 1, 1–19.

MacDonald, G. and Leary, M.R. (2005) Why does social exclusion hurt? The relationship between social and physical pain. *Psychological Bulletin*, 131, 202–23.

Macmurray, J. (1961) *Persons in Relation*. London: Faber and Faber.

Macmurray, J. (1962) *Reason and Emotion*. London: Faber and Faber.

Marcia, J. (1979) Identity status in late adolescence: description and some clinical implications. Paper presented at the Identity Development Symposium, Gröningen, the Netherlands, June 1979.

Marcia, J. (1980) Identity in adolescence, in J. Adelson (ed.), *Handbook of Adolescent Psychology*. New York: Wiley.

Marcia, J., Waterman, A., Matteson, D., Archer, S. and Orlofsky, J. (1993) *Ego Identity: A Handbook for Psychosocial Research*. New York: Springer-Verlag.

Marples, R. (ed.) (1999) *The Aims of Education*, London: Routledge.

Max-Neef, M., Elizakle, A. and Hopenhayn, M. (1991) *Human Scale Development: Conception, Application and Further Reflections*. New York: Apex.

Maslow, A. (1954) *Motivation and Personality*. New York: Harper.

Maslow, A. (1968) *Toward a Psychology of Being*, 2nd edn. New York: Van Nostrand.

McCloskey, M. (1983) Intuitive physics. *Scientific American*, 248(4), 122–30.

McDowell, J. (1994) *Mind and World*. Cambridge, MA: Harvard University Press.

McDowell, J. (2001) *Mind, Value and Reality*. Cambridge, MA: Harvard University Press.

McGuire, K.D. and Weisz, J.R. (1982) Social cognition and behaviour correlates of preadolescent chumships. *Child Development*, 53, 1478–84.

McLellan, J. and Pugh, M. (eds) (1999) *The Role of Peer Groups in Adolescent Social Identity: Exploring the Importance of Stability and Change*. San Francisco, CA: Jossey-Bass.

McNaughton, D. (1988) *Moral Vision*. Oxford: Blackwell.

Mead, G. (1934) *Mind, Self and Society*. Chicago, IL: University of Chicago Press.

Meighan, R. (2002) *John Holt: Personalized Learning Instead of Uninvited Teaching*. Nottingham: Educational Heretics Press.

Merleau-Ponty, M. (1962) *Phenomenology of Perception* (trans. C. Smith). New York: Humanities Press.

Mezirow, J. (1991) *Transformative Dimensions of Learning*. San Francisco, CA: Jossey-Bass.

Miller, D. (1998) *Enhancing Adolescent Competence: Strategies for Classroom Management*. Pacific Grove, CA: Wadsworth Publishing.

Miller, R. (ed.) (1991) *New Directions in Education*. Brandon, VT: Holistic Education Press.

Mitchell, J. (1972) Some psychological dimensions of adolescent sexuality. *Adolescence*, 7(28), 447–59.

Moon, B. (2001) *A Guide to the National Curriculum*. Oxford: Oxford University Press.

Nardia, E. and Steward, S. (2003) Is mathematics T.I.R.E.D? A profile of quiet disaffection in the secondary mathematics classroom. *British Educational Research Journal*, 29(3), 345–66.

Neill, A.S. (1960) *Summerhill: A Radical Approach to Childrearing*. New York: Hart Publishing.

Neill, A.S. (1992) *Summerhill School: A New View of Childhood*. New York: St Martin's Griffin.

Noddings, N. (1984) *Caring, a Feminine Approach to Ethics and Moral Education*. Berkeley, CA: University of California Press.

Noddings, N. (1992) *The Challenge to Care in Schools*. New York: Teachers College Press.

Noddings, N. (2000) Care and coercion in school reform. *Journal of Educational Change*, 2(1), 35–43.

Noddings, N. (2002) *Educating Moral People: A Caring Alternative to Character Education.* New York and London: Teachers College Press.

Noddings, N. (2003) *Happiness and Education.* Cambridge: Cambridge University Press.

Noddings, N. (2005) Caring in education. *The Encyclopaedia of Informal Education,* available at: www.infed.org/biblio/noddings_caring_in_education.htm (last accessed 26 January 2012).

Nucci, L. (1997) Moral development and character formation, in H.J. Walberg and G.D. Haertel (eds) *Psychology and Educational Practice.* Berkeley, CA: MacCarchan, pp. 127–57.

Nurmi, J. (1987) Age, sex, social class, and quality of family interaction as determinants of adolescents' future orientation: a developmental task interpretation. *Adolescence,* 22, 977–91.

Nussbaum, M. (1988) Non-relative virtues: an Aristotelian approach. *Midwest Studies in Philosophy* 13, reprinted in J.P. Sterba (ed.) *Ethics: The Big Questions.* Malden, MA: Blackwell.

Oates, T. (2010) *Could do Better: Using International Comparisons to Refine the National Curriculum in England.* Cambridge Assessment paper. Cambridge: University of Cambridge Press.

O'Connor, M. (1990) *Secondary Education.* London: Cassell.

OECD (1997) *Societal Cohesion and the Globalizing Economy: What Does the Future Hold?* Paris: OECD.

Onwuegbuzie, A., Witcher, A., Collins, K., Filer, J., Wiedmaier, C. and Moore, C. (2007) Students' perceptions of characteristics of effective college teachers: a validity study of a teaching evaluation form using a mix-methods analysis. *American Educational Research Journal,* 44(1), 113–60.

Packer, M. (2001) The problem of transfer, and the social cultural critique of schooling. *Journal of the Learning Sciences,* 10, 493–514.

Pajares, M.F. (1992) Teachers' beliefs and educational research: cleaning up a messy construct. *Review of Educational Research,* 62(3), 307–32.

Parker, J., Creque, R., Barnhart, D. *et al.* (2004) Academic achievement in high school: does emotional intelligence matter? *Personality and Individual Differences,* 37(7), 1321–30.

Pattison, S., Rowland, N., Cromaty, K., Richards, K., Jenkins, P., Cooper, M., Polat, F. and Couchman, A. (2007) Counselling in schools: A research study into services for children and young people in Wales. Lutterworth, Leicestershire: British Association for Counselling and Psychotherapy.

Peters, R. (1966) *Ethics and Education.* London: George Allen and Unwin.

Piaget, J. (1926) *The Language and Thought of the Child.* New York: Harcourt Brace.

Piaget, J. (1932) *The Moral Judgement of the Child.* London: Free Press.

Piaget, J. (1950) *The Psychology of Intelligence.* London: Routledge & Kegan Paul.

Piaget, J. (1965) *The Moral Judgment of the Child.* New York: Free Press.

Piaget, J. (1985) *The Equilibration of Cognitive Structures*. Chicago, IL: University of Chicago Press.

Pittman, K. and Cahill, M. (1992) *Youth and Caring: The Role of Youth Programs in the Development of Caring*. Washington, DC: Academy for Educational Development.

Prentice Hall School Professional Development (n.d.) www.phschool.com/professional_development/assessment/portfolio_based_assess.html (last accessed 16 March 2009).

Pring, R. (2004) *Philosophy of Education: Aims, Theory, Common Sense and Research*, London: Continuum.

Pye, J. (1988) *Invisible Children – Who are the Real Losers at School?* Oxford: Oxford University Press.

QCA (Quality and Curriculum Authority) (n.d.) Curriculum purposes, values and aims. Available at: http://curriculum.qca.org.uk/key-stages-3-and-4/aims/index.aspx (accessed March 2009).

QCA, available at www.qca.gov.uk.

Rawls, J. (1971) *A Theory of Justice*. Cambridge, MA: Harvard University Press.

Riley, K. and Docking, J. (2004) Voices of disaffected pupils: implications for policy and practice. *British Journal of Educational Studies*, 52(2), 166–79.

Robinson, C. and Taylor, C. (2007) Theorizing student voice. *Improving Schools*, 10(1), 1–15.

Rogoff, B., Goodman Turkanis, C. and Bartlett, L. (2001) *Learning Together: Children and Adults in a School Community*. New York: Oxford University Press.

Rogers, C. (1961) *On Becoming a Person: A Therapist's View of Psychotherapy*. London: Constable.

Rogers, C. (1969) *Freedom to Learn: A View of What Education Might Become*. Columbus, OH: Charles Merrill.

Rogers, C. (1979) The foundations of the person-centered approach. *Education*, 100(2), 98–107.

Rogers, C. (2000) *The School of Tomorrow*. Oxford: Open University Press.

Rogers, C. and Freiberg, H. (1993) *Freedom to Learn*, 3rd edn. New York: Merrill.

Rorty, R. (1989) *Contingency, Irony and Solidarity*. Cambridge: Cambridge University Press.

Rosenblum, G. and Lewis, M. (2006) Emotional development in adolescence, in G.R. Adams and M.D. Berzonsky (eds) *Blackwell Handbook of Adolescence*. Malden, MA: Blackwell Publishing, pp. 269–89.

Ross, A. (2000) *Curriculum: Construction and Critique*. London: Falmer Press.

Rowntree, J. (1977) *Assessing Students: How Shall we Know Them?* London: Harper and Row.

Rudduck, J. and Flutter, J. (2000) Pupil participation and pupil perspective: carving a new order of experience. *Cambridge Journal of Education*, 30(1), 75–89.

Russell, B. (1930) *The Conquest of Happiness*. London: Allen & Unwin.

Ryan, A. (2001) The peer group as a context for the development of young adolescent motivation and achievement. *Child Development*, 72, 1135–50.

Ryle, G. (1949) *The Concept of Mind*. Chicago, IL: University of Chicago Press.

Sachs, J. (2003) Teacher professional standards: controlling or developing teaching? *Teachers & Teaching: Theory and Practice*, 9(2), 175–86.

Schoenbach, R., Greenleaf, C., Cziko, C. and Hurwitz, L. (1999) *Reading for Understanding: A Guide to Improving Reading in the Middle and High School Classrooms*. San Francisco, CA: Jossey-Bass.

Schuck, S. and Pereira, P. (eds) (2011) *What Counts In Teaching Mathematics: Adding Value to Self and Content*. London and New York: Springer.

Schutz, P. and Lanehart, S. (2002) Introduction: emotions in education. *Educational Psychologist*, 37(2), 67–8.

Searle, J. (1983) *Intentionality: An Essay in the Philosophy of Mind*. Cambridge: Cambridge University Press.

Seginer, R. (1998) Adolescents facing the future. *Youth and Society*, 19, 314–33.

Seginer, R. (2008) Future orientation in times of threat and challenge: how resilient adolescents construct their future. *International Journal of Behavioural Development*, 32(4), 272–82.

Seginer, R. and Halabi-Kheir, H. (1998) Adolescent passage to adulthood: future orientation in the context of culture, age and gender. *International Journal of Intercultural Relations*, 22(3), 309–28.

Seginer, R. and Lilach, E. (2004) How adolescents construct their future: the effect of loneliness on future orientation. *Journal of Adolescence*, 27(6), 625–43.

Seldon, A. (2007) Leaders in your life. *Times Education Supplement*, 17 August.

Sergiovanni, T. (1994a) *Building Community in Schools*. San Francisco, CA: Jossey-Bass.

Sergiovanni, T. (1994b) Organizations or communities? Changing the metaphor changes the theory. *Educational Administration Quarterly*, 30(2), 214–26.

Shaffer, D.R. and Kipp, K. (2007) *Developmental Psychology: Childhood and Adolescence*, 6th edn. Belmont, CA: Wadsworth.

Shanahan, M., Mortimer, J. and Krüger, H. (2002) Adolescence and adult work in the twenty-first century. *Journal of Research on Adolescence*, 12(1), 99–120.

Shorrocks-Taylor, D. (1999) *National Testing*. London: British Psychological Society.

Sigelman, C. and Rider, E. (2009) *Life-span Human Development*. Beimont, CA: Wadsworth.

Smollar, J. and Youniss, J. (1989) Transformation in adolescents' perceptions of parents. *International Journal of Behavioral Development*, 12(1), 71–84.

Smyth, J. and Shacklock, G. (1998) *Re-making Teaching: Ideology, Policy and Practice*. London: Routledge.

Sosa, E. (2007) *A Virtue Epistemology*. Oxford: Oxford University Press.

Standish, P. (1999) Education without aims, in R. Marples (ed.) *The Aims of Education*. London: Routledge, pp. 35–49.

Stanley, J. and Williamson, T. (2001) Knowing how. *Journal of Philosophy*, 98(8), 411–44.

Steinberg, L. (1987) Impact of puberty on family relations: effects of pubertal status and pubertal timing. *Developmental Psychology*, 23, 451–60.

Steinberg, L. (1988) Reciprocal relations between parent–child distance and pubertal maturation. *Developmental Psychology*, 24, 122–8.

Steinberg, L. (1993) *Adolescence*, 3rd edn. New York: McGraw Hill.

Steinberg, L. (1999) *Adolescence*, 5th edn. New York: McGraw Hill.

Steinberg, L. (2005) Cognitive and affective development in adolescence. *Trends in Cognitive Sciences*, 9(2), 69–74.

Steinberg, L. (2008) *Adolescence*, 8th edn. New York: McGraw Hill.

Steinberg, L. and Dornbusch, S. (1991) Negative correlates of part-time employment during adolescence: replication and elaboration. *Journal of Developmental Psychology*, 27(2), 304–13.

Steinberg, L., Fegley, S. and Dornbusch, S. (1993) Negative impact of part-time work on adolescent adjustment: Evidence from a longitudinal study. *Developmental Psychology*, 29(2), 171–80.

Steinberg, L. Lamborn, S. and Dornbusch, S. (1992) Impact of parenting practices on adolescent achievement: authoritative parenting, school involvement, and encouragement to succeed. *Child Development*, 63, 1266–81.

Steinwand, G. (1984) Adolescent individuation: the culmination of a developmental line. *Journal of American Academic Psychoanalysis*, 12(1), 43–57.

Stenhouse, L. (1975) *An Introduction to Curriculum Research and Development*. London: Heinemann.

Sternberg, R. (1983) Criteria for intellectual skills training. *Educational Researcher*, 12, 6–12.

Sternberg, R. (1985) *Beyond IQ: A Triarchic Theory of Intelligence*. Cambridge: Cambridge University Press.

Sternberg, R. (1997a) A triarchic view of giftedness: theory and practice, in N. Coleangelo and G. Davis (eds) *Handbook of Gifted Education*. Boston, MA: Allyn and Bacon, pp. 43–53.

Sternberg, R. (1997b) *Thinking Styles*. New York: Cambridge University Press.

Sternberg, R. (1997c) *Successful Intelligence*. New York: Plume.

Sternberg, R. (ed.) (1999) *Handbook of Creativity*. New York: Cambridge University Press.

Sternberg, R.J. (2002) Cultural explorations of human intelligence around the world, in W. Lonner, D. Dinnel, S. Hayes, and D. Sattler (eds) *Online Readings in Psychology and Culture*. Bellingham, WA: Centre for Cross-Cultural Research, Unit 5, Chapter 1, available at: www.wwu.edu/~culture.

Sternberg, R. (2003) What is an 'expert student?' *Educational Researcher*, 32(8), 5–9.

Stoll, L. (2009) Capacity building for school improvement or creating capacity for learning? A changing landscape. *Journal of Educational Change*, 10(2), 115–27.

Stoll, L., Fink, D. and Earl, L. (2003) *It's About Learning, What's in it for Schools?* London: Routledge Falmer.

Stoll, L. and Reynolds, D. (1996) Connecting school effectiveness and school improvement: what have we learnt in the past ten years?, in T. Townsend (ed.) *Restructuring and Quality*. London: Routledge.

Stones, E. (1992) *Quality Teaching*. London: Routledge.

Striegel-Moore, R. (1995) A feminist perspective on the etiology of eating disorders, in K. Brownwell and C. Fairburn (eds) *Eating Disorders and Obesity*. New York: Guilford, pp. 224–9.

Super, D. (1953) A theory of vocational development. *The American Psychologists*, 8, 185–90.

Super, D. (1957) *Psychology of Careers*. New York: Harper & Bros.

Super, D. (1980) A life-span, life-space approach to career development. *Journal of Vocational Behavior*, 16, 282–98.

Taylor, A. and Lehmann, W. (2002) Reinventing vocational education policy: pitfalls and possibilities. *Alberta Journal of Educational Research*, 48(2), 139–61.

Thompson, R. (1994) Emotion regulation: a theme in search of definition. *Monographs of the Society for Research in Child Development*, 59, 2–3.

Thomson, G. (1987) *Needs*. London: Routledge.

Thomson, G. (2002) *On Philosophy*. Belmont, CA: Wadsworth Press.

Thomson, G. (2003) *On The Meaning of Life*. Belmont, CA: Wadsworth Press.

Thomson, G. (2005) Fundamental needs, in S. Reader (ed.) *The Philosophy of Need*. Cambridge: Cambridge University Press.

Thornton, S. and Flinders, D. (eds) (1997) *The Curriculum Studies Reader*. London: Routledge.

Torrance, H. and Pryor, J. (1998) *Investigating Formative Assessment: Teaching, Learning and Assessment in the Classroom*. Buckingham: Open University Press.

Townsend, T. (1997) *Restructuring and Quality*. London: Routledge.

UNESCO (2005) Literacy and empowerment: background and issues. Paper presented at the sixth meeting of the Working Group on Education for All (EFA), UNESCO Headquarters, Paris, 19–21 July, 2005. Available at: www.unesco.org/education/efa/global_co/working_group/Background%20paper.pdf.

UNESCO (2006) *Towards an Entrepreneurial Culture for the Twenty-first Century: Stimulating Entrepreneurial Spirit Through Entrepreneurship Education in Secondary Schools*. Paris: UNESCO.

Uttal, W. (2000) *The War Between Mentalism and Behaviorism*. New York: Lawrence Erlbauum.

Wainryb, C., Smetana, J. and Turiel, E. (eds) (2008) *Social Development, Social Inequalities, and Social Justice*. New York and Oxford: Lawrence Erlbaum Associates.

Wallace, W. (2009) *Schools Within Schools: Human Scale Education in Practice*. London: Calouste Gulbenkian Foundation.

Weare, K. (2000) *Promoting Mental, Emotional, and Social Health: A Whole School Approach*. London: Routledge.

Weber, M. (1958) *The Protestant Ethic and the Spirit of Capitalism* (trans. T. Parsons). New York: Charles Scribner & Sons.

Wentzel, K. and Wigfield, A. (2009) *Handbook of Motivation at School*. New York and Abingdon: Routledge.

White, R. (2000) *The School of Tomorrow*. Buckingham, Philadelphia, PA: Open University Press.

Wiliam, D. (1998) *Inside the Black Box*. London: King's College.

Wilson, B. (ed.) (1975) *Education, Equality and Society*. London: George Allen and Unwin.

Wilson, P.S. (1971) Interest and discipline in education, in I. Goodson (ed.) *Learning Curriculum and Life Politics*. London: Routledge and Kegan Paul.

Winch, C. (1998) *The Philosophy of Human Learning*. London: Routledge.

Wittgenstein, L. (1953) *Philosophical Investigations* (G.E.M. Anscombe, trans.). Oxford: Blackwell Publishing. (Other editions: Blackwell 1958, 2001; Prentice Hall 1999; Wiley-Blackwell 2009.)

Wringe, C. (1998) Reasons, rules and virtues in moral education. *Journal of Philosophy of Education*, 32(2), 225–35.

Yates, I. (2003) *Communication, Language and Literacy*. Dunstable: Brilliant Publications.

Yates, R. (1997) Literacy, gender and vulnerability: donor discourses and local realities. *IDS Bulletin*, 28(3), 112–21.

Zhang, L. and Zhang, W. (2008) Personal future planning in middle and late adolescence and its relation to adolescents' communication with parents and friends. *Acta Psychologica Sinica*, 40(5), 583–92.

Index